# TIME TO TE

# TIME TO TELL

DAVID FULTON

ROCKHAVEN BOOKS

# ROCKHAVEN BOOKS

40 Polsloe Road, Exeter, Devon, EX1 2DN

Copyright © David Fulton

First published in Great Britain in 2014 by
Rockhaven Books

All photographs and diagrams are copyright.
Details of copyright holders are available on request.

Biblical Quotations are from the NIV.

Cover illustration by Kenson Low, with grateful thanks.

Printed and bound in Great Britain by
Short Run Press Ltd, Exeter, Devon.

We have attempted to trace the true owner of the copyright of all
material that is quoted in the book. Should we have been guilty of
error or omission please inform us and we will amend future copies
and post the appropriate credit on the Rockhaven Books website:
www.RockhavenBooks.com

My grateful thanks to those who have helped me
and stuck with me in the writing of this book.
For without them, as they say "none of this
would have been possible".

*Initial editing*
Derick, Liz, Jodie, John and Audrey, Lt Col Tim,
Bill and Judy, Jan, Helena and Steve, Martin

*Final editing*
Kate

*For the artwork*
Kenson Low

*For support*
Roger and Garry

*For great patience*
The Fulton family

# FOREWORD

When asking me to write the foreword to his book, David referred to our first encounter.

*The doorbell rang and I invited David in. We had not met before. He explained that he had not had a full night's sleep in six months and that he regularly blacked out in the street and had to be picked up by an ambulance. He went on to say that, some three months earlier, he had been recommended to see me regarding his trauma.* "*You don't know how many times I've walked past your gate. I've even walked down the path, as far as the front door but couldn't ring the doorbell. But I'm here now and feeling more than a little apprehensive.*"

We met weekly for two hours. After one session, in an attempt to empathise with what David was telling me I cut out a piece of plywood, two-feet square, and stood still on it for half an hour to have some sense of being in 'the chimney'. As the sessions progressed David told me of a deep darkness that had been troubling him and that he couldn't face. I asked if it would help him to write it down. That was the beginning of this book. A few weeks later David said to me at the end of one of our sessions, "Next time, would you come with me to a place I can't go to? I've now typed it out but doubt if I could read what I've written. Would you read it for me?"

We set aside the whole morning for our next session – I'm glad we did. Even as an experienced counsellor, the impact was shattering. In fact, I did no other work for the next three days. The fourth day was Sunday, and I needed that 'day of rest'. The outcome of our time together was tremendous – David had found healing. We have never talked about that encounter since. It marked both an ending and a new beginning.

And now it's time to tell his story. Although incarcerated in a prison cell from which there was no escape, David continually escaped in his mind travelling on his boat, his Land Rover, to spend time with his family and his God. Although captive, he knew that, ultimately, "the Truth will set you free" (John 8:32). But be aware, David tells it as it is. When he invited me to read the first draft (my computer read it as I'm dyslexic), I was shaken, even though, as his trauma therapist, I had already heard much of it from David's own mouth some two years before. Surprisingly, hearing it outside a counselling session, I was shocked.

Could this really be true? I found myself judgmental – what about the language he uses? It didn't sound very Christian. Was this the good-natured David I now knew? I then had to ask myself, "Would I have survived in that totally dark prison cell being tortured on a regular basis?" More recently, David has been doing up our boat for Rockhaven Adventure Therapy. As we've become friendly with the guys at the docks, he has loaned them draft manuscripts. It has not been unusual a few weeks' later for them to sidle up and ask, "Is David's book for real? Could anybody really go through that and survive?" The answer is 'Yes'. This is a true story of survival against the odds.

So please, don't jump to judge this man; rather journey with David in his daily, hourly, struggles and enjoy his unusual sense of humour. It has been a privilege to get to know David, to work with his story and to see him using his experiences to help others.

May you too be blessed.

Now it's time for you to read David's story.

Roger Helyar, MBACP
Rockhaven Counselling & Therapy, Exeter

Nº 106595

FORM 4

## THE IMMIGRATION RULES. 1965

# RESIDENTIAL PERMIT 'B'

### FOR RESIDENCE AND EMPLOYMENT - SKILLED WORKER

THE PERSON TO WHOM this Permit is issued, whose details appear below, is permitted subject to the undermentioned conditions to enter, reside and undertake employment in The Gambia from the date of issue until 31st January next following.

### DESCRIPTION OF HOLDER

Other Names:..... DAVID FERLAND

Date of Birth:..... 10th - 09 - 1948

Place of Birth:..... KILMARNOCK

Nationality:..... BRITISH

Married or Single:..... MARRIE

Sex:..... MALE

Occupation:..... CHAPLAIN

(Signed)..... 1 - APR 2008 .....
(Holder)
CODE IMM080

### CONDITIONS

(a) D............... is deposited with the Principal Immigration Officer; or

(b) A Bond in the sum of D................... is entered into and guaranteed by the Standard Bank of West Africa Limited;

(c) The holder is permitted to establish residence in The Gambia for the

sole purpose of entering into employment with PRISONS DEPT

in the capacity of ..... CHAPLAIN

(d) The holder is not permitted to vary this employment, nor to engage in any other form of employment or business whatsoever, whether paid or unpaid, without the permission of the Principal Immigration Officer;

(e) No dependent of holder is permitted to undertake any employment or conduct any business whatsoever, whether paid or unpaid, without the permission of the Principal Immigration Officer;

(f) .........................................................................

(g) .........................................................................

# THE CHIMNEY

*Even though we walk through the valley of the
   shadow of death,
We will fear no evil, for you God are with us,*

Psalm 23

## THE GAMBIA, WEST AFRICA 2009

It was days until they came back at midnight. Nothing much was said. They didn't use handcuffs because of my broken arm. I can't say it was a nice surprise to see *'Hermann Boring'* again, but there he was, sitting in an important looking revolving leather chair behind an important looking desk, looking anything but important. "I said I'd see you again, Major. Are you going to sign this document or not? Though, I suspect not."

"Isn't it great to get something right for a change?" I said to him as I looked up at the clock. "It's first thing in the morning and you're right . . . the answer is no". He said nothing, only raising his right hand and pointing to the door. They pushed me outside to the back courtyard, and into the torture chamber. I was frightened, not for my life, but for my arm. If they strung me up again I could kiss my goodbye to it. They made me strip and forced me towards to *'The Chimney.'* This was a confined, two-foot square space of thundering silence and blinding darkness. Knowing that pain was coming I decided to think of something else, mind over matter and all that!

It could have been hours or days later when there was a banging on the steel door. "I don't hear you Major . . . you should be screaming by now." It was *Reich Marshall Boring.* I said nothing. I made no sound. I had no idea how long I'd been there, so many hours must have passed. I looked up and the sky shone blue through the opening at the top of the chimney. I did note though, that the pain, which enveloped my entire body, was less acute than the excruciating pain of the previous occasion I had visited *The Chimney*. He banged again, "No one can stand the tunnel more than twenty four hours, and you've been there thirty eight already, speak to me. Are you dead, like your Christian God Jesus?" "Thank you for your concern" I said, "but Jesus and I are very much alive as you'll find out one day asshole." Not exactly a good answer, but my speaking seemed to satisfy him, he wouldn't have to explain my death to the British Government. A final bang on the door and he shouted, "There's a little surprise for you later that will maybe make you think again," and with that I heard him retreat.

By the light from the top of what they called the tunnel, (because they don't know about chimneys), I could see that my legs had swollen up grotesquely, as had my left arm. My body had assumed a concertinaed position, my legs numb but unable to fold up owing to the restrictions of the twenty-four inch square cell. The pain just went on and on, but again I stopped thinking of myself, and realised there were probably millions of people suffering much worse. Gradually a blanket of night covered the top of the chimney and with the darkness came the mosquitoes and cockroaches. I had almost given up hope of getting out of there, when suddenly the door opened and I fell out. The NIA guard didn't seem an unkindly man, and said, "Forty-four hours Tubab, that's a long time," and with that he turned on his heel and walked out, leaving me alone.

It was difficult to know what time it was, probably between one and four in the morning. I lay on the unfinished concrete floor covered in my own excreta and urine, feeling nothing but pain and humiliation. There was an oil lamp burning on the desk at the far end of the room that cast a pale yellow glow over the place. I needed to get water. It had been two days since I last had a drink, but I couldn't see how I could move with only one capable arm. As I lay there, I had a very strange feeling that was sending shivers down my spine. Something wasn't right.

Now, although I am a committed Christian, I am not someone who hears God very well. He normally speaks to me through the Bible and often through my thoughts. However, on this occasion, it was as if God said to me, very clearly, "Death is here". There was something in the air that I just couldn't make sense of, a smell that left a coppery taste in the back of my throat. Was it evil? No evil I knew, but what was that smell? Then suddenly, I was four years old in the local butcher's with my mother. While she was waiting at the counter, I wandered off into the back of the shop. I was fascinated by all the hanging carcasses; cows, sheep, and rabbits. That was the smell, dead meat. I stretched my neck and scanned the place as best as I could in the semi-darkness. Gradually, as my eyes got used to what light there was, I saw what looked like a bundle of rags about fifteen feet away in the corner. Using my one good arm, I forced myself to slide up the grey concrete wall. I looked over and saw that it was actually a body. As I tried to sharpen my focus, the head moved and it made a groaning sound.

I could barely move, but I had to investigate further. I needed to get over there . . . somehow! Slowly, and with great difficulty, I managed to roll onto my right hip. Using my right arm, I dragged my body (which was now lightweight) over to the man. He seemed a big fellow and like me was naked. He was in an even worse mess than I was. I could see white bones sticking out of various parts of his body. As I continued to drag myself toward his head, I realised to my horror that I knew him. It was James. James was one of my chaplains whom I brought to faith in Christ some years previously. Shortly after he converted from Islam, he changed his name from Mohammed to James. He hadn't had it easy as a Christian convert, but it was obvious that with me out of the way the extremists were extracting their pound of flesh. "James! James," I managed in a husky whisper, "James its Dave." He watched me as I dragged myself closer; his eyes were wide and staring, never blinking only staring, pleading.

I came to the top of his head, he was a big man, about six four and his head was like a cannonball, always shaved and shining. I put my good hand under his head to lift it onto my swollen lap when he moaned and coughed. Seeing that he was starting to choke I laid it back down and tried to check his airways. Putting my finger in his mouth, I was shocked to discover there was something stuffed inside and I drew it out. It was one of his testicles, and his tongue was missing. At least, that's what I realised when I looked down and saw that he'd been castrated.

I felt as if my life had stopped, as if I was watching the whole scene from above me. This was not real; nothing that was happening was true. How could it be? How could God allow this? His eyes followed mine as I looked at what they had done to him and yet cruelly still kept him alive. Then I realised the eyes had no eyelids. They had cut them off. Both his legs had been broken many times over. His arms were also broken, and in the dim light, I counted six ribs protruding through the skin. He seemed beyond pain but he knew he was going to die. He tried to say something that I can't really describe; part gurgle, part words, but I already knew very well what it was. It was what I would have said, if I had been him. "Finish it." How could I? How could I not?

I looked about me. Over by the door were my prison shorts and t-shirt. There was a tap, (that had recently been reaffixed to the wall), plus the necessary handle, and an iron bucket by the tap. I dragged myself over to the clothes, and draping them over my shoulder headed towards the tap. My mind was as clear as a bell. I realised that if I succeeded in what I aimed to do, that it would be tantamount to committing suicide. I didn't know how much time I had, or indeed why I wasn't already on my way back to Mile Two Prison. All I could do was focus on the job at hand. I managed to reach the tap, and to my relief the bucket was already full of water in which I soaked the clothes. Before doing anything else, I gulped some of it down. I hung the wet clothes over my shoulders and began dragging my body back towards James again. Looking behind me, I could see a trail of blood mixed with water dripping from the clothes. While I could feel nothing at the time, due to the numbness in my lower limbs, I realised that I was scraping the skin and flesh off my hip as I hauled myself across the rough concrete floor. *So what Dave," I thought, "you'll be dead soon anyway, what's a little blood?"*

Reaching James, I told him what I thought he wanted me to do. I told him that if I was right, he should look right with his eyes, and if not, then he should turn his eyes left. This, as I write it, might sound clinical, but it was anything but. Tears were rolling down my cheeks, this was the last thing in the world I wanted to do. My heart was breaking. I was angry with myself for putting James in this situation. I was angry with James for not keeping his head down. I was angry with the extremist Muslims who had done this to him, and to me. I have to say that I was also angry with God who could have stopped it. Still could, but I knew He wouldn't. I made one of the toughest decisions of my life that night, and even now, as I write I struggle to come to terms with my actions.

He looked right, then to the centre and right again. For me time stopped. The moment had come. I started to recite Psalm 23 for both of us.

The Lord is our shepherd, we shall not want.
He makes us to lie in green pastures,
He leads us beside still waters, He restores our souls,
He guides us in paths of righteousness for his name sake.
Even though we walk through the valley of the shadow of
    death,
We will fear no evil, for you God are with us,
Your rod and Your staff, they comfort us.
You prepare a table before us in the presence of our en-
    emies.
You anoint our heads with oil, and our cup overflows.
Surely goodness and mercy will follow us all the days of our
    lives.
And we will dwell in the house of the Lord forever.

Amen

I covered his mouth and nose with the wet clothes. When I looked into his eyes I sensed the gratitude as well as the regret for I knew he believed as I did, that we'd both be dead within the hour and nobody but God would know what had taken place. I believe it was late June 09, or maybe early July when James died, I don't know which. May God forgive me for what I did, for I doubt if I ever will.

What had transpired in that dark dungeon was not spoken of, not one word. I pulled myself back over to the bucket and washed myself as best as I could and removed any blood that was on my clothes. They came in without so much as a glance at James and two men gripped my upper arms and dragged me out. I must have felt pain – especially in my broken arm, but I can't recall it. Still naked, I was thrown into the back of the pickup, and taken back to Mile Two, where on arrival, they dumped me, unceremoniously in the courtyard. Some prison guards carried me inside. I felt as if I wasn't wholly there, like things were happening to me while I was wandering about in slow motion, as if in a mist. The guards treated me as kindly as they could, and I remember thanking them and telling them that I forgave them. When the cell door clanged shut, I started to pray. Although I believed that I had lost my salvation because of what I had done, I still had a sense that God was there and listening.

Mental Wellbeing and Access
Waverley House
St. Luke's Road
Torquay
TQ2 5NU

Telephone: 01803 290782
Fax: 01803 290782
Web: www.devonpartnership.nhs.uk
Your Ref:
Our Ref: GC/mjs

Department: WB&A Torbay 1
Ask for: Graham Carr

Date: 24 February 2011

Dear ███████

Re: ████████████████████████████

I assessed David Fulton on 23 February 2011 following receipt of a referral on 7 February 2011 from Dr Claire Grindal, Clinical Psychologist at Torbay Hospital.

Mr Fulton was a Chaplain in the Gambia and was taken into captivity in 2008 and systematically tortured for a period of two years before escaping and being smuggled out of the country by the Foreign Office. Please find enclosed a letter from the High Commission detailing David's experiences and other corroborating information. It felt pertinent, during the assessment, not to explore David's experiences in detail as I believe he should be assessed by a senior psychology clinician. During the assessment David told me that the problems he is experiencing are that although he has made fantastic physical recovery since his escape he continues to experience nightmares and flashbacks relating to the events, the longest lasting up to ten minutes. Most recently David's flashbacks result in him being back in his dark and small cell. Consequently David finds he is very emotional and struggles to be able to express how he is feeling and his experiences. However he is able to document them in a book which he is finding very cathartic. David has also found that in writing down his story, he is able to bring out details that he has been suppressing. David's faith is important to him and he tells me that during his ordeal over the last couple of years it has kept him strong.

**Risk**
David tells me that he has no thoughts of harming himself or other people.

**Plan**
I am referring David to you as I believe he has had a significant traumatic experience and the most appropriate intervention at this point would be a thorough assessment from the Psychology Service.

If you have any questions, please do not hesitate to contact me.

Yours sincerely

Clinical Team Lead
Mental Wellbeing & Access Team

████████████████████████

# The Sunday Times

**From** Times Online
December 6, 2008

## UK missionaries David and Fiona Fulton jailed in Gambia

**Tristan McConnell in Accra**

A British missionary couple have appeared in court and been charged with sedition following their arrest a week ago in The Gambia, a largely Muslim nation and popular package tourist destination.

David Fulton, 60, and his wife Fiona, 46, were reportedly offered bail of £125,000 each which they have been unable to pay. They were arrested last Saturday accused of inciting rebellion against the government.

Police said the Fulton's had sent letters critical of the government to individuals and groups. The couple were paraded on state television earlier in the week.

President Yahya Jammeh seized power in a bloodless military coup in 1994 and has ruled Gambia with an iron fist ever since. Journalists and opposition activists receive death threats and are regularly arrested, beaten and detained without charge, according to human rights groups.

The couple moved to the mostly Muslim West African country 9 years ago after initially visiting as tourists. They live in Serekunda, a town close to the capital, where they were arrested last Saturday.

Speaking from the capital Banjul a missionary colleague, Kofi Mensa, told The Times there was confusion surrounding the whereabouts of the couple. "I am trying to find out where they are. I have heard nothing from them but think Fiona may be at the police headquarters," he said.

Mr Fulton – who became a Christian while serving a jail term in the UK for armed robbery – is thought to be locked up at the overcrowded Mile Two prison outside the capital.

A friend of the couple who did not want to be named said Mrs Fulton was being well treated, but there were concerns for her husband. "We don't think he's fared quite as well," said the friend. "He's not eating."

Pastor Martin Speed of Westhoughton Pentecostal Church in Bolton, with which the couple has links, said: "The work he is doing is not political. He's sharing his Christian faith with people.

"There does seem to be a growing difficulty for Christians in the country of Gambia," he said.

Mr Fulton helped establish a Gambia branch of the Christian organization Prison Fellowship International. A newsletter published by the Fellowship said Mr Fulton had fallen foul of Gambia's government in the past.

He was "arrested and banned from the prison system" after an inmate complained that he was trying to convert detainees. The Fellowship newsletter reported that Mr Fulton became a Christian while in prison in Britain.

Mr Fulton also served in the British army before becoming a missionary and moving to Gambia with his wife and their two children who now live in England. After being banned from the Gambian prison system Mr Fulton became a military chaplain, a role that may have put him on a collision course with the unpredictable President.

Mr Jammeh is prone to outlandish claims and bouts of paranoia that see alleged plotters thrown in jail.

In recent years the eccentric 43-year old retired colonel claimed to have a secret cure for AIDS – his prescription is a green herbal paste and a diet of bananas. Mr Jammeh has visited the sick and dying waving his hands over their heads and chanting incantations rather than supplying anti-retrovirals.

A United Nations official who questioned the efficacy the President's 'cure' was thrown out of the country.

Rights groups were outraged earlier this year when Mr Jammeh told a rally that he would make the country's ban on homosexuality "tougher than the Iranian laws" and threatened to behead homosexuals giving them 24 hours to leave the country.

The skinny West African state clings to the banks of the river Gambia and its narrow Atlantic coastline dotted with resort hotels has become popular with British holidaymakers seeking a cheap tropical break.

A Foreign Office spokesperson confirmed that two British nationals have been arrested in The Gambia.

# MY PRAYER

In my suffering Lord, help me to enter into your suffering on the cross.

In abandonment and desolation, grant me supernatural faith, hope and love.

When I have been given the Judas kiss, arrested and tortured by extremist Islamist's,

Grant me the consolation of your unconquerable will.

When my fellow missionaries, out of fear and self-preservation say like Peter of old "I don't know this man",

Grant me the gift of forgiveness.

In being beaten, crippled, starved, humiliated, abused and electrocuted, grant me the grace to return hatred and bigotry with love.

When I cry "Let this cup pass from me" and it doesn't, let me respond with your words "not as I will, but as you will."

When my cross is too heavy to carry and they talk about my death, grant me the grace to persevere to the end.

In what seems to be never ending misery, May I never lose sight of you my Lord, my comfort, my strength, my victory,

Amen.

# INTRODUCTION

"Write a book," they said, "a book?" I said, "I don't think so." "Why?" Because some of what I would write will be unthinkable, almost unbelievable. I read once about a Polish Jew, who having escaped from a Nazi concentration camp managed to get to America, to tell them of the atrocities perpetrated against the Jews by the Nazis. He wrote a book that he wanted to use as a platform to tell the world about his experiences, and to warn them, but he wasn't believed and ended up committing suicide. I will not be doing that by the way. If you believe what I say, fine. If you don't, well, that's up to you.

I do understand however, that being so far removed from my experience, that what I (and others) went through, (and indeed are still going through), may be difficult for you to take in. Nevertheless, here I am at, a keyboard taking the first step in what may be a year or two of work, (the first month probably trying to work out how a computer works). I fear that it will be fraught with pain and emotion, saying, what in truth I don't really want the world and its uncle to know. It will put my life, and my family's life under a microscope, and who'd deliberately volunteer to do that? A policeman friend of mine said, "Everyone has skeletons in their cupboard." Would you want yours exposed?

If you're reading this, then I guess I'll have gone ahead with it, for better or for worse. I know this is something I have to do, not just for myself, but also for others. I want to encourage Christians who think they are losing the plot, not making the grade, not living up to what other people expect of them. Christians who have blown it badly and feel that even death is preferable to shame and disgrace, and believe me, I've been there. This is for other Christians who feel dissatisfied with the cards they've been dealt, especially those in a leadership position, whether major or minor and for whom everything seems to be going pear-shaped. One of the problems I have is that in general, I struggle with testimony books. They just don't do it for me. I seem to end up feeling like a second-class Christian.

Equally, I also hope that this book will speak to you if you are not a Christian. Maybe some of you who feel that you are too bad to be shown forgiveness by God will think, "Hey, there is hope for me. If he can get through it with God's help, then so can I"

My life has mostly been lived on the edge. I was born in Scotland, a twin, the eldest of two boys by half an hour. I've been described as an outspoken adventurer and I suppose that's reasonably accurate. I have been many things in my life, but sadly never an intellectual. At school, I wasn't the brightest bulb on the Christmas tree. I am a bit of a loner and very self-reliant. I haven't a lot to be boastful about, but neither does modesty suit me. I've soldiered; I've been a single handed sailor, (but not a candlestick maker).

I've been an armed robber and a prisoner (the two should, and do go together,) and that's when I came to faith in Christ, in prison. I've driven rallies in a Lancia Stratus and driven all over Africa in Range Rovers and Land Rovers. I've scuba dived in the Seychelles and the Caribbean and jumped out of aeroplanes in England, (not using the same equipment I have to say). I've played rugby in Scotland, The Seychelles, Germany and The Gambia and I've skied down mountains in Scotland and Norway. I am a mechanical engineer and a fair cook. I have five children and six grandchildren, although I feel far too young to be a Granddad. I have been married twice, divorced once and have been living for almost twenty-nine years to my, mostly wonderful, long-suffering and resilient wife Fiona, who is not perfect, thank God.

I've just read the last paragraph and it seems to portray me as a perfect six-foot Adonis with a cleft chin, who's never let anyone down and breezes through life with women falling at his feet. Well, let me put the record straight. I'm five foot nine, *Mr Average* and, to my eternal shame, I am sorry to say that I've let plenty of people down in my life. I don't have a cleft chin, (though I've had a broken jaw), and women don't fall at my feet. Personally, I believe they used to see me as a challenge, now they just see '*Me*', and as for the things I've done, I don't claim to have excelled in any, but probably because of my enthusiasm, I score just above average. So I'm no Christian James Bond, OK? Good, I'm glad that's clear.

Many years ago, when Fiona and I were not long married, I found myself called upon to try to talk an Iranian man out of jumping from the roof of the local hospital. Thankfully, he didn't jump, and actually came to stay with us. One thing he said to me that has stuck in my mind was this; "David, it's not the length of your life that's important; it's the breadth of it, and what you can get into it." I remember thinking at the time that he summed up my unspoken, unwritten, unsought philosophy. I've always been a dreamer and I have always followed my dreams, I still do. What a terrible thing it would be: to know, that you have lived all your life, but never followed your dreams.

Anyway, Fiona and I believed that something drew us to go to The Gambia. We'd been there on holiday and felt that even as lone voices, we could make a real difference there. I have to admit to not wanting to leave our "comfort zone". I had a small automotive business and we had our own home in Torquay in Devon, England, which is a beautiful part of the country. We had two children, Iona and Luke, and I guess you could say we were settled and comfortable, and yet, early in 1999 we began preparations to move to Africa. I had flown out to The Gambia, and found land where we would build our house in the village of Kerrsering, (about an hour's drive from the capital Banjul). While I was doing this, Fiona was at home, where she sold our house, which was the last thing holding us back. Therefore, on 10th September, my birthday, after all the preparations were completed, we flew out of London Gatwick, bound for Banjul.

This book is about our time spent in The Gambia, West Africa, and it pulls no punches. It's a country which is 96% Islamic and has one of the worst records of human rights abuses and crimes against humanity in sub-Saharan Africa, and that takes some doing. The dictator President Jammeh is an extremist Muslim and a practitioner in the dark arts, (witchcraft). He is also an international drug baron, trafficking cocaine bought from his friend President Chavez of Venezuela, (now dead), and shipped across the South Atlantic to Guinea Bissau, then by road to The Gambia and on to Holland. This is how he is able to keep the country and his presidency going, using the huge profits from drug money, (told you it pulled no punches!) This report from a Prominent Gambian security officer can attest to this fact:

### BamSerign Mass

**Kibaaro News can today prove with confidence that Gambian President is deeply involved in drug dealing. Malang Saidy, a former officer of the National Drug Enforcement Agency (NDEA), armed Kibaaro News with substantial evidence proving the secrets of President Yahya Jammeh's Bank of Allah.**

It is also well known that he is a gun runner, smuggling guns to the Casamance rebels and fuelling the civil war in that part of Senegal.

We had some great times in The Gambia as well as many scary times, and then at the end, a horrific time. I guess I was living on a pedestal of others making. As a Church leader in The Gambia, a major in the army and a white man, Gambians looked up to me, and as a missionary, people back home in the UK respected me. Everyone had certain expectations of me; however, I am going to be open and honest with you because clearly, like everyone else, I am far from perfect.

I hope you will be able to identify with some the surrealism of what I am about to tell you. You might judge me, and/or empathise with me, but I want to share with you the horrific events of what happened to me during those two years of darkness and onslaught. Therefore, if anything, I hope you believe.

Now, I know what you are thinking, "Will this book put a stop to any chance Dave might have had to star on that popular Islamic TV program, Friday Night at the Mosque?" Well I have to say that it probably will, except for the last episode *"The stoning.* I think that at this point it's good to say that I have many good friends who are Muslims, men and women who are honest, trustworthy, hard working and happy with their lives. It's the extremists who are the evil people, and I guess that applies to the lunatic fringe in any religion and indeed those in any position of power.

I'd like to tell this story just like it is, warts and all. To tell it retrospectively, with my wit, sharper and more defined and as my memory serves, as though I was sitting with you in your lounge, or on a plane, maybe even by your hospital bed. So please enjoy. Be blessed and encouraged.


## NOVEMBER 2008. KERSERRING, THE GAMBIA, WEST AFRICA

That November Saturday morning started like most other mornings in The Gambia. The weather was almost perfect, blue skies, the sun splitting the trees, a nice 36°C, too warm for some, but after a very hot and humid rainy season, 36°C was OK for us. After breakfast, my wife Fiona walked with our two-year-old daughter Elizabeth to visit a friend. She'd have to walk along the dirt tracks to the next village, probably about three miles away. I went upstairs to my office to start preparing for the Sunday service at the Veranda Church where we were joint leaders and which met on our veranda. I was also trying to finish the preparations for my last Christmas service as "Chaplain for the combined armed forces and service personnel of The Gambia", or "CAFASPOTG" for short (only joking). Fiona and Elizabeth were due to fly home to England on the 2nd December to be with our daughter Iona who was expecting her first baby. We were also excited about going out for a meal that evening to celebrate our friend's birthday with them. How easy it was, to be deceived, into thinking that all was well with the world.

I guess I'd been working for about an hour when our dogs started barking and there was a loud hammering and shouting at the outer gate of our half acre compound. Rushing downstairs to see what all the commotion was about, I opened the front door of the house, when the two big, 18ft, compound gates burst in.

Despite Alue, the compound boy's pathetic attempts to keep them closed, a gang of men came streaming through and I recognised some of them as "NIA", which is The Gambia's secret police.

NIA stands for National Intelligence Agency. Now there is an oxymoron for you if I've ever heard one.

Of those who came storming across the compound, four were regular police, one was an Imam, and the rest were NIA (secret police) As they pushed Alue aside and ran towards me, I braced my arms across the front door and shouted, "Show me your warrant". Some of them pulled out side arms and one of them put an automatic pistol to my head and said, "This is my fucking warrant."

Now, when someone pulls a gun out a gun or a knife, threateningly in familiar surroundings, "i.e." a safe environment, it produces instant shock, (or so I'd once been told). A person's body temperature, blood pressure and muscle tone all crash and a disabling paralysis results", not at all like one sees on TV. Well that's exactly what happened to me. In retrospect, I am embarrassed that I only put up a token resistance, trying to stop them entering the house by standing in the doorway to block their way.

I knew the Secret police had been following me and there was always the chance that this sort of thing might happen. Indeed, I'd dealt with two attempts on my life before, and by God's grace I'd dealt with them successfully, but I guess this was so totally unexpected in my own home. I'm no stranger to guns, I had five guns of my own, two .22 rifles, a Remington 12 bore repeater shotgun, a 4 10 shotgun and a Walther PPK side-arm. In fact, truth be told, I've always loved guns (it's a man thing ladies), but when they were being pointed at me I was beginning to develop this love/hate relationship.

There were nine of them, excluding, the Imam who was the chief spiritual Islamic leader in the Gambian Islamic Council, and who was obviously in charge. They carried an assortment of weapons that they were nervously pointing in my general direction. What they had to be nervous about beats me; they were the ones with the guns.

I was forced at gunpoint to sit in our lounge where my shock

28

turned to stubbornness and I couldn't help but notice that the men were looking about them in awe at the interior of the house. While to us it was just nice, to them it would appear like something out of *"Homes and Gardens."* I think that got them even more angry and they started shouting at me that I was exploiting Gambians, that I was only here to make money and to bring down the government. I was grateful that Fiona and Elizabeth weren't in the house, because it was becoming a bit ugly.

Things were really getting out of hand and they were taking it in turns to try to slap me. It seemed to make matters worse that I was just sitting there fending them off and smiling! Yep! Smiling! You see, I honestly didn't think I'd done anything wrong, because I hadn't. The secret police had arrested me several times before, and released me without charge, simply because there was no charge they could level against me.

Two of the police officers stood before me with guns pointed while the others ransacked the house. After about an hour, they brought into the lounge: my uniform, guns, and a load of A4 sheets they had printed from my computer. There were about one hundred of them and they were selected emails that I had sent over the last few years to family and friends. "Sedition, sedition" the Imam started to shout and the others took up the chant, "Sedition, sedition."

I said I had to go to the toilet and was taken there by an ordinary policeman whom I knew. "Want to join me?" I said, as he put his foot in the door I was trying to close. "No sir," he replied, "I just don't want you to escape." "I promise not to, how's that?" I said and he withdrew his foot. Locking the door, I sat on the toilet seat and texted Fiona: "Come home, the police are here, but as far as they are concerned, you are just a housewife and mother. Deny everything." I remember a bit of information I was given a thousand years ago, "If ever one finds oneself in this sort of situation then deny, deny, deny."

I flushed the toilet and returned to the lounge. They had placed the guns on the sofa and I half expected them to accuse me of some firearms offence, but they said nothing. I'm sure they already knew they were legal and I had the correct documentation.

It was then, probably at about 11am, that Fiona and Elizabeth arrived back at the house. Fiona was surprisingly calm and laid back. She sat down with me and after a chat together; they took us to a police station, about four miles away. During the interrogation, they asked us to write a statement, but all I did was copy some of the emails, which they put in front of me. I still couldn't see where all this was leading, the emails were just letters to friends and family asking for prayer, nothing about inciting any coup attempt, even though I could have been involved in one if I'd wanted. It seemed to me that they were losing interest when the Imam said, "Take them to Banjul police station" We were herded into the back of an old Renault car with two policemen, never to see our home again.

Half an hour later, we arrived at Banjul. They took us to the "serious crime" office, and told us, that we were going to be there until further notice. Our friend and fellow church leader John came with some food (as none is supplied), and despite not having much of an appetite, we ate what we could and kept the rest for breakfast. They produced a thin mattress, and we settled down for the night. I felt sorry for Elizabeth, although at two years old she thought it was great fun to be sleeping on the floor with mum and dad. We spent most of the night fending off mosquitoes and trying to guess what the morning would bring. As Fiona and I talked, we truly believed that this was at the least a misunderstanding and at the most, something that would pass over in a short time, and so after praying together we managed to fall asleep.

Well, morning came, as mornings do, and as it was a Sunday, nothing much happened until about midday. Then two men came and told me to give my wife enough money to buy some food as they were taking me away for further questioning, but I would be back soon. I gave her about 300 Dalasi and was bundled into the same old Renault and taken to the NIA headquarters. I wasn't to see Fiona and Elizabeth again until we appeared in court some days later. I say some days because, from that time till the time I managed to get out of captivity my nightmare began, and the word time had little or no meaning.

# THE BEGINNING

They took me to NIA headquarters. They started to question me about an abortive coup attempt in 2006, and another in 2008, both of which I knew about. Actually, I could have taken part in both, but thankfully at the time was able to resist the temptation. However, the coup plotters were all senior army or immigration officers, people I knew well because of my involvement with the military, and my role as chaplain, so of course my mobile number was on all of their phones. The questioning was quite easy when it started, and I said nothing. Then this one particular senior officer came in, stood behind me and said, "You are charged with sedition." Then to the others, "beat the shit out of him until he signs a confession." I turned around in my chair, and this was the moment, (looking back), that I realised that this was not just a bad dream. It wasn't going to go away. In fact, it was probably going to get worse. Not one man, but two had come in. The first, who had given the order, was a brute of a man, and quite fair in complexion for a Gambian. His name was Hydria. He was second in command of the secret police. The other was an Imam. This fellow I'd see plenty of over the next two years. I nicknamed him "Bin Ladin." His face was twisted and pockmarked, and later when I was being tortured, he was *always* there, and he was *always* smiling. Now, I have to say that this man had some ugly smile. He was unshaven, and had teeth so bad that they looked like a row of condemned houses. All in all, he was not a pretty sight.

They cuffed me with my hands behind my back, threw me on my face in the office, and proceeded to put me in leg irons, which are similar to handcuffs but went round the ankles with about twelve inches of chain so that the wearer, in this instance me, could slowly shuffle along. They took me down a flight of concrete stairs, at the bottom of which, was a small area lit by a single candle. I assumed that either the electricity had failed again, or they were doing their bit towards combating global warming.

They took me to a cell called "Babba Dinka," which in the local language means "*the crocodile pit*". They removed my bonds and told me to strip off my clothes and give them my wristwatch. "Not in this lifetime fella," I said. "Quiet," the big guy shouted. He started to hit me with a baton and beat me to the ground. The two men who had brought me there proceeded to give me a kicking. I curled up on the filthy concrete floor in the foetal position to protect my delicate bits. "OK, OK" I shouted, before they really started to enjoy themselves. As they opened a cell door, the stench that escaped out of it was so bad that even the guards took an involuntary step back.

They threw me into the cell, naked as the day I was born. I was in total darkness, but I wasn't alone. There were a number of other men, well I assumed they were men, none of whom I could see but could hear breathing, coughing and groaning. No one spoke when I arrived. "Salam Alykum" I said. There was no response. "Hullo?" Nothing. I felt along the wall by the door and bumped into someone who grunted and pushed me away. "Sorry fella," I said, "didn't see you there." That came as no surprise as I couldn't see my hand in front of my face. "How many are here?" I asked. "Shhhh!" The sound came from someone next to me and a voice whispered, "The cell's bugged." Now, that I knew already, as I could feel that there were cockroaches crawling over my feet and mosquitoes were buzzing about at full volume. I whispered back, "Ok, I understand," but not understanding in the least.

Finding a place to sit, I nursed my wounds until I could stand the stupidity of it no longer. Groping along the wall at head height, (feeling somewhat vulnerable it has to be said), I found the door. "Guard, guard, let me out, I want to talk with your boss." "Shhhhhhh" was all the response I got, and that from inside the cell. They didn't come and my impatience grew, but then, patience had never been one of my strong points.

The time dragged by and I must have slept a little, because when I awoke there was a stirring that seemed to denote a new day, but because of the total darkness I never knew. Again, I began to bang on the door and again, was ignored by those outside and castigated by those inside. Eventually, someone came, and dragged me out into the passageway. They put me back in handcuffs and leg irons, and led up the stairs and along the corridor . . . still naked. "Why don't you give me my clothes back?" I asked, but they only clouted me on the back of my head for my troubles. They took me into another office where they made me stand in front of a desk, empty, except for what looked like the world's oldest PC. The buff coloured plastic was dark and dirty and the vents at the back were so black, it looked like it ran on diesel. I stood there for about ten minutes before the powers that be, deemed to see me. On the wall clock, it said 9.15, but I didn't know if that was am or pm. I guessed that it was probably Monday morning and that maybe things were moving forward.

Yes! In came the boss man and threw my watch on the desk. He told the guards to free my wrists and legs. My clothes, they dumped at my feet. He spoke in Jolla, his native language. "Take him to the toilet and get him cleaned up."

*"Ah! Progress"* I thought as they pushed me out of the office and into a small filthy local toilet, (a hole in the floor), with a broken sink and a bucket of water. To my surprise, on the sink were my own razor and a bar of good soap. The kind Fiona buys, (please make a mental note of this, as the detectives among you will see the significance of it later.) Maybe Fiona has returned home, and she's sent these things in. I thought that was encouraging.

# FIRST COURT APPEARANCE

Sure enough once I was dressed and presentable again I was taken out to a pickup, the very one that I knew had been following me for the past few years. They bundled me in and we headed to town. "Where are we going?" I asked, "Home?" "Shut up" the guy on the right shouted in my ear. Well, I guess there wasn't time for any more conversation as we pulled up outside the main police station which is next to the court. Again, I was bundled out of the pickup and into the midst of a crowd of people. There was also a gaggle of reporters. A gaggle? Is that what you call a group of noisy, nosy reporters? Well, whatever the case, there were television cameras, reporters, and photographers; as the Americans say, "The whole nine yards." Thankfully, though I could also see some friendly faces: people from the Veranda Church, both black and white, as well as some local Muslim friends, folks we knew who were just concerned for us.

They led me into the police station where I was reunited with Fiona and Elizabeth. They were in the same clothes they'd been wearing when we were taken into custody, so I realised that they had not been released and had been with the police since Saturday. Fiona and Elizabeth came running up and hugged me. During the hug Fiona said, "We've been charged with Sedition but we're innocent." "I know," I replied, "but I'm not sure that makes a lot of difference." "Well, we plead not guilty" she went on, "but we have to get a lawyer." Now this was going to be easier said than done. The British High Commission came up with a list of lawyers. A policeman friend of ours was there to support us and allowed me to use his mobile phone to contact some of them. One Christian lawyer whom I knew quite well was in London . . . great! The next was another Christian lawyer who was at another court in the same building. I can't mention his name as he's still there, but when he came to see us and read the charges he was too scared to take the case on and whispered in my ear, "They'll kill me, or disappear me." The poor man was shaking with fear. "OK, no problem," I assured him, but in reality, it was a problem.

At last, someone who we thought was a friend, managed to get in touch with a man, believed to be the best lawyer in The Gambia, Antaman Gaye. He was in another court, but said that he would come to see us as soon as he was able. We waited probably about two hours with relative freedom and Fiona, Elizabeth, (who by now had realised that something was wrong) and I clung onto each other. Fiona desperately worried about me, and I, desperately worried about Fiona and Elizabeth. Everyone wanted to see us and talk to us, but we only wanted to be with each other. We did though thank those who came to see us, and passed out instructions as to who to contact and what they could do for us.

All too soon, they took us out of the police station to the magistrate's court, which was in the building next door. The street was bustling with people, which is typical of most African towns. We made our way over the storm drains, pushing through market stalls selling everything from bananas to used car parts. The local press were there with their old-fashioned cameras clicking away.

Almost thankfully, we pushed our way into the old colonial style building and up a set of stairs to the courtroom. Fiona and I had to stand in the dock with Elizabeth. They read out the charge to the crowded courtroom, namely; the publication, supposedly by us, of "sixty seven seditious emails' criticising the President and the government. The magistrate then asked us "how do you plead?" "Not guilty" I replied. "Not guilty" repeated Fiona. I looked at Elizabeth who Fiona was holding. She said nothing.

Our lawyer stood and said that he hadn't had time to look into the case and applied for an adjournment which the magistrate granted. "One week from today," he announced and abruptly stood up and left. Antaman Gaye came to see us and more or less assured us that the case against us would not get far. He called it a nonsense charge and we had to agree there. Little did we know whose side he was on. They then took me back through the gaggle, to the pickup, and this time I had a longer journey to Central Prison, the notorious "Mile Two."

# MILE TWO

Mile Two! The name still sends shivers down my spine especially when I think of the Confinement wing which houses all the "special prisoners"; convicted, unconvicted, detained without trial, political, life and death sentence men. Good men who dared to stand up for what is right, who told the truth about the Dictator Jammeh and are languishing even now. If they incarcerated a dog in here, it would be dead within a month.

Fiona and I had worked in Mile Two prison from 2000 to 2005: I was the Chaplain for the prison service and Executive Director of the fledgling "Prison Fellowship the Gambia" which we were instrumental with others in starting. Fiona worked as a volunteer teacher in the female wing in Mile Two, and the juvenile wing at Joshwang prison and as Executive Secretary of Prison Fellowship. We also took Church services in the three prisons in The Gambia, the third of which was in the interior. I never understood why we were never allowed into Mile Two confinement wing, but now I knew. Anyway, when I went through what is laughingly called reception, I was stripped of my belt, watch, wedding ring, my shoelaces and then as an afterthought, my shoes. I can only imagine that this was in case I tried to bribe my way out with the gold ring, failing that, garrotte myself with the shoe laces, hang myself with the belt or kick myself to death with my shoes whilst timing the whole thing with my watch.

I digress. In reality, nothing prepared me for the horror of the confinement wing. My guards and I approached the rusty steel door set into a fifteen-foot concrete wall topped with razor wire. Obviously, they were watching us as the door swung open at the first knock. The sandy ground was wet, dirty and stank to high heaven, and as we walked further in, I noticed that a septic tank was overflowing. "Shit," I said and one of the guards turned round and said "Yes" and we moved on. There were three concrete cellblocks, and they took me to block number five, (that has you confused, doesn't it), well, me too. It could only happen in The Gambia, but I was in cellblock number five, the worst one. Technically, I was on remand, and should have been entitled to remand privileges such as they were, but I hadn't counted on David Colley.

"Who's David Colley," I hear you ask. Well David Colley is, or was, the Director of Prisons for The Gambia, and I was his arch-enemy. Back in 2002, I reported him to the Minister of Interior for sexually abusing a Christian female officer. In 2005 I took up the case of thirty seven men in the remand wing who had been in prison from between nine and twelve years without seeing the inside of a courtroom. The result was that I went with the DPP (Director of Public Prosecutions), and the Chief Justice, (both Nigerian Christians), and thirty-seven men walked out of there, depriving David Colley of 70 Dalasi per day or D2, 100 per month. For each man, that equated to D77, 700 per month, or D932400 every year for all thirty-seven men. At that time the Dalasi was D31 to the pound, so he'd be losing over £300,000 a year, most of which went into his pocket. Let's just say he was well ticked off!

Despite having a Christian name "David" he was about as much a Christian as Attila the Hun was, in fact he called himself a "chrismuss", half-Christian, half Muslim, depending on who was giving charity to the prison at the time.

Now where was I? Ah, yes . . . Mile Two. They weighed and measured me, 196 lbs; height 5ft 9ins, "looks fit" pronounced as medically fit.

# HOME

After reception I was taken to the filthy stinking cell block number five and like the inner sanctum of the temple is the Holy of Holy's, so this was the smelliest of smellies, the inner sanctum of Mile Two's confinement wing. There were three passageways dimly lit with three 40w bulbs, and with cells on either side. The cells on the two outer rows had windows, the rest didn't have any light or ventilation save a barred hole in the door about 1ft square. They took me to the end of the centre row, and told me to strip. I'm not saying that I was used to it, but I knew better than to argue and others I'd seen while walking through the confinement were naked. So after stripping off my clothes and putting them on a nail in the wall in front of the cell we had stopped at, the officer got out a rope of keys (one hundred and ninety, I learned later), and tried what seemed like every one in the padlock. It was then that I noticed that eight of the doors, four on each side of the passageway, were smaller than the rest and had no grill in the door, but before I could speculate further, the guard found a key to fit my padlock and opened up. "Get in," he ordered and I ducked my head and entered what was to be my home for almost the next two years.

I crouched through the doorway into the cell and stood up banging my head on the ceiling, I couldn't stand up straight. The cell was only about five foot high, but as I turned to complain, the door slammed shut in my face and I was in total darkness . . . total darkness, not a chink or a crack of light anywhere.

Now, there are three things that intimidate me in life: The first is being alone with a beautiful woman that I don't know. The second is a fear of heights. Not flying though, I've even been trained and piloted a light aircraft with no problems, but standing on the edge of a cliff or looking out of the window of a skyscraper makes my stomach do somersaults and I experience vertigo. I'm also terrified of confined spaces and that I have to confess to experiencing panic then, just a little. No, that's not true. I panicked quite a lot!

I hammered, kicked, punched and thumped on the door. I shouted for the guard to let me out. Always the eternal optimist, that's me. When nothing happened, I calmed down and tried to assess my situation. I was naked but stifling hot. The smell in the cell was disgusting, urine and excrement, and the foul air was rank and damp. It was so thick it could almost be tasted, tangible, choking. I started to crawl around the cell. There was excreta everywhere, and it wasn't long before I was covered with it. The walls were dripping in slime. The cell was six feet long by four feet wide and five feet high. There was what seemed in the darkness, to be an old 2.5 litre paint tin, which I assumed, was the toilet. There was an old one-gallon oil container with water in it and as I groped around, I managed to find a nail in the wall, there was nothing more, no seat, no bunk, no mattress, no blanket, no nothing. I could hear however I wasn't alone, there were rats scurrying about the cell in the darkness. How many I didn't know, but one rat is a rat too many as far as I was concerned, and then I was bitten on my bum, and what is euphemistically called my private parts. Ants . . . Biting ants, the floor was alive with them. I jumped up and bashed my head on the roof again. "Shit" I roared, and groped my way to the door again. "Is there anyone there?" I shouted, banging on the metal door. I was starting to get angry; there didn't seem to be an upside to this place. However, at least I wasn't in a cell with a 6ft 6ins black man called "Big Bubba" as a cell mate, who wanted to be my *special friend.*

I felt there was no use getting my knickers in a twist. I needed to do something positive and the first thing was to clean up this place. I found the water container and set about cleaning the floor using my hands to sweep the water and excreta from the back of the cell towards the door. Even though no light came in through the bottom of the door, I was sure the water was going out, as it seemed to recede carrying the dirt and ants with it. It turned out that there was another plus to my cleaning. The water, (about a gallon), lay in puddles on the corridor floor and the guards were not amused. I could hear shouting (in the local language) and then the rattle of keys as someone painfully went through every key trying to open padlock. After about five minutes, the door swung open and a senior officer was standing behind the guard. He was a small, dapper man. His uniform was clean, but he was standing in what had come out of my cell and he wasn't a happy bunny. "Fulton, what are you doing?" he shouted. Just "spring-cleaning" I replied. "I thought about having a little get together here tonight with some friends." "Look at this mess," he said, pointing at the passageway. "No problem," said I, "just as soon as I finish the cell I'll clean up out there." I really thought that would earn me a slap, but he said to the guard, "Let him clean up if he wants to," and marched away as if he was on parade. Well, I thought, what do you know, round one to me? Wrong! As soon as the senior officer was out the way, the door slammed shut, and I was back in the darkness again, this time with no water.

I had a week until the next court appearance and I hadn't a clue what was going to happen now, no idea about feeding times, when or if I could shower; empty what they euphemistically called my *Chamber Pot* and so on. What I could do though . . . was pray and think, and so that's what I did. The praying was OK, but the thinking wasn't easy. Far too many negative thoughts for my liking and in some ways I had the worst cellmate imaginable . . . myself. I went over and over the events of the past few days and couldn't see anything I could have done which would have altered the situation for the better. However, that didn't make me feel any happier. There was a noise at the cell door. I thought that it would open soon after, but instead there was a grating of metal and a hatch at the bottom of the door, which I hadn't noticed before slid up. I was there like a shot, but before I could say anything, someone pushed a steel bowl through, and the hatch shut again. I picked up the bowl and realised that this was food and that I was hungry.

There were no eating utensils, and filth covered my hands, so I guessed it was back to basics. I wiped my hands on my hair to clean them as best as I could, and I probed into the bowl with my fingers. There was boiled rice and what felt like a small fish head, probably about the size of a mackerel's head and that was it. *Hmm,* there'll probably be something else soon, I thought. Wrong again! Getting things wrong was going to be the norm for me for a long time to come. I started by picking at the rice which hadn't been cleaned prior to boiling and still had gravel and God knows what else in it. I felt my way round the fish head and I really couldn't manage to eat it. My stomach started heaving, so I just ate the rice. After about fifteen minutes the hatch opened again "bowl," demanded a voice, then a moment later, "bowl." "I haven't finished," I said through the hatch. "Pass out your bowl now, or there won't be any food for you tomorrow," came the reply. "*Tomorrow*", I thought. "*Tomorrow*," surely there will be more before tomorrow." I told you there'd be plenty of "wrongs", and this thought was another one; because it looked like I'd been fed for the day. Anyway, I passed the half-eaten food out and the hatch slid down with a grating noise.

I had a feeling that this was going to be a long and lonely day and night, as I settled down on the rough concrete floor now thankfully clear of biting ants, and I tried to recall some of the emails that had gotten us into this mess, and why anyone could have taken offence at them. I don't know if I slept or I reminisced, but my mind went back to the time when I took an inspection team of three Immigration officers with me into the interior, I was going to an immigration outpost to do an Alpha course.

The Alpha course could be described as, "*an introduction to Christianity.*" I used it a lot when talking to Muslims about my faith. It is non-threatening, just putting forward the Christian perspective. I firmly believe that people should know the alternatives (and I believe the Christian Bible to be the truth). Sadly, in my opinion, the indoctrination of many people, since birth, has been into a religion that is at odds with the Bibles message of love and forgiveness. I believe that as adults these people should be in a position to make their own decisions.

# MORE THAN AN INSPECTION TRIP
## August 2006

I remembered we all met up at Denton Bridge at about 6am to catch the tide. After we'd been under way for about half an hour, sailing east into a spectacular sunrise, the Deputy Director of Immigration came up to the flying bridge. I could see that he was in awe of the Nautilus. She was my 45ft steel hulled boat, which

I used to go up the river Gambia into the interior and to the immigration posts. "This is so wonderful," he said, "I can see why you love our country so much."

The tide was with us even though we were on the river. The River Gambia is saline for about one hundred miles inland and tidal all its length. It's often like an inland sea, sometimes more than ten miles wide and the incoming tide is faster than the current going down. The weather was perfect with a breeze from the stern. I was in shorts and t-shirt while the others were in uniform. This is an anomaly about The Gambia and indeed about many African countries. There are so many service men and women all in uniform whether on or off duty. I think it's an authority thing.

There was nothing to do but enjoy the trip and spectacular it was. The sun was rising in the east over the bow pulpit, dispersing the morning mist that hung like a curtain over the river. The wildlife was awakening to the crisp new dawn, the freshest time of the day. Then the sun arose in its full strength, the heat was a taste of what was to come from the cloudless sky. Sometimes, I'd go below to the galley, and make tea and cheese sandwiches. (If I'd been selfish I'd have done ham sandwiches with a glass of wine and have had it all to myself). After about fourteen hours steaming, we left the main river and headed up a tributary (locally known as a bolong) as far as Nautilus could go without running out of water. She has a draft of 1.5 metres and the tide was quite high, but wasn't full when we dropped anchor in the tributary with the mangroves ten metres on either side. This meant we had about eight hours to get to the outpost in the small tender (which was my mission), and back before the ebb tide left us high and dry.

From the stern of the *Nautilus,* the immigration officers helped me load the tender with an old TV set, 20ltrs of petrol, a 2.5kva generator, and a video player with tapes. About 10 bottles of drinking water and my 12 bore Remington Repeater shotgun with cartridge belt. If this happened in the UK we'd probably have been arrested on terrorism charges, but this was Africa and if there had been anyone watching (which was unlikely in the mangrove swamps) they'd probably have shrugged their shoulders and thought it was another coup. Lastly, I changed into my uniform and strapped my Walther PPK side arm on, *the name's Fulton, Dave Fulton*. We cast off from the Nautilus and headed through the narrow bolongs that feed the main river. It's an almost magical experience. I've done it scores of times and I never fail to be enchanted by the birds in the mangroves and the fish jumping for flies and mosquitoes on the surface of the water. The bolong meanders its way to the river from the Casamance and only experience keeps me from a wrong turn, which would lead us up a dead end or onto a sandbar, and in the early days, I often did. The trip in the 16ft tender is about ten nautical miles and my passengers were now just starting to relax. Like most Gambians, they can't swim and feel vulnerable in a small boat. This wasn't the time to mention Crocs or Hippos, but while I had one hand on the tiller throttle of the 15hp outboard engine, the other was cradling the 12 bore on my lap, which was loaded with my home-filled solid shot cartridges. The Bolong narrowed until it was only eight feet wide and we started to attract plenty of mosquitoes and tsetse fly. They swarmed above us like kamikaze pilots diving to their certain death, but determined to inflict damage before they died. One day, I'm going to ask God why He created these insects.

The bolong turned sharply to the right and suddenly widened into a small keyhole lake with a village and outpost at the far side. There were about fifteen mud and grass houses, and a more solid wooden structure, which was the immigration post (Outpost 4), and a wood and corrugate shop with a faded Coca Cola sign. There were three dugout canoes drawn up onto the mud, with nets hung on a bamboo fish drying rack behind them. The immigration post was there first, and then would come a few of their wives and children, followed by fishermen to supply the post with food, and of course they would bring their wives and children. There would be a foreign trader ready to start a shop supplying rice, soap, sugar, green tea, candles and cheap batteries for the Chinese radios that found in every far-flung village in West Africa.

My first impression when I saw this outpost and village four years ago was "that it was like something from the film Out of Africa." Now as then, about twenty or more naked children rushed screaming and shouting excitedly into the water to greet the boat. Men and women stood to watch and the immigration officers were scurrying about to tidy themselves up at the sight of the top brass in my boat. I became aware that the screaming had changed, not only in volume, but also from excitement to terror. I knew instinctively that it was a croc; the children were scrabbling and fighting with each other to get out of the water. I had just cut and tilted the outboard motor to beach the tender and was kneeling on the stern seat while the boat was moving towards the beach under its own momentum. I lifted the Remington and cocked it, nothing was to be seen, but that's the way with crocs.

Just then, we ran onto the mud bank. I kept my balance with the gun ready, but still nothing. All the children were out and the adults were looking for the menace. Everything went quiet. It was as if even the forest creatures were holding their breath. Then about fifteen feet away there was a swirl of muddy water and a long V-shaped wake and it was gone. While we unloaded, the tender one of the immigration men stood guard with an AK 47, not that there was much chance of the croc returning, but it looked good for the inspection team. They went on to do their rounds, but I have the impression that they were just glad to be out of the boat and on to dry land and that a cigarette and some attaya (green tea) were all they had really wanted.

I set up the TV and video with the help of the men from the village while the rest got out their mobile phones and 12v battery charger for when I started the generator. Everything would be recharged during the two and a half hours that the genny would be running even the small freezer in the local shop would be cool for a while. While it was nice to help the villagers and it was a good PR exercise, my reason for being there was to explain Christianity and to preach to the Gambian service men and women, and over the years, I found the Alpha course a wonderful tool. I visited sixteen outposts up and down the country, all of them, only accessible by boat from the river. We started the genny, and switched the TV on under the shade of a mango tree

44

for everyone to watch. It's in English which suited the service men and women, but the villagers watched it as well. What can I say? I think it summed it up for me when I saw one man look at Nicky Gumble's image on the screen, then look round behind the TV and with a puzzled expression on his face said, "Its witchcraft".

I ran through three sessions of Alpha, which pleased the shop-keeper and those who were charging batteries. Over the next three hours, I had the privilege to lead twelve men to faith in Christ. It wouldn't be easy for them, so I didn't make it easy for them to make that commitment. I told them that their families would most probably disown them, their wives and children taken from them and I've known some men to be stoned (with proper boulders). If they were going to give their lives to the Lord, then it had to be 100% or not at all. It couldn't be because they felt emotional, not because it seemed a good idea, not because a white man suggested it, but the real McCoy. That afternoon twelve men entered the kingdom of light from the kingdom of darkness.

Time was getting on and there is no saying more true than "*time and tide waits for no man*". We had to go, and go now. All the equipment was loaded on board the tender and when the D.I.G. and the two officers and I were in, the men pushed us out into deep water, where I lowered the outboard and pulled the starter rope. It started first time and with the tiller hard over we turned around and headed for the narrow channel. Again, I cradled the 12 bore on my lap; my concern was about hippos. Most people don't realise that hippos kill more people in Africa than any other animal and they're very territorial. We entered a narrow stretch of water with no room to turn nowhere to run. "Keep the 12 bore handy" said a little voice in my head.

With no time to waste, we headed for the Nautilus at about ten knots. "Won't be long now," I said, but just then there was a bang and the piston came out through the block. Now I don't know how many of you are technically minded, but let me assure you that this was not good. In fact, it was terminal: very terminal. There was a pregnant pause. "Oops," I said, "now this could be a problem. Nevertheless, we had two paddles, and only about eight miles to go, plus the tide was with us going out . . . *Easy*. What I didn't say was that we only had two and a half hours to do it in, or the outgoing tide would leave the Nautilus high and dry, so we had to get our fingers out and get a move on. There was a whimper from one of the men and he was pointing into the water. Crocs, and biggish ones at that. I explained that if we kept paddling fast it would keep the crocs away. In reality, I hadn't a clue how it would work, but it was better than drifting down slowly.

There's nothing like a couple of crocs watching you, licking their lips and deciding what wine to have with black meat, or whether to have the white man for dessert to focus the mind. The paddles were going so fast that I wondered if we'd have gone much faster even if the outboard was working. We took turn about with the paddles, ten minutes on and ten minutes off, but it was always going to be touch and go as to whether we reached the Nautilus in time before she grounded out at low tide. However, as she hove into view she was still swinging from the anchor.

"Make for the stern ladder," I shouted, as I made my way towards the bow. I went forward carefully as the crocs were still circling us like Red Indians round a wagon train. Slinging the gun over my shoulder, I took the bow rope. "As soon as I make fast, I'll go on board and get her started and into deep water, if you guys can transfer the stuff into the big boat that would be great." I tied up to the stern ladder, climbed aboard heading for the wheelhouse. As I was unlocking the saloon door, there was an almighty scream. *Shit,* I thought *the crocs have someone*! Leaving the door, I readied the shotgun and raced back aft. I couldn't believe what I saw; I took it in at a glance. One of the immigration officers was hanging backwards with his leg trapped through the two top rungs of the ladder. He had one hand holding the rail and the other holding the generator. The two officers in the tender were trying to take the weight of the generator, but there wasn't enough room in the bow and with everything and everybody forward the water was lapping in and the crocs were wringing their hands in anticipation." "Permission to abandon the generator sir?" he said, I just could not believe it; it was like something out of a comedy. "Let the bloody thing go," I shouted, (I just can't imagine myself saying, "permission granted)" and he did. It fell back into the tender on top of the two who were struggling to take its weight, and the lot fell into the thwarts of the tender and thank God not straight through the hull. I threw the gun on the aft cabin roof, and grabbed the man and hauled him up. "Shit," (and I am sorry for the language, but I'm just telling it like it happened, so,) "*Shit,*" I thought, "*this is a bummer.*" "Hey you guys get your arses up here and see to your mate." As they were sorting themselves out I quickly took in the amount of blood that had saturated the man's trousers and of course as he'd been hanging upside down it looked to me that his upper leg and groin area was worst affected. "Cut his trousers off," I shouted as the others were scrambling on to the deck, "I've got to get the boat into deep water"

Quick as a flash, I was on the flying bridge starting the engine and raising the anchor at the same time. As soon as the hook was clear of the water I pushed the throttle full forward. "Bugger," (this seemed to bring out all the wrong, but descriptive words in me) she wasn't moving. Reverse full, forward full, reverse full, we were slowly moving, muddy water everywhere, but she was dragging herself into deep water, yes! It only took a minute to find two fathoms of water where I dropped the anchor, cut the engine and dug out the first aid box. Making my way aft, I was appalled to find the deck awash with blood, and the DIG and his sergeant looking down at their moaning comrade. They had cut his trouser leg off and the blood was pouring onto my recently painted deck (no consideration, youngsters these days). He was lying on his back with his left leg extended and the shinbone was sticking out from his leg through a large triangular flap of skin, just like the piston on the outboard. Therefore, to prevent any more mess on my deck, I took off my belt and used it as a tourniquet on his upper leg and almost immediately, the blood slowed down to a seep.

You didn't need to be a Harley Street surgeon to know that it was a compound fracture, which was a good job, as I wasn't one. I wasn't even a back-street one. Anyway, something had to be done, and done quickly. He was moaning with the pain and I could empathise, as a few years previously I had a compound fracture to my left arm while playing rugby. OK, a moment to consolidate, look at options and see what's to be done. We were about twelve hours from the nearest medical centre, which is the problem with bush work. I believed that a tourniquet just wouldn't be good enough for that amount of time; even working it slack to let the blood flow and tight to stop it. It didn't seem to me that the artery was severed, just a lot of veins at and around the damage, where the skin and flesh was torn. *Right,* I decided, *it'll have to be a DIY job.*

This would require the full medical kit, but *my* full medical kit wasn't much to write home about. However, I did have a doctor with me, and a wonderful instruction manual. Opening the locker in the galley I took out a half bottle of Dr. Johnnie Walker's Black Label, a first aid box and a book called *"Where there is no doctor."* Once upon a time, many years ago, I trained as a Paramedic. You know the kind of thing, stitching up knife wounds, digging out bullets, splinting stuff that needs splinting, sticking needles in people just the common stuff . . . nothing out of the ordinary, but this one did present a bit of a challenge. The guy's leg was a mess, and he had lost, (by the look of my deck), quite a bit of blood. He was in shock, and as I said before, it was bush work.

The first thing to do was get the bone back where it should be, "are you allergic to alcohol?" I asked. He rolled his eyes upwards, which I took to be a no. "OK", I said, "let's do it anyway." I opened the bottle and put it to his lips and he took a mouthful, gagged, coughed, but like a good Muslim licked his lips so none would be wasted. I, (against every Scottish instinct) poured some (sparingly) over the wound. "OK," I said to the two officers whom were looking at me aghast, (Muslim to the core) "you hold him under the arms and you grab his left ankle." Having done this, I asked the DIG to "pull." There was a scream and he fainted, (the patient that is, not the DIG) best thing all round really. I tried to push the bone back into place, but it just wouldn't go. "Come on," I shouted! "Pull!" but still nothing.

Now, at this point, maybe it would be good to paint the picture a little clearer. The temperature was about 37°C, humidity was high, flies were swarming about us and the blood, in clouds so thick that I thought there was an eclipse of the sun. The sweat was pouring off our bodies and the crocs were hugging themselves in anticipation and enjoying the starter of blood that was running off the deck into the water. We're not talking sterile conditions here. Anyway, try as we might, there was no getting the bone back, they pulled, I pushed, but it just wouldn't go. So I prayed.

"Ahh," I hear you say, "Shouldn't you have done that first?" Well there's always a smart arse who, sitting in their civilized lounge, in their civilized country, sipping a civilized cup of coffee, that has all the answers. Anyway, I prayed, and into my mind came something I read in a book a long time ago and if my memory served me right it for use only in extreme situations. Now on a scale from one to ten, how extreme was this? Hmm? I'd say 9.99 recurring. I turned to my operating theatre staff, and with a "back in a minute" ran along the deck, through the saloon and into the galley, where I grabbed two towels and a long screwdriver. I immersed the towels in the sink, which was full of water and rushed up onto the deck again. The patient was still out for the count, and the deck was still awash with blood and my two helpers were still in exactly the same position as I left them. I know my mind should have been more focused, but I stopped and stared, looked and looked again, it was as if time had stood still, with only the things in my hand to prove that I'd ever left them a moment ago, weird.

Anyway, I said, "OK, we do this once and for all." I made a thick pad out of the smaller of the two towels and placed it on his leg over the protruding bone, and then taking the other towel, I wrapped it round the leg encompassing the pad. Inserting the long screwdriver through the outer towel, I wound it taught with the screwdriver. "Now pull," I shouted. "Pull or he'll be a cripple for life. *He'll probably end up one anyway*," I thought. I turned the screwdriver until the pressure of the pad was bearing down on the bone and I kept turning. Click. Was that it . . . Just a click? The sweat was dripping off our faces; it seemed too easy after the earlier struggle. "Is that it?" the DIG asked. "Don't know," I said, "best we have a look," and I started unwrapping the towel and peeled it from the wound. Plainly, for all to see the bone was back where it should be and we were euphoric. They warmly patted my back, but I shrugged off the congratulations, "Thank God" I said, "not me, modest or what?

It wasn't long before I got him stitched and splinted. Hospital was still a priority, but there was time to sit on the deck amid blood and water and finish the whisky between us. Dr J Walker working another wonder, forging a temporary truce between Christian and Muslim and sealing a friendship that was to last years, not to mention a job well done.

We got under way and I made a call on the radio for a medi-vac, but it was another nine hours before an army Land Rover met us at a village jetty and took our man away for further treatment. I wanted to go on into the interior, but the others were having withdrawal symptoms from excitement and opted to return. They were now stressed to the point of wanting more whisky, and that was my cue to capitulate, (I'd only one bottle left).

There was no hurry on the way back, and it was a good job as nothing was in our favour. The tide was against us, the wind was against us and the atmosphere on board had soured, you could cut it with a knife. The two guys were angry that those men had come to faith in Christ and it was sixteen long hours to go before we moored at Denton Bridge.

## MAKING FRIENDS

I awoke disorientated, sore and itchy. I hadn't a clue where I was, I didn't even know if I was awake or still sleeping in the void of total blackness. I put my hand in front of my face and could see nothing. I felt my sore and itching body covered in mosquito bites, but in my head, I felt it could have been a dream. Dream or not I was hungry and thirsty. So I groped about for the water container, but it was empty and I was still hungry and thirsty, a condition I was to get used to. The heat was unbearable and I realised that there didn't seem to be any ventilation, which caused a moment's panic. There was nothing I could do about that so I started doing exercises, fifty push ups, fifty half squats and fifty sit ups, resting for the count of two hundred then repeating them until I was exhausted. Outside my cell, I could hear people talking and the sound of banging. *Could they be building a gallows?* Then all was quiet for about two minutes before the Islamic chanting started at about 100db plus. I don't know if I'm giving my age away here, but I remember 8 track tape players that went on and on and on and on, you know what I mean, well it was like that. I banged at the door and shouted, "Shut that row off, or I'll . . ." What? What could I actually do? So, I shut up and hoped it would stop sometime soon, but it didn't.

Hours passed and no one came near me until at some point, I guessed in the afternoon, the hatch slid up and a pale shaft of light spread over the cell floor, and a bowl of food was pushed in. I dived to the hatch and held it open. "I need water and the toilet" "I'll be back for the empty bowl in ten minutes, give me your water bottle then," he replied. "At last, someone who'll help me," I thought. When the hatch shut, I was plunged into darkness again, and picking up my bowl, I felt inside, ah, rice and another fish head. No imagination these Gambians or maybe they have a job lot of fish heads. Anyway, I was seriously hungry and I had only ten minutes to eat so I got stuck in. A mouthful of boiled rice with what seemed like gravel, and later I found out was mostly gravel then I picked up the fish head. Yuck! I started to nibble what flesh I could get off the skull, but there was precious little of that, then more rice and more rice, but with nothing to drink, eating boiled rice wasn't easy. You didn't have to be a rocket scientist to know there was little in the way of goodness in this meal, but it filled a space for the moment and anyway, I didn't believe I'd be there for long.

True to his word, the inmate opened the hatch and shouted, "Bowl!" As I slid the bowl out, I also slid out the empty blue plastic gallon oil container. "OK," he said as they disappeared, "I'll be back". The hatch slid shut again, and I was left wondering what would happen next. More than an hour passed before the hatch slid open again. "You OK?" the man said as he pushed the water container through the gap. "I think so," I replied, "but I don't know what's going on, can you talk?" "Yeh, I'm the mess boy, what do you want to know?" "When do they feed us? Where's the toilet? What day is it?" There were a million questions I wanted to ask but this guy wouldn't know any of the important ones. "You are fed once a day between three and four in the afternoon, fish head and rice every day. You get to empty your "chamber pot" once every two days and that's when you get your water and I don't know what day it is." "What is your name?" I asked. "Don't you remember me sir," he said, "I'm Captain Sanneh (name changed to protect him, he's still there) 2006 coup plot, I'll try to help you, but don't eat the food unless I bring it because they will try to poison you," and with that, the hatch was shut and I was left sitting on the floor, stunned.

# THEY CAME IN THE NIGHT

There was a loud rattling of keys that went on for five minutes. Eventually when the door swung open, a voice entered the cell "Right Fulton on your feet, you're coming with us." There were two men, both wearing wraparound sunglasses, both in mufti and were accompanied by one prison officer. The two were obviously secret police and had been watching the wrong spy movies. "Where are we going," I asked. "To hell," one of them said. Now I thought he meant "To hell with you" but later I was to find that he really did mean, "*Hell*"!

I got dressed and then was shackled hand and foot as before and taken out into the courtyard where there was a battered old Toyota pickup. "In," one of them demanded. "Was that a please?" I enquired, *Biff!* I really should try to curb my efforts to educate Gambian thugs.

The driver, obviously a former kamikaze pilot, hurtled through the streets taking corners on two wheels. Whilst being thrown from side to side, I managed to see the clock on the dashboard.

It read 2:15 and as the sun wasn't shining I guessed it was a.m. *clever huh!*

I knew where we were going now, so I didn't ask, and I was right, we went straight to the secret police headquarters. This is the secret police's secret headquarters that everyone knows about and isn't much of a secret. In we shuffled, and this time they took me outside to a courtyard. Facing us was a large concrete building. It stood on its own, about 20 metres square and seemed unusual from the outside, as it had no windows. As soon as we went inside the smell hit me, it looked like an abandoned slaughterhouse minus the charm and there stood Bin Laden the Imam.

At first glance, the room looked to have gymnasium apparatus scattered about, and what I took, to be a row of lockers at the far end. How can I adequately write of the dread that I felt in the pit of my stomach when I realised that this was where torture was commonplace. How can I illustrate the horrors this room had seen and anyway how would you believe me? There was a special odour, a mixture of death and disease and of human waste and the dankness of whatever organisms were growing on the dark concrete walls. They loosened the handcuffs on my left wrist and put another set on the same one. *Strange* I thought, but before I could get into an interesting and engaging conversation with my guards, I noticed what looked like a Neanderthal standing against the left sidewall. It was dressed in chic banana republic trousers, Che Guevara t-shirt and boots that made Doc Martins look like ballet shoes. "It's a zoo," I exclaimed. "What?" the guard said. "It's a zoo," I repeated, "or maybe a museum, with live exhibits." I pointed to the Neanderthal who was playfully bending what I took to be an iron bar, back and forth. However, the guard obviously didn't get it as we both shrugged. They pushed me towards what looked like a large frame in the centre, not unlike the support for children's swings in a park. The top beam was about twelve feet high and had two pulley wheels on it about six feet apart with a rope hanging through each of them.

"Strip," the Neanderthal shouted, I turned to the guard who had brought me here. "It talks," I exclaimed, "but it isn't very smart. How can I strip with these on?" I held out my cuffs and pointed to the leg irons. Now, I could almost hear the cogs turning as he mulled over this latest problem. There was a battle going on inside his skull. Then a decision was made that would enable him to keep his authority and dominance intact, but would also move things forward, he took off the leg irons. I was then able to remove all my clothes, as the handcuffs went through the sleeves of my short-sleeved shirt. There I was again, as naked as a newborn baby, but not quite so blasé about it.

Two more guards came in and despite my struggles on went the leg irons, and held by both arms. They forced me towards the frame, where they closed the open end of the handcuffs, which were dangling from each wrist and threaded the rope through them. Then two guards pulled on the ropes hauling me up into a spread-eagled position. It felt like my arms would be torn from their sockets as the pain shot through my shoulders. The pain in my wrists was almost unbearable so I tried to grab onto the handcuff chains that linked me to the rope. "Whack, whack," my fingers were beaten with a long baton that one of the guards held. I suspected that others had tried to take the weight off their wrists before me and they'd made this long baton in response. The little finger on my left hand snapped and this forced me to let go. As all my weight jerked on my left hand, both the thumb and the wrist were dislocated. They held me in that position, just off the ground, when the Neanderthal sauntered up to me. "When I am finished you will sign a confession," he said in remarkably precise English, making it all the more surreal. "You will beg me to stop and I won't. I will stop only when *I've* had enough, not *you*. Do you understand?" I told him to go away and the second word was off. Well I can't say that I ever got to like the fellow whose name by the way was Casper, and who I would have gladly made a *'friendly ghost'*, yet I did respect his devotion to duty and he certainly enjoyed his work.

What I'd thought was an iron bar was in fact a piece of black two inch diameter rubber hose. I was under no illusions as to what he was going to do with it, but I didn't expect to be doused with water before he started. He was right-handed and his first strike was like an electric shock across my buttocks, the next a little bit higher and so on until he was at my shoulders. Everything in me wanted to scream, such was the pain, but I refused to give them the pleasure. I probably moaned, but any screaming I did at him or at them, I kept inside me. He stopped . . . more than a little frustrated, just short of me losing consciousness. "Have you anything to say?" he demanded. I looked at him. He wasn't even out of breath! "I have to warn you," I said through gritted teeth, "I'm a black belt in Origami." Whack! How I hate people without a sense of humour. He went back to work again, and at some point I must have passed out. At least I think I must have done, because when I regained consciousness I was on the floor of the chamber and can't remember untying myself and climbing down from the frame. After that day, I could no longer look on, or refer to that room, as anything other than a torture chamber.

I don't know how long I was left there, I tried to assess my injuries, but apart from my dislocations and little finger it didn't seem that anything else was broken. One thing that was concerning me was that there was no feeling in my left thumb and forefinger and there was numbness in the rest of my hand as if I'd had a novocaine injection. There was plenty of bruising though and because of the lack of feeling; I was able to put my thumb and wrist back where they should be. How were they going to explain this when I went to court on Monday? I wondered if I told the court what had happened to me that the full weight of the law would fall on them. How naive. Eventually four of them came for me and they lifted me bodily and took me outside where they dumped me, still bound and naked, into the back of the pickup. The night, or rather early morning (probably about 3am,) was warm. There were the usual African night noises of crickets chirping and dogs barking, but the fresh air was what I appreciated most. It was wonderfully reviving.

However, the feeling uppermost in my mind was that I'd won. I was alive. Round one to me: but how many rounds were there in this match? Unable to see over the sides of the pickup, I counted the corners and the length of straights and I knew we were heading back to Mile Two. The horn blasted and the big steel gates opened allowing the vehicle into the prison yard. When we stopped, they unceremoniously dragged me out, and threw my clothes down beside me. The pickup drove out while two prison officers came over and took off my handcuffs and leg irons. "Can you walk?" queried PO Maneh (not his real name, he was one of the officers I knew from when I worked there, and is still there). He was full of concern, and for the first time since they had taken us into captivity, I felt like someone cared. They carried me into the guard hut, and then helped to my feet. "Can you walk?" he asked again. "Yep" was all I could manage and with his help I walked back to the confinement wing and then on to my cell where I allowed myself to collapse in the darkness. I think that was about 4.30 on Tuesday morning, but I wasn't too sure.

The Gambia was always full of challenges and excitement for me, and every day was different. It was no use writing a "to do" list in the morning as things were constantly changing. Emergencies were commonplace and often while on my way to take a service at one barracks I'd be called on to deal with a problem at another. Once, I was called to the airport to mediate in a situation where a Dutch woman coming off a plane was caught with cannabis. Another time, one of my friends was shot, but by the time I got there, it was too late and he died in my arms. Every week they'd be two or three extreme situations and of course my work was exciting in itself, going up river in dangerous conditions, dealing with the families of service personnel who'd come to faith in Christ. I was told by a counsellor friend of mine that I was addicted to adrenalin, that I just had to put myself in situations 'Where angels would fear to tread' and on reflection I have to admit that he was probably right. However, to date this was without doubt the most difficult and dangerous situation I'd ever found myself in. Worse, I couldn't see a way out, but I'd work on that.

# POISON

I slept fitfully but when I awoke, the pain hadn't gone away, I didn't need any light to know my back and buttocks would be a fetching shade of black and blue, which I understood was all the rage in Mile Two this year, so, what now? Well I had six days till the court case started, so I thought maybe I'll catch a rat or two which was reinforced by a nip on my foot that was bleeding after being dragged, I presume while unconscious. How many other bites I had received while asleep I didn't even want to think about, but I was determined not to have any more. My rat hunt in total darkness wasn't very fruitful, but at about mid-afternoon the hatch opened and in slid a bowl of food. The person who delivered it said, "Good food today" and down went the hatch. "Where is the mess boy?" I shouted at the door without any answer. I was ravenous and felt inside the bowl to find good size fish, rice and vegetables; I scooped up a handful then remembered to say grace just before putting it in my mouth. "Lord thank you for this food, may it do me good and no harm, Amen." Then, for some reason before I ate, I prayed that Fiona and Elizabeth would have enough to eat and while I was at it, I remembered the rest of the family. Finally, I put my hand in the bowl. Bang, bang, the door shook with the urgency of the knocking. "What is it," I shouted. "Don't eat the food, didn't I tell you?" came the loud whisper (you know the kind of loud whispering I mean). "I haven't," I loudly whispered back. "Tip it out and I'll collect the bowl in five minutes. Wow! It was then I remembered Sanneh's warning; surely not? The repercussions for them would be enormous, but I tipped out the bowl in the corner of the cell and didn't lick my fingers.

Five minutes or so later the hatch opened again "Give me the bowl and then pretend to be sick," said Sanneh. "I'll report that you're ill." "But I'm not," I protested, "What will I do when they send a doctor?" It was nice to hear laughter in that place, but there was something false about Sanneh's because I hadn't told a joke. Hours passed and all I had to do was reflect on my predicament. I probably dozed off, as I was a bit slow when the hatch quietly moved up a crack and a tin of some kind slid under the door. "Enjoy," came Sanneh's loud whisper, before the hatch closed. I crawled over to the door from where I was sitting propped up against the back wall and felt around for whatever I was supposed to enjoy. My hand touched something that I immediately recognised as a tin of sardines. "Thank you," I whispered loudly, "thank you."

I didn't know what to do, should I open it and scoff it immediately? God knows I was ravenous enough, or should I wait until the doctor came to see me and have me shot for feigning an illness? Anyway, the hunger won and I decided to eat it now, but that was easier thought, than done. How many of you have actually opened a tin of sardines'? Even with two good hands, it's not the easiest job in the world, and dangerous . . . very dangerous!

Well, my small but obvious problems were that my hands were bruised and swollen. My left hand had a broken finger and I was in total darkness, but as my late mother use to say, "If things don't change, they'll stay the same" So having no wish to remain hungry I attacked the said tin. I don't want this passage to deteriorate into a lesson on how to break into a tin of sardines, but I was surprised, nay, shocked to find that my finger wouldn't fit inside the ring pull on the lid. I needed something to insert in it and there was nothing in the cell. Ah! Then I remembered the nail in the wall, *right, where was it again?* I remembered coming across it when I was feeling my way round and exploring the cell, but I couldn't for the life of me remember exactly where. However, as I probably had a year or two to spare I decided to re-explore the cell and eventually found it cemented into the wall, probably at one time it was used to hang and bleed rats so they would be Halal. Anyway, what could I use to prise it from the wall? Then I remembered I had a tin of sardines that could if I was of that mind, be used to knock the nail from side to side to loosen it. It was the work of moments and I had the nail in one hand and the sardines in the other. What joy! Using the nail as a tee piece through the hole in the ring pull, I was able to prise off the top.

Gingerly I prodded the contents to discover three tiny fish in oil all of which went down smartly, oil and all. I propped myself against the wall and listened to the squeak of the rats and was, if not content, at least fed for another day.

No doctor came to look at my nonexistent illness and I remember thinking *"This is like being in a 'do they' novel. Ordinary people like me don't get themselves into this sort of predicament, do they?"* Sleep came and with it the realisation that I was probably the only person in the world who thought I was ordinary. It seemed that the reason I was here was simply because I'd put myself in "harm's way" and the more I thought about it I realized that it has "ever been thus" I can't remember a time when I was content to be a spectator, and when I went for something, I gave it everything I had. I was here because Fiona and I truly believed that we should sell up everything and go to The Gambia to tell the Muslims that they were going to hell in a handcart. Of course, quite typical of me, I never went to Bible school and believed that by God's grace and my experience we would do just fine, but by the look of things we weren't doing "just fine". Was there any hope of getting out of here? Well, this was most certainly a learning curve and I had hoped it had bottomed out and was taking an upward swing.

When I was in my teens, I went to Marr Collage in the town of Troon in Scotland where they tried their best to educate me. A Godly man and my English teacher W.K Morrison once said to me: "To know you must learn. To feel you must experience. To dream you must hope. The way forward must come from the remembered knowledge of the past, the pain of the present and the hope of the future." At the time, I hadn't a clue what he was talking about, but now? Yes. I hope. There is always hope for a Christian, hope, and the assurance that God is on our side. As the Bible says, "If God be for us who can be against us?" Well the truth of the matter is "almost everyone," *"But" what it means (and this is a mighty big but), they can't win.* Even if they killed me, they have still lost. I was going to heaven and they were going to hell. "Final score: Christians 1 Muslims extremists 0". Actually the score should have been more than one, as they'd tried to kill me twice before. There was one occasion where it was closer than most and I'll tell it as I remember and piece it together as it was recounted to me through confessions and family narrations as well as my own experience.

# INTENT ON MURDER
## June 2005

The Barracks room was hot and steamy in the tropical night, there was only one candle burning and even that added to the heat. Mosquitoes and flies were buzzing about the room where Sgt. Mohamed Bah and Private Modu Samba huddled together. Their coal black faces were shining and the sweat was running off them, more because of excitement than the heat. They were used to the heat. "When he comes tomorrow we will kill him," said Bah. "It must look like a mugging, so we will take all the white man's money." "We'll be rich," the other conspirator added. "Yes he will die and Allah, blessed be his name, will reward us with a place in heaven and many virgins." "Remember," said the Sergeant "we're not doing this for the money; it is Allah's will that this infidel dies."

I had just finished the service in Fajara Barracks and headed out of the main gate in the old Nissan Patrol I had at the time. Returning the salute from the sentry, I drove out turning left on to the road. I noticed a beat up Renault 4 taxi parked by the road-side on the right of the gate, and at the time, I never gave it a second glance, as they were as common as muck. I drove on, but after about two hundred metres, there was a severe wobble on the steering wheel along with noise and drag from the nearside front wheel, which forced me to pull up close to a chain link fence. I got out, and found the wheel was hanging off with only one of the five wheel nuts holding it on. I got out the jack and spider (multisized wheel brace), jacked the car up and tightened the remaining nut. This was Africa, these things don't faze you. I took one nut from each of the three other wheels and it was as good as new. I'd just let the jack down and knelt to retrieve it from under the car when I was aware of someone behind me. I glanced up and there was a soldier. "It's OK," I said, as I thought he'd stopped to help, "I've done it now." However, as I turned back to get the jack, I caught a movement that in retrospect must have seemed out of place, because I started to turn towards him again when *"Crack"*, I was hit a glancing blow on the head which almost caused me to pass out. As I went down, he tried to hit me again with what I was to find out later was a two foot long piece of 3x3 hardwood. Although everything seemed to be getting darker by the second I knew that, I couldn't slip under, and managed to raise the wheel brace to parry the blow. Both the wheel brace and the hardwood club spun away and the man tripped on the jack handle, which was sticking out from under the car and measured his length beside me.

As I struggled to get up another man who was also in DPMs was falling on me with a knife in the classic underarm grip. Instinctively I gripped his wrist with my left hand, his fist with my right and twisted as he fell. How the knife didn't go through my hand I don't know but there was a snap as something went in his arm, (or wrist as it happened) and the knife turned towards him. Now, the rest is what must have happened, as I have no recollection after I heard the snap. As he continued to fall on me the momentum drove the knife up below his chin, through his mouth and into his brain and he landed on top of me bleeding copiously and inconsiderately on my head. I have had a little training in this sort of thing (the fighting not the bleeding), and indeed I've trained others in un-armed combat. However, looking back, I really believe that God was somewhere in this.

Now, while all this was going on there was an army truck full of solders heading for Fajara barracks, which I'd just left, and as they reached my Patrol an hysterical woman ran in front of it waving her arms to make it stop. As that happened a soldier, (the one who'd clubbed me), ran away down the track. Some of the solders in the truck recognised my Nissan Patrol and came over to see what was wrong.

They found two solders; one black and one white, covered in blood one on top of the other and both seemingly dead. We were thrown into the back of the Patrol where I came to just as the doors slammed shut and no doubt, I'd have been taken to the mortuary. "What's going on?" I mumbled "Ahhh!" That shook them. "We thought you were dead," a Sergeant replied, not in the least apologetically. "The rumours of my death have been grossly exaggerated," I quoted one better than myself, "Pardon?" "Oh, never mind, where are you taking me?" I asked, "The RVH," he replied. "Not on your life," I responded with some vigour, "Take me to Westfield Clinic, at least I'll stand a chance." Now to clarify things, the RVH is the Royal Victoria Hospital, which at that time was not a good place to be taken, and I'm being charitable, (people have been known to go in as visitors and come out in a box). At Westfield Clinic, I was looked over by my friend Dr Peters and he mentioned, not for the first time, that I should give thanks to God for my thick skull. Four stitches in my head and concussion. That wasn't so bad, I've been carried off the rugby field with worse. I phoned Fiona, she got a local Gilly-gilly bush taxi to where I was, and she drove me home.

I found out later that there was a concern at the British High commission about any repercussions. After what had happened, and what I had done, any reports in Gambian newspapers could have read something like this:

*"British Military Chaplain, David Fulton was involved yesterday in a fight with a Gambian soldier and after a struggle, the fully trained, well fed and healthy British Chaplain, killed the poor undernourished, untrained Gambian."* Although quite a distortion of the truth, the press never let that get in the way of a good story, do they?

Anyway, I decided to phone the CDS and find out what was going to happen about it. He was very apologetic and told me that there was an alert on all border crossings and ferries to catch the soldier who had escaped. He informed me that during the search of the men's rooms, they had found some extremist Islamic material, some illegal small arms, and some correspondence with an Imam, known for his extremist views. Apparently, these weren't men from The Gambia, but Senegalese Jolla tribesmen, from the area of the Casamance. There were, (and still are), quite a large number of Jolla Casamance soldiers in the Gambian army, and as no Gambians were involved in the attack, I wasn't to worry about a thing. Indeed, I was to be 'congratulated' for dealing with this threat to moderate Islam in the Gambia. They intended to keep it 'in house' and there would be nothing in the news. Wow! That was a relief; I could now relax and hurt in peace. Eventually, they caught the other soldier on a ferry and brought in front of a court martial. Days later, when I gave evidence at that court martial, I pleaded for him not to be executed, (as was the norm if he was found guilty), however, my appeal was rejected and he was found guilty of attempted murder. He was shot two hours later by firing squad.

# I CAN DO THAT

"Chaplain," said Major Njie a few days later, when I was well enough to go back to the barracks, "The CO wants to see you." I headed wonderingly to the CO's office. "Come in," Major General Mbye shouted, "How are you feeling?" "I'm OK sir; it only hurts when I laugh." "Well this'll make you laugh," he went on, "the family of one of your attackers needs to see you." "Why"? I asked him. "Don't know, but they sent a boy who came to see me and he said it was a matter of life or death." "They probably want me to pay for the funeral," I replied, "but I don't see any harm in seeing them." "Good," he retorted, "the boy can speak broken English, he'll show you the way." "Thank you sir," I said, "permission to carry on?" "Granted," he mumbled and went back to his paperwork.

"Where?" I exclaimed . . . "The Casamance, are you mad,

that's in Senegal." The boy of no more than twelve years old was quaking in front of me. "It's another country and, well, it's a long way to drive"

"I walked on my feet for two days," he whispered in Pidgin English.

"Two days . . . but why?" I enquired.

"The peoples sent me, they are my Father and they will dead be."

"OK," I told him, "come with me." What I gathered from his Pidgin English was that as a matter of life and death I had to see his family. We walked round to my car where I had maps and drew one out which was the southern part of The Gambia and from the border through the Casamance to the border with Guinea Bissau. "OK fella where do you come from?" I challenged him. "Kafountine," he replied. "Yeah, but point it out on the map," I said. "I don't know paper like this," he replied, "but I know where on my feet." *"Hmm,"* I thought, *"this is going nowhere fast."* OK fella, what we'll do is this; I'll make the preparations today and we'll meet back here and we'll go to see them tomorrow, Yeah?"

"We will see them not living," he said in his mixed up English, and hunched his shoulders while walking away."

"Hold it," I shouted at him as he walked. "What do you mean not living?" He came back and looked up at me, "I mean not living" he said, as tears welled up in his eyes "they will be not living."

I looked at my watch 09.15hrs. "Get in," I told him, "have you eaten today?" "No boss." "OK, we'll get some fruit on the way. Oh; By the way, what's your name?" "Mohamed," I should have guessed.

I phoned Fiona to let her know what had happened, that I may be away for a while, maybe even overnight, and we set off. "Darsalami," he said. That was a town near the border and we reached it within an hour. Then it got interesting, as at the south side of the town he pointed to a track, which was barely wide enough for a bicycle, never mind my Nissan Patrol. Nevertheless, he was insistent that this was the only way he knew, so I put the

Patrol into four-wheel drive and pushed my way through the bush, grateful for the bull bars.

After a while, I asked him where the Immigration and Customs post was. "Back," he said, pointing diagonally behind us. "Of course," I thought, "he'd have no paperwork and no I.D. so he'd have to have crossed the border into The Gambia illegally, which meant he'd have to go back in illegally, which meant in turn that I was in Senegal illegally and would have to come back illegally. (Did I ever mention life was never dull?).

Well, as we were well into Senegal by now it was best to keep going, and we did for about two hours. We turned off the narrow track onto a wide dirt road heading west and I was able to get out of second gear. After another half hour, we reached the coast and the road turned south again. Another half an hour passed and he pointed across a bay to a town on the distant peninsular; "Kafountine!" He exclaimed excitedly. "Kafountine," I rejoined, relieved. I looked at my watch; *12.10hrs, 'maybe I'll manage to sleep in my own bed tonight', I thought.*

Kafountine is a nice town of medium size, probably about five thousand people with some tourist hotels. We however, were not heading for the hot spots. It was to the shantytown area that Mohamed led me. The kind of houses that could be found in The Gambia, Sierra Leone, Nigeria or indeed any West African Country. We travelled along narrow dirt streets flanked with rough unpainted concrete walls often eight feet high. Half-naked children played football with a ball made of rags tied in a rough round bundle, their bare feet hardened against the rough ground.

I had to sound the horn to clear the way for as soon as the Patrol was sighted we were surrounded with kids. They jumped on the running boards and the rear step, and as I slowed down, some even climbed on the spare wheel and up onto the roof rack. Mohamed jumped out and started shouting at them in local language and one or two dropped off, but most just hung on till we arrived at a compound with double gates which were closed. Mohamed, having run in front of me, started to open the gates. The children jumped off and left us, as if the car had just had an electric current passed through it. When the gates were open I drove into a compound that had a sandy area wide enough to turn the Patrol, which was bounded by what could be mistaken for stable blocks, but in fact were houses, one or two bedrooms and parlour. Mohamed walked to the veranda of one of the blocks and gestured for me to pull up there. I stopped the car and got out not knowing what to expect. Then I heard a wailing noise, almost a screeching. I was led into the parlour of a mud blockhouse where a man and woman were sitting on the floor, and that was where the wailing was emanating from.

The boy pointed to me and talked through the noise and gradually it died away. "This is my Mother and not my Father," he said "but the same father and mother as my brother who tried to dead you." (A long time ago, I decided not to try to work out relationships in the West African extended family system, so I just nodded.)

"They need to be sorry for the son's badness," "The son's badness?" I repeated, "What badness?" "He tried to dead you," said the boy, looking at me as if I was a bit thick, "Ah . . . that badness. It's OK, he didn't succeed." "But he tried to succeed and they," he said, pointing to his parents, "say you sorry."

I wasn't getting anywhere, I just couldn't get what all this was all about. Why should I? What was this life and death situation I was told about? There was a commotion outside and I turned to see many people milling about, so in exasperation I went outside to the veranda in case the car needed moving. It looked as if the whole of the village was there, but one man stood out from the rest. He was a dignified looking fellow and better dressed in his long flowing robes. "You are English?" he said, I didn't want to get into the English-Scottish thing so, to my eternal shame, I said "Yes." "I am Mohamed," he replied. "I am the compound Imam, who are you?" It took me but the work of a moment (that's a metaphorical moment you understand) to explain the whole thing to the Imam who took it all in at a grasp. "Ah," he said excitedly, "I was the very one who sent the boy to summon you." Well, I've had a summons or two in my time, but this was the weirdest.

"So what's happening with them?" I asked, pointing to the room I'd just left. "They won't eat as their son has shamed them and will fast till they die." "What? That's a bit over the top," I exclaimed. "It's their shame," he replied. "The son can't ask for your forgiveness, so he will go to hell unless the parents grieve to death for him." "That's crazy," I replied. "I'm sure that's not in the Qu'ran."

"There are many sects in Islam and different teachings some seem strange, but are nevertheless," (and he really did say nevertheless), truths to the followers." "Right," I went on, feeling I was making some headway, "what can I do?"

"Forgive them of course, forgive them if you can," he pleaded. "I've got no problem with that," I said. "In fact I'm a committed Christian and that's part of Jesus' teachings." With that piece of spiritual input, a small girl came up to me with a can of Fanta Orange and it was only then I realised how thirsty I was. "I'll go and speak to Mr Bah while you relax for a while," said the Imam. Well, as my wife will tell you I always do as I'm told, so relax I did with an ice cold Fanta, it was all becoming clear now and life suddenly got better.

We all met back in the house half an hour later where I formally forgave the family for something they hadn't done and I started to edge my way towards the front door. "I can't be taking you back till the eating has happened," little Mohamed said as he blocked my exit. "What is an eating?" I enquired. "Oh, never mind, I can find my own way back thank you"

"No the eating." he said in exasperation, "the eating." I turned to the Imam for help. "He is meaning a feast, a celebration, the eating." "Well that's all very well," said I, "but I have to get home for my dinner, my eating." "You must stay," he persisted "It is expected, it's an obligation". Just as I was wondering how long it would take to boil a pan of rice and fry a fish for a meal, three children came in wrestling with a large sheep, or was it a goat? I can never tell the difference, unlike God, coz the Bible says he'll sort out the sheep from the goats.

Now that's all very well, but this sheep or goat needed to be sorted out now. I won't bore you with the horrors of being the chief guest and being expected to cut the animal's throat, or the hours of bleeding, skinning, butchering, beheading and eventually cooking over an open fire on a spit. By nine o'clock, we were ready to eat and by that time, I'd given up all hope of getting back that night. Oh, I could have made it in about five hours, but as there was and still is, quite a vicious civil war going on in the Casamance it wasn't advisable to travel after dark. Moreover, I'd have to cross the border by the back door, so to speak, having entered inadvertently by the side door in the first place. I thought it expedient to spend the night there and travel back in the morning.

I slept in on a grass-filled mattress made from many old cement bags and was surprisingly comfortable. It wasn't till the next day I realised that it was Mr Bah's own bed and he gave it to me to use that night. Morning came and it was with great relief and no little joy that I wound my way through the jungle tracks using only the sun on my right (east), and a compass when the trees blocked out the light, to wend my way home. I hadn't a clue when or where I crossed the border, but after about four hours driving I passed through a village which had a police checkpoint and two Gambian policemen who saluted me as they waved me through. An hour later saw me home with Fiona and the children. I felt terrific, I'd done some good and I had a leg of sheep, (*or was it goat?*), in the back of the Patrol for dinner.

## SURPRISE SURPRISE MILE TWO

I was still in my cell thinking about that incident when I noticed something had changed, but I couldn't work out what it was. The Islamic chanting was still blasting out, I was still hungry, I was still sore and bleeding, and Mosquitoes were still buzzing in my ear. Have you ever noticed that about mosquitoes? One seems to try to get right into your ear to distract you and while you are, the others are biting lumps off your "private parts". So what had changed? Then I realised that while I had been musing I wasn't, (as was my habit), automatically kicking the rats off my bleeding ankles. (Please believe me when I say "bleeding ankles," I'm not swearing). Well, I thought, maybe they have a way in and out of the cell, so I decided to investigate. I'd only moved about two feet from where I had been sitting when my hand pushed the first rat. It was dead. Then after sweeping my arms over the floor, I found another three of the little rascals. Dead as doornails, I wasn't under any illusions as to how they shrugged off this mortal coil. I scrabbled about until I found where I had dumped the contents of the bowl, gone . . . not a grain of rice or a fish bone left, all eaten by the late rats.

It has to be said that it was then that realised that the people who were against me, for whatever reason, would stop at nothing to get rid of me. It's not often that I've felt fear in my life, but that day, not a week since my capture, I felt a chill of fear going down my spine that I've only read about happening to other people in books. Now I was starting to get so paranoid that whenever I heard a movement outside the cell I thought they were coming to shoot me. After a few hours had passed there was the familiar rattle of keys as they went through the bunch to find mine which was probably second to last. The door opened and three guards stood there and when I said, "Can I help you?" They nearly dropped. I realised that they had expected to see me either dead or writhing on the floor dying. "Go and find a Bible and read the Gospel of Mark chapter 16 verses 15, 16, 17 and 18," I said. Bang, the door shut without another word. Now I guess I cheated a bit, because I didn't 'eat' the food, but the Bible doesn't say how we will be protected. Who knows? Maybe someone did get a Bible and read where it says *Christians will be protected from poison*. I have no doubt that Sanneh's warning was God-inspired and in this case, he decided to use a Muslim acquaintance of mine to save me from the poison that killed the rats.

I had four days left before court again so I was reasonably sure that I'd be left alone till then as I might be marked and that would raise questions. I was wrong again. That night the keys rattled for the usual five minutes until one fit my cell's padlock and the door swung open. "Out," said a man I'd never seen before. He had to be secret police; the wraparound-mirrored sunglasses were a dead giveaway. I pointed to the specks, "Do you wear them in the shower?" I asked with an innocent expression. "Out," he repeated.

We went through the same routine. I got dressed in my own clothes, which hung on the nail outside the cell. They cuffed my hands behind my back, and locked on the leg irons. I shuffled down the passageway and out into the confinement yard, then to the iron door that leads to the main prison yard. This time it was pitch black, the power had failed. The prison should have had an emergency standby generator, but the Director David Collie had sold it.

I stumbled towards the pickup of which the driver had left his headlights on to light our way. I smiled to myself when I saw how dim they were, (not the men, the headlights, well, maybe both). Anyway, we got to the vehicle and they told me to get in the back. Now children, do not try this at home without an adult to help you, coz it's not easy and try as I didn't, I managed to appear as if I was as weak as a kitten and they had to help me in. It wouldn't start, which seemed to surprise them. The driver cranked the engine over, but the battery was almost dead. "Want a push?" I enquired helpfully. "Shut up," came the somewhat frustrated and angry response, as some prison guards were coerced into shoving it round the yard till it started.

It was the NIAs not so secret headquarters that we went to, and this time we went straight to the torture chamber. They took off the handcuffs and leg irons and ordered me to strip, and then Godzilla came in, still twisting his thick hosepipe into knots. I watched him warily; he never for one moment took his eyes off of me. Worst of all he was smiling from ear to ear. Here was a man that truly enjoyed his work.

I once heard it said, "You can judge how evil someone is by their smile" and that night I knew the truth of it. This man was truly evil and sadistic; I was sweating like a glacier in a heat wave. They pushed me towards what looked like gray painted lockers at the back of the room and I stopped in front of the doors. I looked around wondering what was coming next. There were six doors, each one about eighteen inches wide and at the end of which, a tap was set into the wall and a drain in the floor. The concrete floor was wet and slippery and seemed slightly sloped towards a drain by the tap. Darkness prevailed except for an oil lamp on a desk with a chair pushed under it. The gorilla chap I'd decided to nickname Godzilla opened a locker door and pushed me towards it.

*What was I was meant to see there?* I wondered. The answer was nothing; I glanced in and realised I was meant to go in there. "No way," I shouted and spread my arms and legs so I couldn't be pushed in as they were trying to do. "No bloody way," I shouted again and the harder they pushed the more I pushed against them. Then there was what seemed like a crippling blow to my back, and they threw me to the side and I lashed out behind me. Another blow hit my arm and my side went numb, I was on the floor and looked up.

Godzilla and one of the other guards had cattle prods and pushed them at me stopping only inches from my body. I stood up with my back against the wall and my one serviceable arm out-stretched as they herded me back to the open door of what was in fact a tiny cell. One more prod saw me thrown in by the kick of it, and the door slammed shut behind me. I was standing on a grill of quarter inch reinforcing rods welded into three-inch squares. The cell was, as well as I could measure two feet square, but about ten foot high tapering to the top which was open to the sky and had a grill similar to the one that I was standing on.

Now, I was totally confused. It was pitch black, but I could see a star or two from the open top that seemed to me to be like a chimney. What were they up to? I was so confined that I couldn't sit and the grill I stood on was biting into my bare feet, not at all comfortable. After about an hour my calf muscles started to spasm and I got terrible cramp in my legs and buttocks so that I could no longer stand properly but neither could I sit.

I prayed and prayed that this agony end. I prayed that Fiona wasn't suffering any torture. I prayed that moves were afoot by the British High Commission and British Government to put an end to this nonsense, but felt nothing except a sense of abandonment by God and man. As the hours passed, I lost all positive feeling except pain from my waist down and I knew by the smell that I had urinated down my legs and felt shame and humiliation.

The sky in the square of light above me had turned blue when eventually I could support my body no longer and it collapsed, or rather concertinaed against the rough concrete walls. Just when I thought, I'd had enough, an excruciating pain shot through my legs and back. The pain occupied my body like a solid thing, so all consuming that I could no longer pray. All I could think was pain and then my bowels emptied.

I remember quite clearly through the pain that this was a mental turning point, even so early on in my captivity. They would not win this fight. There would be no more passivity on my part. If this was evil, then I would never give in to it. There was no question of that in my mind. I was determined to survive, but if I were to die, it would be on my terms and not theirs. I wanted to sleep, but the pain shot through my body at regular intervals and sleep never came. With night came the darkness, and with it the buzzing and biting of mosquitoes and large cockroaches climbing up my body from the sewer beneath the grill I stood on.

There was also another noise. It was almost like singing, but how could it be? I tried to concentrate, but it was so faint. *There it was again!* "The Lord's my shepherd I'll not want; He makes me down to lie, in pastures green he leadeth me, the quiet waters by." I was sure I'd lost it, but then the next verse started, "My soul He doth restore again" and so I joined in "and me to walk doth make, within the paths of righteousness, even for his own name sake." Whoever was singing couldn't sing worth a damn, but it was so sweet to my ears. When we'd finished the same voice shouted, "Who are you?" I shouted back "Dave Fulton, who are you?" "Patrick," he replied, "Patrick who?" I said, (hoping this wasn't going to deteriorate into one of these Knock, knock jokes.) "Patrick, Auntie's driver, is that really you Dave?" "Yes it is," I shouted back. "What are you doing in this place, are you a prisoner?" I just heard a faint yes when my door was hit by an electric shock and I was jerked rigid for two or three seconds, then as the power was cut I slumped into an even more concertinaed position and silence reigned again.

Time stopped. I had no idea how long I was there, it could have been hours or days, but it was dark when the door opened and I fell out. Shockingly, my body had swollen grotesquely from the waist down, and my knees, elbows and shoulders were grazed and bleeding from rubbing on the rough concrete. My upper body however, was still functioning, as I'd been able to cross my arms and raise them up and down above my head to keep the circulation going. I lay there on the concrete floor and watched the guard as he walked out of the room. I was desperate for water and dragged myself over to the tap, which was at the end of a three-foot pipe, and was attached to the wall with brackets and I couldn't believe it, there was no handle to turn. Someone had taken it off, and left it hanging on a nail about six feet up the wall.

I tried and tried to prop my body up to enable me to reach the handle. I looked for something to knock it down with, but all to no avail. By this time nothing else mattered but water and I grabbed the tap and heaved, nothing happened except I dragged myself nearer to the wall. I shuffled my body round until my swollen feet were against the wall and I managed to bend at the waist and grab the tap before I fell back again. I pulled, but nothing seemed to happen, I pulled again, still nothing. I knew I had only strength for one last heave. It came away in my hands, not the pipe, but the tap, and the water sprayed upwards and outwards as I fell back on the floor. I opened my mouth swallowing as much water as came from the sky and allowing it to clean me. Well as you can imagine I wasn't the most popular person in the whole world with the NIA. In fact, and call me Mr Sceptical if you like, I suspect I've been scored off their Christmas card list because of that. However, I revelled in the water, drinking it and letting it sooth me.

I got a few kicks and slaps, but the sense of victory and of doing something against them, (albeit by accident) was enormous. I was unable to walk and had to be carried out to the pickup to be transported back to Mile Two. Again, I was able to look at the cab clock through the rear window as they shoved me into the back of the pickup 03.50hrs. I had seen daylight only once through the top of the chimney, so that meant I'd been in there for twenty four hours, yet it seemed like twenty four days.

# ONLY A WEEK?

Back at Mile Two, it was Saturday, one week to the day since we were taken into captivity and I was thrown out of the pickup with my clothes dumped beside me. The prison officers were aghast at my condition and four of them gently lifted me back to my cellblock and into my cell. They didn't shut the door and soon there was a prisoner there tending to my injuries. He bathed my injuries with warm water and gave me rice and fish that I seemed instinctively to know was safe to eat. When the day shift came on two senior officers, who I knew from my time working there came to see me. "We're sorry that all this has happened to you Sir, but there's nothing we can do, we're under orders from the Director to keep you in the punishment cell." I tried to speak but couldn't and he went on, pointing to the fellow who was tending to me. "This man's an inmate, but he's also a medic, he'll be there for you, "and with that they walked swiftly away.

It was Saturday and I was to appear in court on Monday and was in two minds as to know whether it would be good for me to be carried into court looking as I was, or to walk in with my head held high. I remembered a saying that a Welsh friend of mine often used, "I'd rather be envied than pitied." I was determined in my mind to walk into court that following Monday. Fiona had enough to worry about without seeing me as a cripple. The week-end was long and sore, but gradually the swelling went down, and as it did so, the pain seemed to change into an all-enveloping dull ache. They fed me the usual fish head and rice, and I really prayed over it.

As you can imagine many thoughts went through my mind, as

indeed did many Scriptures. I am blessed that since I was a child I've been brought up to believe the Bible and I have, even before I gave my life to Christ, had no doubt that the Bible is the word of God and as such I was able to hold onto the promises that God has given me through the Bible. The one that I recall bringing to mind and believing that day was Psalm 9: 9&10 – that he was my refuge and my stronghold and he won't forsake me. What a solace.

On the physical side though, there were two big problems. Firstly, my toilet was an old paint tin of about maybe six inches in diameter. At the risk of sounding crude, it couldn't be used to defecate in without urinating on the ground in front of it, (not that I 'went' that often), but you see the difficulty. Secondly, I wasn't able to squat, kneel or bend my feet and legs; they were like lumps of frozen meat for the first twenty four hours and I had to relieve myself where I lay. Even though I was back in total darkness, I *was* able to do what I could by way of exercising the legs. Of course, there was no church for me on Sunday, so I spent some of my time praying, exercising, and singing hymns. I seemed to major on one song that we often sung in the Veranda Church, "One Day at a time sweet Jesus" and I belted it out even louder than the Islamic chanting on the loudspeakers.

> I'm only human, I'm just a man
> Lord, help believe in all I could do
> And all that I am,
> Show me the stairway I have to climb
> Lord for thy sake teach me to take,
> One day at a time.

I was ready for court on Monday morning. Well when I say ready, I mean I wasn't in the sauna, or in the middle of a full English breakfast. I was sort of, just there, ready. Again, the clinking of keys and what seemed to be an interminable wait till they found the right one second from last. "Why don't you start at the other end?" I shouted. What a waste of time and breath. Now this was a big moment for me. Was I able to walk, or was I going to fall on my face? The swelling was gone and I felt relatively well, so as the door swung open I stooped through and stood up straight. Three guards were watching me and I believe were quietly pleased that I was OK. However, that didn't stop them cuffing my arms behind my back and chaining my legs once I was dressed.

I shuffled along to join another fourteen men in the main yard who were going to court. A few recognised and greeted me, others were antagonistic towards me, obviously delighted to see a Tubab (white man) being treated so badly. I was the only prisoner in bonds.

They told us to board an old ramshackle truck, but while everyone else clambered up and over the tailgate, I was left like a lemon, standing there in my chains unable to get up. One guard shouted at me "Get on Tubab." I gave him (what used to be called, an 'old fashioned look)' but said nothing. There was obviously a problem, but what to do? The guards surrounded me, scratching their heads. They looked at each other, while confusion reigned. While I wanted to get to court to see Fiona and Elizabeth, I was really enjoying the hot sun beating down and the clean fresh air, but at this rate, we'd be late for court, which is not unheard of. "If you were to unlock me I could climb on," I suggested. However, after a huddled conference, they lifted me bodily into the truck.

Up to about, halfway to the top of the tailgate I deliberately made my body limp, a dead weight. "Grab him," shouted the guards to those already in the truck. Nobody moved. "Hold him then." Apathy, then I started to fall; I would have loved to have a video of it as I landed on top of the guards to the cheers from the inmates. "Unchain him," the squad leader shouted, "we'll be here all day else." There was a scramble for keys and I was unchained and slowly climbed into the back of the truck followed by about ten guards.

# COURT

It only took fifteen minutes to reach the court where I was able to see Fiona and Elizabeth. They were in good spirits, and thankfully, their treatment had been reasonably good. They were holding them at the police station. Here, at least they could receive extra food and visitors. However, I believed it was a cruel thing that they were suffering and I had this thought confirmed much later. The confinement of Fiona and Elizabeth was purely to ensure my compliance. The authorities knew that I was more than capable of escaping if Fiona and Elizabeth were out of the country. To hold me . . . they held them. We had about an hour together before they called us to stand in the dock. We pleaded not guilty again so our lawyer asked for and received one week's adjournment. I had another hour together with Fiona before they took me back through the bunch of reporters and local TV cameras to prison. Fiona was concerned for me and of course I for her. She, despite my efforts at normality could see that I'd been abused, but I assured her that it wasn't too bad.

# BACK IN PRISON

Back in Mile Two I was thrown into my cell and left to my own thoughts. I have to say that I wasn't happy with what I was thinking. "Where were the Christians?" Isn't this a great time to stand and be counted, or were they like those in the time of Peter when he was imprisoned, (Acts 12) and the Christians locked themselves away? Were they hiding in case of arrest? Guilty by association was probably uppermost on their minds, but at least they prayed. Were the Christian leaders in The Gambia, many of whom I'd helped get out of serious situations over the years keeping their heads down, but praying? I know I was probably being uncharitable, I suspected that they were doing nothing, but by doing nothing, one becomes an accomplice. I want to repeat that, "By doing nothing, one becomes an accomplice" which may seem a better option to some than becoming a victim.

Anyway, I guess that I was struggling with the enforced loneliness and utter darkness and that was making it difficult to live with myself. I went over and over what had happened and I just couldn't see how they had managed to get hold of my emails, or indeed how the emails could have been construed as seditious. (Sedition was publishing material, which would or could lead to rebellion or breaching public order). All I had done as far as emails were concerned, was write the truth to family and friends so they could pray for various situations. To my knowledge nothing was published, so what then? We must have been betrayed, but by whom? It was all too much: I felt I was going crazy so I tried to sleep but sleep never came. What had I done to warrant the personal attention of the President? WHY? WHY? Why was I being victimized whilst held in prison? Why, was the Islamic Council on my case with such a passion, and most of all, why had God allowed it? Well, if the truth's to be told (remember that little sentence in the introduction about being honest?) I really knew the answer to most of the whys.

# WHY?
# I'LL TELL YOU WHY

David Collie the Director of prisons and to whom I was arch enemy Number One, was the reason for my maltreatment in Mile two, but the Islamic Council and the President were behind the rest. It seemed that by preaching the Gospel and standing up for social injustices I'd opened Pandora's Box, taken out a can of worms and thrown it at a hornets' nest. One of the early things that ticked off the oppressive Islamists and the President was my stand against FGM (Female Genital Mutilation), even on one occasion stepping in armed and with other soldiers just in time to stop young girls going through forcible female circumcision. At every opportunity, I would make my views and the Christian take on this known, even though others, (White European Christians) told me to mind my own business. The President is a supporter of this barbaric practise and has had high profile Gambian women's activists put in prison for denouncing it. I am fully aware that my primary purpose was evangelism, but the Bible says that "faith without works is dead" and when one has the opportunity to voice the Christian perspective and do something practical I believe that one should, regardless of the consequences. Sleep must have come, though I could never find a comfortable position. When I'd lie down, the floor was so lumpy with the unfinished concrete that I felt like one of those Indian men who lay on a bed of nails for fun. Inevitably, I'd wake up in a semi-slouched position, which meant I'd dropped off to sleep sitting in the corner of the cell. However, this time I was awakened by shouting and jumped up and banged my head on the ceiling again. There seemed to be an argument of some sort in the corridor, but I couldn't make out what it was about above the noise of the loudspeakers and their damnable Islamic chanting. Then the keys started to rattle. "Try the last one first," I shouted. Why did I bother? After five minutes, the padlock snapped and the door flew open. "Out," said the NIA man with the wrap round mirrored shades. "What's the time?" I asked as I stooped through the door nursing my head. There was no reply, but he threw my clothes at my feet. "I take it we're going for a car trip," I said conversationally. There was no reply again, he just stood back against the wall with his arms folded glaring at me (at least I think that's what he was doing behind the mirrors).

After I'd dressed and was chained I was pushed and prodded out into the yard where two senior prison officers were arguing with an NIA operative. We stopped and even though the argument was going on in Wolof, I knew enough of the language to understand that I was the subject of their heated conversation. It was pitch dark again, probably about midnight and it seemed that the prison officers who I knew, and only a month ago would have considered me a friend didn't want me to be taken from the prison, (neither did I, by the way) but the NIA were saying that they had the authority to do so. "Where is the written Authority," asked the ASP (Assistant Superintendant of Prisons). "We are answerable only to the President, and so will you be if you get in our way," was the reply. *Aha, the President does have his finger in my pie. Maybe I can bite it off.* You see, knowledge is power, and although I was seemingly powerless, that was in part due to my lack of knowledge. How can you fight if you don't know who your main enemy is? "Sorry sir," ASP Mendy (not his real name) said to me "we can't stop them." "That's OK, thanks for trying," I told him as they shoved me into the back of the pickup.

# SIGN HERE

When we arrived at the secret police headquarters, they took me into what looked like a mini conference room. It had greenie/brown gloss-painted walls, a sort of natty shade of phlegm. A trestle table in the centre that had parquet flooring style linoleum tacked to it with panel pins driven in to half their length, and then bent over. There were six tubular steel chairs pulled up to three sides; while at the top of the table were two over stuffed easy chairs. Pushing me forward shades said, "Sit". Not one for chatting was he! Well as you would expect I shuffled towards the table, skirted the side and plonked myself on one of the easy chairs. There was an almighty roar and I got the feeling that he wasn't best pleased at my choice of seat. He was making his way round the table when three men came in.

The first was Bin Ladin, smart as ever in last year's bottom sheet and his nearly-beard uncombed. A smaller, dapperly dressed man followed. His face was so black that it had a purple sheen, and this blackness, accentuated by his brilliant whiter than white shirt and striped look alike regimental tie. His head was shaven and he looked like and could have been an international executive. I took an instant dislike to him.

Then in total contrast, there was what was probably the ugliest man I'd ever seen in my life, and I've been to Wakefield! He had to stoop to get though the door, but when he came through, he stayed in the stooped position. His face looked like a horseshoe turned upside down, the mouth had a permanent scowl and he had a scar on his brow from the corner of one eye up to the hair line, then down to the edge of the other eye. As if some beast had blunted its teeth on him then chewed his ears. It was the nose however, that was his most striking feature; it was so huge that it seemed designed for some purpose altogether more grand than merely being breathed through.

"Leave us," the dapper man said to shades as he glanced at his watch, which I noticed, read 2.45am. "Wait outside." Shades slunk out, almost bowing as he went. "Now," he continued, looking at me. "How are we today?" "I don't know how 'we' are," I replied, "but I've been better in myself, thank you doctor." "Oh, I'm not a doctor," he said kindly, no, (he said it smarmily), "but I can help you." "Oh," I said back, "but you have an advantage on me, you know who I am and I don't know who you are. I'm chained up and you're not. However, if you've got a "get out of jail free card" then I'm prepared to give you five minutes of my valuable time." He smarmed again, "I can get you and your wife and daughter on the next plane to the UK, you can keep your house and your boat and you'll be allowed to return to The Gambia whenever you want."

"That sounds good," I said, "but how come I get the impression that this isn't out of the kindness of your heart?" "Ah! Yes," he said, "there is something you can do for us before you go, a few forms to sign and an interview on television." "Television", I exclaimed, feigning joy, "I've always wanted to be on television, can I star in Bay Watch? I'll be the under six foot non-swimmer without the tan and the less than white teeth." For some reason his smarm was slipping, but with considerable effort he dragged it back and drew a sheaf of papers from out of his suit jacket pocket. "Sign these and your ordeal will be over." I looked at the bundle. "Ordeal" I questioned, "ordeal?" This isn't an ordeal: being married to my first wife, now that was an ordeal." Oops, the smarm was slipping again, but to give the fellow his due, he was game. "What are you like," he said, "can't you take anything seriously . . . Sign!" You know, I think maybe he had a point; I really have to take things more seriously. "I'll look at the papers," I said, "but my hands need to be free, don't you think?" It was as if for the first time he saw that I had my hands cuffed behind my back, so to put him more in the picture, I leaned back and swung my manacled feet onto the table. "Get this man unchained!" he screamed and gathered up the papers and stormed out the room. Round One to me, but Round Two was soon to begin.

Shades came back in and with bad grace removed the cuffs and leg irons. Smarmy returned ten minutes later, fully composed. "Now," he began flourishing the papers, "I want you to read these and if you sign them you and your family can all be on the flight home this afternoon." I took them, there were three separate lots of two A4 sheets of paper, each stapled together. The first was a confession I should sign stating that I had been involved in the attempted coup plot of 2006, and that the British Government were complicit in it. I took the staple out and put it face down gently. The second was a letter supposedly from me involving a Government minister whom I knew and was an opponent of President Jammeh in the same coup plot. This one I also placed face down on the table. The third was the piece-de-resistance, and showed how little they knew me. It was a letter, again supposedly written by me on a computer, *'would that be the laptop I was hiding in my cell?'* I wondered, claiming that I have converted to Islam and denouncing Christianity as a false religion. I held this one in my hand in front of me and said to him, "I can understand the other two, but why this one?"

He answered quite coolly, "It will discredit your work here over the last ten years, that," he said pointing, "That, and the television interview." "If I don't sign what will you do?" I asked. "I will have you shot," he said matter-of-factly. There was a stunned silence. I was amazingly calm; I just sat there and said, "You know, I think I am going to opt to join a select group of Christians who I have admired all my life. I've often wondered if I were them would I have the courage to say no, so to you my fella I say NO," With that I proceeded to tear all the papers before me into shreds.

Laughed . . . They nearly did. Smarmy showed his true colours and dived across the table to hit me. However, this time my arms were unshackled so I blocked his punch and put him in a wrist-lock forcing him face down his full length on the table. Others were coming and as I put on more pressure, he shouted on them to stop.

All this was instinctive and maybe not altogether wise, and it soon dawned on me that I was on a hiding to nothing in the end. I think the Americans have a phrase for it: 'A lose, lose situation'. It was almost laughable and I could feel my face breaking into one of those ear-to-ear grins as I contemplated the scenarios. "If I let you go will you let me go?" or "Promise not to hurt me and I won't hurt you." It was hardly a hostage type situation was it. I'm sure like me you have watched on TV footage of Jews kneeling beside open graves and being shot in the head by an SS or Gestapo executioner. I have often said to myself that I'd have taken a few of them with me if it were me and here I was in a situation where I was going to be shot by the looks of it, and the best I could manage was a wristlock . . . sad.

I suppose at the end of the day it wasn't what I was going to do, but what God wanted me to do. How is it that my emotions, my thoughts often go against what I know God would want, and I still try to justify them and debate with God as to how I maybe knew best, just this once?

I sighed and let him go. He staggered away and the others piled in. It seemed to me that these guys were getting better at putting my shackles on but their customer relations needed a little polishing, that was for sure. Two of them put on my leg irons and holding them dragged me feet first out of the room and down to the torture chamber. I could tell this wasn't going to be good. Even as I tried to take the weight of my body on my shoulders and avoid my head banging on the steps, a prayer I'd heard somewhere came into my head, "Lord, when I die tonight, may I die like a man, may I not disgrace myself or let you down. Amen."

Eventually we ended up back in the torture chamber, where they took off my shackles and told me to strip, which I did. They shackled and cuffed me again behind my back and this time they tied a rope to the handcuffs, then passed it through the chain of the leg irons. They led me to the centre of the room and they tightened the rope in such a ways that my wrists, which were behind my back, were forced to join with my ankles and I had to kneel. My back bowed to such an extent that I thought my spine would snap. Then Smarmy arrived. "Comfortable?" he said "More comfortable than you'll be spending an eternity in hell," I replied.

"This is the round that will get rid of you for good," he said, showing me a live round from an AK 47. It's not the biggest bullet in the world, 7.62mm if my memory serves me right, but it looked enormous to me. He showed me an AK 47 and said, "This is the gun that will kill you." Then everything went black as they pulled a stinking cloth bag over my head and pulled the drawstring tight around my neck. I gagged at the smell inside the bag; someone had vomited where I was trying to breath. I heard a round being loaded into the magazine and the noise of it being pushed into place. Then the metallic snicker of the charging handle as they pulled it back, and someone put the gun to my left ear. There was nothing to say, no witty remarks, only the thoughts of a family left behind, of what might have been, then BANG.

Everything went white. I mean blinding, lightning white! After the initial bang, I didn't feel or hear anything. There was a sensation of floating down in slow motion towards the ground like a feather or a leaf falling from a tree. I knew by instinct that they still kept me bound, and my body arched backwards, but I felt or heard nothing. My body settled on my right side and there was an uncanny sense of watching all this from another dimension, as if I was a spectator. I quite clearly remember thinking, *'that wasn't so bad, dying is easier than living.'* Then as I lay there, (for how long I don't know), a buzzing noise started about two feet above my left ear and I knew I wasn't dead. Strangely enough, I was disappointed; I wasn't going to heaven quite yet.

Later I discovered that they substituted a blank round for the live one and it was the subject of great hilarity in the NIA. Less hilarious for me was the damage they had inflicted on left eardrum . . . It had been blown out.

I was carried out to the pickup and taken back to Mile Two and my cell. My head was bursting but there was no medical help so I lay in the darkness listening to what movement I could hear above the Islamic chanting. Eventually I perceived by the routine noise outside the door that it was now dawn on the Wednesday morning. The other prisoners, those allowed to go to the latrine, stopped by my door "Are you alright sir? We heard they took you away again last night." That was when I realised that I couldn't hear out of my left ear. "I'm not too bad," I replied. "I've a blinding headache though." "We'll get you something," they said. "Dr Johnnie Walker's cure-all would be good," I replied. "It's good to hear you've still got your sense of humour major," they said through the laughter.

# FELLOW PRISONERS TO THE RESCUE

I had to wait until room service brought the food in the afternoon when there was a container pushed through with it. "What's this?" I asked the mess boy. "It's an infusion sir," he replied, just before he dropped the hatch. "An infusion," I thought, "I think I'll give it a miss." Well as the day moved into evening and on to night, my head was still bursting. I'd prayed for healing, I'd commanded the headache to leave in Jesus' name. I'd even thought of casting out the spirit of headache (just joking). However, yes you've guessed it I still had a blinding headache.

'Maybe if I can sleep it'll go away,' I thought and as I tried to get comfortable on the concrete floor I almost knocked over the concoction they'd left for me. More out of thirst than anything else, I drank it. It was awful: it tasted like rats urine and who's going to contradict me on that, eh! Anyway I got it down and within ten minutes the headache was gone and when I lay with my head pillowed on my right ear to sleep I couldn't hear any mosquitoes or the Islamic chanting, just the buzzing of the tinnitus. That night with heartfelt prayer, I really thanked God for my life, as indeed I have done every day since.

I was left alone for the next two or three days, but found the tiny cell so dark and claustrophobic that I was almost panicking and had to restrain myself from banging my head against the wall. I wasn't going to let them know of my claustrophobia, as that would be another weapon in their armoury that could be used against me.

The days seemed to drag on in this never-ending darkness, the very air seemed thick and hard to breathe. Time and real life ceased to exist and things long known, long understood, became ethereal. I'd force myself to pray and I'd sing hymns to try and lift my spirits. The darkness wasn't only the lack of light but the utter darkness of the lack of hope that, I have to confess, sometimes overwhelmed me.

This confinement wing contained men I had known well in my capacity as Chaplain to the Gambian Servicemen. Most of them had been senior officers in the army or Immigration and were now in prison either for attempted coups, or for speaking out the truth about the President and the government. There was at least one man an hour outside my cell trying to cheer me up and that was the start of how I believe God allowed these Muslim men to be instrumental in sustaining me whilst there, yes, and even saving my life.

One morning a prisoner, a Muslim, banged on the door and told me it was Sunday. He said I should demand to my right to attend the church service. I duly banged on the door until a guard came. "I have to pray at church," I told him, "as a Christian I should be allowed to pray in church on a Sunday." Now in Islam, it is of the utmost importance that a Muslim attends Friday prayers in the mosque, so it was with this in mind that I insisted that I attend Sunday prayers in a church. "I'll ask the PO," he said and left. Actually, I didn't hold out much hope of going to "church service" as it was held in the main yard. Indeed, formerly as Chaplain to the prison service, I had taken countless services there. The church building was a room that doubled up as a classroom during the week used by WEC missionaries to teach the Mandingo men to read and write their own language.

Well, much to my surprise the guard came back and started his fumbling about with keys and eventually, when the door opened he told me that I was to dress as I was going to Church Service. I was elated, not just to be leaving my cell without being tortured, but that I was going to be meeting with other Christians to worship God. It was another pleasant surprise when I lined up with other men who were prisoners in the confinement wing and who were Christians. They in turn were glad to see me as they had heard all about what had happened to Fiona and me. There was one Ghanaian called Freeman who had stabbed his brother in a fight that got out of hand. There were two men from the Casamance, Joseph and Fabbea, who'd been captured in The Gambia having strayed over the border. They were Casamance rebels or freedom fighters as they called themselves in the Casamance struggle for independence from Senegal.

Then there was one former Gambian Government accountant, who supposedly embezzled millions from the President, Hmm! The last group were Nigerians, five of whom were in for kidnapping. There was no love lost between Gambians and Nigerians, but as time went on we came to see that they were set up. So including me that made ten of us lined up in twos to be marched out of the confinement wing to the main yard and the church.

Going through the main yard we were greeted by the Christian brothers there, many of whom I had known during my time as Prisons Chaplain and were still doing their sentence. A white man came up to me and introduced himself as Michael. He was doing three years for a financial scam, and never professed to being a Christian, however it was good to talk to a fellow Brit. On entering the church Ebrima Fatty the leader of the Christians came and embraced me. "Sorry Pastor Dave," he said and when I looked at him, the tears were rolling down his cheeks, "they've finally got you." "Yes," I replied, "but it'll be alright, I haven't done anything wrong." He smiled, "Nether have half of these," he said and gestured about him, "in this country it's guilty till proven innocent. Believe me my brother; if it's the Islamists who've put you here they won't let you go easily."

More men filed into the room and sat on the benches in front of rough wooden school desks. "Can you lead us Pastor?" enquired Fatty. I think I should let you know at this point that I am not a Pastor: in The Gambia, church leaders are all wrongly called Pastors and I've found that it's a waste of time trying to correct people. "OK," I replied, and stood up in front of the blackboard. I had a flashback of only a few years ago when almost every Sunday Fiona and I stood in this exact spot leading some Praise and Worship before I spoke. "Well gentlemen," I started, "I can say that it is an unexpected pleasure to be with you all this morning. You know what's happened and might be confused, but if we believe that God is in control then we have to believe that he allowed this to happen for His purpose. However guys, I can't say that I understand what that purpose might be at the moment."

Just then, Frances Mendy, one of the Prison Fellowship Chaplains came into the room. "Dave," he exclaimed and rushed over to embrace me. "We've all been praying for Fiona and you." Of course, the service had started and it wouldn't have been right to chat just then, so I made to sit down. "No," he continued, "you carry on, you're my boss." This was a reference to the early days of Prison Fellowship (The Gambia) when Fiona and I were instrumental in its inception and of which I was Executive Director for five years.

I then spoke for a while and we had a time of open prayer where much of the time was devoted to praying about my court appearance the next day. There were guards hovering around all the time, which was unusual, as Muslims won't normally be seen near the church service. After about two hours, the service ended and they herded us prisoners back inside the confinement wing. It was common knowledge among the inmates that allowing me access to the church was a privilege that hadn't been sanctioned by the senior staff who weren't in at the weekends. Those guards, who allowed me to go, did it because they knew the injustice perpetrated against us, and believed that if questioned, they had good reasons to allow it on religious grounds.

Back in my cell, I felt as good as circumstances would allow. I had seen and fellowshipped with other Christians. I had won a victory in getting to church in the first place and believed that I had set a precedent for future Sundays if I was still here.

Monday morning came, and by that time, I was starting to feel weak from lack of food and exercise. However, yet again I was determined that Fiona wouldn't see me in any state that would worry her. The police came for me and this time, when I was dressed they didn't put me in handcuffs and I was taken in a police pickup with four policemen, one of whom was in the prosecutor's office and I knew well, as I had led him to faith in Christ some years previously.

# A NO WIN SITUATION

What he whispered to me on the way to the court was chilling. "Sir," he began, "they plan to charge you with all sixty seven emails as sixty seven counts, that's sixty seven separate charges if you continue to plead not guilty, I don't know what to suggest . . . you need to speak seriously to your lawyer." What with the shooting incident and my weakened condition, my mind seemed confused. I felt angry with myself for not being decisive; this was so unlike me. However, before I was able to get the scattered thoughts in my mind into any sort of cohesion we arrived at the court.

It was so great to see Fiona and Elizabeth. They were well but concerned for me. Fiona was shocked at my condition, which was a surprise as I thought I had "scrubbed up well". There were others there, some from the Veranda Church some neighbours and acquaintances, some folks who were wringing their hands with glee and of course, the ubiquitous press. We had a meeting with the lawyer and asked him what his prognosis was. He informed us that the maximum sentence for one charge of sedition, (which was what we had at that time) was one year in prison plus a fine. Yet, he went on to say that, such a sentence was unheard of and it was more likely that we'd get a suspended sentence and deportation or a fine and deportation. This was because we were British, and because the international interest in our case was growing, and because everyone here in The Gambia knew we were innocent.

Fiona was still adamant that we continue to plead not guilty, but as we talked, we realised that the President and the Islamic Council were behind this. From our work in the prisons, we were aware that the government could drag out cases. With each charge requiring a court appearance, this could last weeks. If they charged us with, sixty-seven separate counts that would be at least sixty-seven court appearances. You don't have to be brilliant as math to work out that number of charges spaced over six weeks each, was four hundred and two weeks or over seven and a half years. We were left with a choice, plead guilty which we were loathe to do, and serve a maximum of one year in prison and get it over and done with, or spend over seven years on remand, which we probably wouldn't survive, and end up being found guilty anyway.

We spoke to the lawyer and asked him to try for another adjournment in the hope that international pressure would help sway a favourable verdict, and to give us time to pray. I could see that the magistrate wasn't happy, but in the end the case was adjourned for another week and I was taken back to the prison by the police.

By this time, I was starting to feel the effects of the starvation diet of a fish head and dry rice once a day, plus having only one gallon of water for all my needs every two days was just ridiculous. At that time, the British High Commission seemed to be doing nothing, save giving me bits of paper telling me what they couldn't do for me. However, the day after the court appearance they showed me a document, which shocked me. It was a statement, which they advised me to read out in court apologising to the President, the Islamic Council and the Gambian people. "What," I said, "never, all we ever did was tell the truth." "I can't advise you one way or the other," said the man from the High Commission, "I'm not allowed to." To be fair to the BHC, their hands were tied, bound by red tape and in countries like The Gambia, (those with an evil dictatorship,) there is little they can do. I told him that I doubted if we'd read it in court as it wasn't how I felt and he left. "Useless, the lot of them," I muttered.

Having said that, there was one man that I believe was the Deputy High Commissioner at the time, who came to see me a few days later and brought a bottle of water and two salad sandwiches that his wife had made for me. He handed them over but one of the guards said that I couldn't have them unless he took a sip of the water and a bite out of each of the sandwiches. I said to the guard, "Do you think the British are trying to poison me?" "No," he replied, "but maybe there are drugs in there to make you feel happy." So the DHC duly took a sip of water and two small bites of sandwich, shook my hand and left.

They led me back to confinement clutching my treasures, mouth watering in anticipation of the feast. At the confinement gate I went through the customary search and the guard, pointing to the water and food, said, "What's this?" I explained that it was from my High Commission, but he grabbed the plastic bottle from me and split it against the wall before I had time to react. I was stunned and maybe a little late reacting, but I dropped the sandwiches and grabbed him by his uniform shirt and drawing him towards me head-butted him. Some will say "what a bad witness" and you'd be right, but it didn't half make me feel better.

Well I didn't realise there were so many guards in the place and that they'd choose this time to be passing close enough that they could all get the boot in. They forced me down by the sheer weight of bodies and all I could do was to curl up in a foetal position and shut it out. It was like a sort of mental anaesthesia: I could bleed; I could suffer, but hardly feel the pain – that would come later. There was a slackening off, and I heard someone shouting and then it stopped. A senior officer who I'd never seen before was remonstrating with the guards and physically pulling them off me. "Sorry," he said, "these men are from the bush, they have no education." Unable to speak I nodded and tried to stand. "Help him up," he commanded and the men rushed to do his bidding. Two others picked up my sandwiches that having been trampled into the sand and tried to brush them off. "You have them," I said and started to limp my way back to the cell, which I was beginning to see as a place of refuge.

Back at my cell, the officer took my clothes away to be cleaned, after he'd told me that the guards would be disciplined. I didn't argue but laid on the floor and tried to do stretching exercises so the muscles wouldn't stiffen up. That week passed slowly and apart from various former senior servicemen coming to talk to me through the hatch, and my once daily meal of fish head and rice, I was left alone.

# INSTITUTIONALISED?

That week should have been good except for what was to become the norm, the anticipation of the NIA coming in the middle of the night to take me away for torturing. I've heard it said that; "anticipation is worse than the event". Well, in my case that wasn't true. I was aware enough to realise that my cell was becoming like a womb to me, a safe place and no matter how much I prayed that I wouldn't become institutionalised I could see that it was happening, but I was determined to fight it.

I started to make choices to be a pain in their ass, and so as strange as it may sound, some days I'd decide not to eat their food by refusing the bowl when it was slid through the door. This would cause a stir and an officer would come to see me. "Are you on hunger strike?" "No," I'd reply, "I've gone off fish heads." Sometimes, when I was taken to the latrine to empty my paint tin, I'd refuse to go back into my cell and several guards would be required to push me in. There wasn't much I could do, but I felt

I was gaining some victories. The mess boy told me when Sunday morning came around, and I started banging on the door and shouting, "you have to unlock me for church service." I banged and banged until at last I heard the keys jangle over the Islamic chanting and eventually, the cell door opened. "Church service," the guard shouted and I was out of there like a shot. It was so good to put on clean clothes that I had found, hanging on the nail, in a plastic bag. As I dressed I threw the bag into the cell, and this was the start of my scavenging career in Mile Two.

Again, they lined us up in twos, and marched us out of the confinement wing, into the main yard. The inmates in the main prison were curious about how I was managing and it came as no surprise to them to find out that I'd a bruise or two on my arms where I'd covered my face with them during the kicking, and I was limping. Nevertheless, it was great to be out of my cell and free to some extent and having fellowship with other Christians. This Sunday no Pastor had come in and it looked as if the guards would take us back. However, Fatty spoke to the sergeant saying that I was qualified to lead the service and he agreed. How I missed the guitar as the singing was dreadful without any music and there were no hymnbooks. Another slight drawback was that there were four or five different nationalities and languages.

Fiona and I used to bring in Mission Praise and as I had the music edition, we always started on the right note. Anyway we did what we could and I'm sure there were a few chuckles in heaven and maybe even in hell. No, of course not, there is not and never will be chuckling in hell . . . the Bible says so. I spoke on taking responsibility for our own actions, as I could see there was a degree of self-deception in many of the men. While there were those of us who were in there for telling the truth and doing the right thing, most of the men from the main yard and all the Nigerians from there, were in for big and bad crimes. However, they were saying that as they were now Born Again Christians "the old had passed and the new had come" and they should no longer be incarcerated. That's not what it says in my Bible.

However, I have to say that these guys can pray, even though we all know that God's been around a while, they do seem to be under the illusion that He, in His old age, might be hard of hearing and so they tend to pray very loudly. I wondered if they thought that God was a bit forgetful as they kept reminding Him of what he had written in His word, albeit out of context. All too soon, the service was over and the guards marched us back to the confinement wing.

The time passed slowly but at last Monday arrived. It was to be an important day for us, as we'd individually been thinking and praying about what to do. As usual in my chains and cuffs, I shuffled and staggered out of the confinement wing and into the main yard. Again, we were confronted with the fact that I couldn't climb up over the tailgate while shackled. Now, I have to say that at this point I could have got up there like a rat up a drainpipe if I'd needed to, but I wasn't going to let them know that.

The guards scratched their heads and, shouted at each other and me. The inmates already on board the truck laughed and jeered. The truck driver revved his engine and covered the whole scene in black diesel fumes, which poured out of a broken exhaust pipe. It was like an extract from a comic farce or a pantomime. I half expected someone to shout out *"Behind you!"*

"Get them off," shouted a senior officer. "I beg your pardon?" I shouted back, exaggeratingly holding up my slack trousers. A sergeant pushed his way through what was becoming a crowd of prison guards, people who were on their way to have a visit and of course me, Mr Innocent. This was all part of my non co-operation tactics, so I'd not be led quietly like a lamb to the slaughter.

# STITCHED UP

When I got to court, Fiona and I discussed things and our friend Patricia gave me a chicken sandwich and a can of Fanta that I devoured while we talked. It seemed that a deal had been struck by someone, presumably the BHC, that if we read out the apology then we'd be on the next plane home. However, the magistrate wouldn't allow that until the case had started. Our lawyer reiterated his belief that we would get a suspended sentence and deportation order if we read out the apology and pleaded guilty. We recognised the foolishness of the charges, and being somewhat naive, agreed, and after weighing up all the options reluctantly decided to plead guilty.

"All rise," the court official shouted. We rose and they led us to the dock. Our lawyer told the court that we would like to read out a statement, but the magistrate said that for the record, "we weren't allowed to do this prior to a plea of guilty." We would have to change our plea or the case would start at the next sitting with count one.

The Magistrate asked, "How do you plead?" We had no reasonable alternative. "Guilty." The magistrate then allowed me to read out the apology that neither Fiona nor I agreed with, but we were lead to believe this was "the deal" done with the government to allow us to fly home that very day. The prosecution presented their case, namely the sixty-seven seditious emails. Also mentioned by the prosecution was that this case became known, after a "concerned citizen" reported to the Islamic Council and the NIA that Fiona and I were sending emails to the UK and other countries. They said that these emails, could be used to bring down the government and he had a copy of one, which he sent to the authorities. Almost at once, the magistrate, to my surprise announced, "Case adjourned till 28th November for judgement."

Back in Mile Two, I was inundated with enquiries about what had happened and without exception everyone castigated me, firstly for my guilty plea and secondly on reading the apology. I sat in the darkness of my cell and wondered if I had done the right thing, but I really couldn't see an alternative. Though my mind flashed these alternatives; to plead not guilty, that would mean the possibility of years on remand while the Islamist extremists extracted their pound of flesh. To plead not guilty would mean the possibility, even the probability of us both dying while in captivity. To plead not guilty would mean us being apart from our children for years. No! I believed we had done what was best, and the worst-case scenario would be one year in prison, of which we had already served one month and one week. With remission, that one year should be eight months ten days from date of arrest. That meant that we should be out in July 2009. On balance, despite the criticism of others who were either life or death sentence people, I believed we had it right.

# IT'S DYING TIME AGAIN

In some ways, there was a feeling of security in knowing that one part was over, and at least the process had begun. I truly believed that justice and fairness would prevail and it would be on the level playing field of a courtroom. Later that day or was it night? I started to feel cold, but the ambient temperature was over 35$^c$. I was sweating buckets but shivering as well. I knew the symptoms, malaria, so I knew that I was probably going to be vomiting in a short while.

I started to thump on the door, but in my weakened condition, I couldn't make myself heard above the Islamic chanting. There was nothing I could do but lie in the darkness and within minutes, I was throwing up the food I'd been given when we were at court. Then the diarrhoea started, but inconsiderately the vomiting didn't stop. The malaria lasted several days, and though the guards knew about it, and the inmates complained on my behalf, they did nothing. They left me to wallow in my own filth. Indeed, I believe they left me to die.

There were times during these few days when I thought, '*this is it*'. It wasn't the first time, and it wasn't to be the last. I've heard it said; life doles out second chances with a sparing hand; but I've proved that God is very generous with second chances and third and fourth, indeed ad-infinitum.

A medic who was an inmate came to see me. "I've been told

not to treat you," he said through the hatch. "The order to leave you to die has come from the top, I mean the very top. Sorry, but if I help you it'll be me filling your shoes, maybe your grave," and with that he left. However, by God's grace, gradually I recovered, but I was as weak as a kitten and as filthy as a pig in a sty. A quote came into my mind when I realised my conditions and that the pig of a President was behind my persecution "If you wrestle with a pig, you both get dirty, but the pig enjoys it".

The 28th came, and the guards allowed me to go to the latrine and, using a bucket of water, had a shower and a shave before getting dressed. This time when bound hand and foot and taken to the truck, I couldn't have climbed on board if my life depended on it.

# WITH HARD LABOUR

At court, Fiona and our friends were shocked at my appearance and she had to support me when I came in. I noticed Bin-Ladin prominently ensconced where the magistrate could see him. "All rise," shouted the court clerk. When the magistrate sat down, I knew something was wrong. His whole demeanour was that of agitation, anger, even hate towards Fiona and me. We stood in the dock, Fiona propping me up while the magistrate took out a sheaf of papers.

He started to read, totally out of context, extracts from an assortment of emails. He ranted and raved about us trying to undermine the government, (which wasn't true.) He said that I criticized the President, and that I said in an email that he was a 'paranoid schizophrenic, (which was true.) He accused me of "pooh poohing" the President's good works in healing aids, asthma and hypertension, (which was true.) He went on to accuse me of gaining access to high security military installations and equipment in The Gambia, which was a laugh as it was me that beefed up the security of these establishments and anyway, what "high security equipment?" We're talking the bottom of the third world pile here, where AK 47s are considered high tech.

There was something weird about his mannerisms; he had that guilty look, like a Bishop caught in a whorehouse. During his tirade, Fiona whispered in my ear, "I feel sorry for that man." It has to be said that I did feel something for him, but sorry . . . Not me.

For about an hour, we stood there listening to all this nonsense, but at last, just as I was beginning to think I'd have to sit on the floor, he came to an end and the court hushed. "I sentence you both to one year in prison with hard labour and a fine of 250,000 Dallasis (£6,250) each." Wow! There was a buzz in the court as the magistrate leapt out of his chair and almost ran from the court. "A year," I said to Fiona, "the maximum.

# SO NEAR AND YET SO FAR

For the first time in a long time, Fiona and I were in the same transport, but this time we were both heading for Mile Two Prison. We were processed and given our prison clothes, I had a pair of shorts and tee shirt in a fetching blue to match my bruises. Fiona was given a smock top and a lapper made of denim and a headscarf in the same blue that later matched the shadows under her eyes.

We were asked if we wanted to appeal, but both agreed that it was a waste of money as we'd be out in seven months with remission and an appeal could take more than one year. I thought I'd be taken to the main prison, but it was made clear that I was still the President's personal enemy, and David Colley's arch enemy, so as such was taken back to the confinement wing.

Before we were separated Fiona gave me a book she'd been carrying, it was three books in one by Charles Swindoll. 'The

*Grace Awakening, Hope Again and Simple Faith'.* Miraculously they allowed me to keep it and it proved a real blessing to me for the whole time I was in captivity.

They then took Fiona to the female wing where she had worked as a volunteer some years earlier, and where some of the women still knew her. I was being marched through the confinement wing. There was only about 100 yards between us in distance, but it seemed like thousands of miles at that time.

Many men quietly commiserated with me, quietly because I was now officially an enemy of the state, one of them. They stripped me and threw me back into my old cell, same cockroaches, same mosquitoes and the same ants. I couldn't say it was good to be back.

# MERRY CHRISTMAS 2008

At some point in the week, it was Christmas day, though I hadn't a clue which one until the hatch opened and the mess boy slid in a bowl of hot fried rice, a chicken leg and some cabbage. "It's OK to eat it sir," he said, "this is from the Christians outside and here's a Christmas present from them also." Saying that he passed in a plastic bag and slid the hatch shut. It opened once more seconds later "Merry Christmas!" he said and the hatch closed again. I paused. "Merry Christmas," I said to myself in the darkness. I thought of my family. "Merry Christmas" I said to them as tears started to roll down my cheeks. I brushed them quickly away. Just for a moment . . . only one moment, homesickness and self-pity were as acute as a bullet's strike.

"Get a grip," I told myself aloud and gave thanks for the food. I can truly say that never did a Christmas dinner taste better and as I felt inside the bag there were some boiled sweets, a carton of fruit drink, soap, toothpaste and a packet of biscuits. I felt especially blessed by the fact that, we had been in at the start of the introduction of Christmas food and presents, in Prison Fellowship in the year 2001. We asked the churches for money to give every prisoner in The Gambia a gift of soap and biscuits. Now here I was, seven years down the line, benefiting from it.

# COMFORT FROM A CORPSE

Once convicted I believed that things would settle down and I'd worked out that we should be free by the end of July coming, so it was just a question of getting our heads down and getting on with it. I was left alone for days on end and while it was sort of good that I had a date to aim my survival at, I was cognisant of the fact that I wasn't going to survive even till July on the diet that I was receiving. So, what was I going to do about it?

My enquiries through the mess boy revealed that Fiona's conditions were a lot better than mine were. She was in a communal cell, which had a proper toilet and shower. She was with people. Fiona is a gregarious person and despite everything she was going through, I knew she'd be helping the women in the Female Wing one way or another. It's what she does, simple as that. The other prisoners received three meals a day. In the morning, there'd be porridge of sorts for breakfast, or bread and tea. There would be fish and rice for lunch and couscous for dinner. I was relieved to know that Fiona was eating the food that while not good or nourishing, would at least keep her alive. It may sound selfish, but I was able in some way to leave her in God's hands and not worry.

I don't know whether it was lack of nutrition, vitamins or sunlight, but I came out in boils which covered my body and many became septic. This not only added to the discomfort, but also gave me a challenge as to how to get rid of them with no medication. What I needed was a razor blade, but how was I going to do that? Our friend Patricia sent me in twin blade Bic razors, but when I used one I had to exchange it for a new one, Oh well, something would crop up . . . it always does.

I suppose that at some point New Year's Day came and went, but time had no meaning for me. There was only endless night, total disorientation, discomfort, filth and stifling heat. My cell may have only been tiny, but it could have been enormous in the vastness of the dark. Sleep came without any knowledge of whether it had lasted ten minutes or ten hours, as I awoke to the same conditions and in the same condition.

One day the cell door swung open. "Can you have a look at this man?" a prison officer asked me. I crawled out into the corridor, and with the help of the wall, I managed to stand up. "What is it?" I enquired; glad to speak English to someone. "This man," he said again, pointing at the cell next to mine with the door open. I went to the cell and looked in. The place was swarming with large blue flies and mosquitoes.

The smell was even worse than in mine: then I realised to my horror that it wasn't worse, it was only different. As I bent down to go inside, I saw a white man there kneeling with the top of his shaven head against the wall as if he was praying. When I put out my hand to touch him, it came away with some putrid skin and flesh on it. I recoiled back and up, banging my head on the ceiling, which caused me to fall on my knees beside him. I knew there was nothing I could do. He was dead . . . very dead.

I scrabbled out quickly and sat outside his cell and told the guard what I'd found. He didn't know what to do. I refused to go back to my cell and he couldn't leave me alone, so we chatted as I tried to regain my composure. "Who is, or was he?" I asked. "A Hollandees," he replied (Hollandees are what the Gambians call people from Holland, Dutch to us.) "So when did you last speak to him or feed him for that matter?" I continued, "Long time, he never gave his bowl out, maybe four days," he said. "Oh my God: Four days!" I exclaimed, "Did no one think to see if he was alright?" A shrug was all I got and after a while, another guard arrived. This man's only crime was that he had been a homosexual and therefore jailed under the Presidents brutal regime.

The alarm sounded and a lockdown implemented. I was still

in the corridor seemingly forgotten, when senior officers arrived with two mess boys and a wooden door. "Bring him out Tubab," one of the officers said, and as I was the only Tubab there, I assumed he was talking to me. "Yeah, right, you do it," I replied. I'd seen this guy before, his rank was superintendent his nickname was Jimbo and he was a buddy of the Director.

He'd always struck me as being hyperactive and now he started shouting and hopping about from foot to foot, as if he'd been born with two thyroids. "Bring him out and I'll allow you to shower and exercise outside." Well, while that might not sound much to you, to me it was like the promise of heaven.

The mess boys, one of whom was Sanneh, handed me a filthy old blanket and when I went back in he followed at a respectful, or was it a cowardly distance. I put the blanket round the man's shoulders and tried to draw him sideways, but he would not budge. I realised that his head seemed to be stuck on the wall. "Give me a light," I said to Sanneh and he repeated it in the local language.

After a minute, I was given a plastic Bic lighter and it wasn't until I tried to light the thing that I realised that my hands were practically useless with small things like the lighter, they lacked any sort of dexterity. Shaking like a leaf, eventually, I got it lit and saw through the mist of flies that there was blood congealed on the wall from his head down to the floor where it lay thickly spread between his legs as if he'd urinated it. Beside me Sanneh vomited and staggered out the cell.

I pulled the man, (who I was told later was called Hans), back from the wall, and then on to his side. Rigor mortis had well set in and he stayed in the kneeling position, and there was a neat hole in the front of the top of his head. When I looked at the wall, I could see by the light of the flame a nail protruding from a crack in the cement. I tried to pull the nail out with my left hand, but with my little finger on my left hand still broken, and the lighter in my right, I couldn't get a grip, so I had to leave it. "Slide the door in," I shouted into the passageway. They put it flat on the ground and shoved at the cell door, but it was too wide. "Drag him out Tubab," came a voice from the passageway. "I need another blanket to wrap him in," I shouted back. "Wait," he said, and while everyone was waiting, and avoiding looking into the cell, I switched the lighter off and worked the nail loose, then in the darkness slid it and the small lighter up my anus.

Another quite clean blanket was thrown in and I stuffed it in the corner of the dark cell, rolled Hans onto his knees again, then back onto the original blanket, off which I tore a piece to wipe my hands clean of the slime. I was then able to clamber over the body, out into the passageway holding the end of the blanket and breathe reasonably good air again. The mess boys were dragging the body along on the blanket and I said to Jimbo, "Can I have my shower now?" "Fuck you Tubab," he shouted, hopping from foot to foot. You know, I wasn't in the least surprised. "Lock him up," he said to the guard over his shoulder as he walked away. At this point I'm sure you'll be impressed with my self control, but in fact I just wanted to return to my cell with my booty.

The guard who had originally come to get me wasn't a bad man, most of them weren't, and as soon as the passageway was clear he said, "You've got ten minutes to clean up while I go for a smoke," and with that he left me alone. I staggered as quickly as I was able back into the late Hans's cell. I grabbed the blanket and then got back to mine where I extracted the nail and lighter and put the lot in the same corner as the door so that a cursory glance would reveal nothing amiss. Then I got my almost full paint tin toilet and emptied it. Back in the cell I picked up the gallon container and filled it to the brim, emptying it over me about a dozen times, scrubbing myself with the piece of blanket. When I was finished and my water container was full and back in the cell, the guard still wasn't back. So, never one to miss an opportunity I staggered along the passageway and asked through the door of a fellow I knew, "Have you a razor I can borrow?" I hadn't shaved in days. "Sure, he replied and passed me out a sliver of soap and what must have been the rustiest, bluntest, razor blade in the world. It was one of these two-sided jobs that I'm sure he'd been using to try to cut his way out through the bars.

However, "beggars can't be choosers". I shaved, washed my hair and handed the blade and an even smaller sliver of soap back. "Keep it," the fellow said, "Thanks" I replied, and then the guard returned to lock me up. A blanket, a lighter, a blade, some soap, another nail, another victory. "Thank you God," I said.

Time passed slowly and for some reason they stationed a guard outside my cell door to stop anyone talking to me or trying to help me in any way. I was physically uncomfortable, in pain and hungry, but strangely, or maybe not so strangely, I felt blessed with a supernatural peace, which I believed was the result of people praying.

I asked the medic, who was the only person allowed to speak to me, how I went about getting vitamin tablets. "There are none in the prison," he told me, "but if you send out a prescription they have to allow them in." "How do I get a prescription?" I asked. "Ah now, there is a problem," he replied. "There are no prescription pads left since last week." "So what do I do?" the saga continued. "I have some old ones they don't know about, I'll give you one, but you need to get a pen and fill it in as if it was written here."

It took two days, but he was true to his word, and a single piece of paper arrived through the door along with my food. When I'd eaten and the bowl was ready to be taken away, I was in position by the hatch in order to see what I had been given. In the light when the hatch opened, I saw where I needed to fill in the medication and sign it, but sign it with what? David Fulton? President Jammeh? Mickey Mouse? Life sure wasn't easy. One thing was for sure, I needed a pen. "Lord," I prayed, "how do I get a hold of a pen in here?"

Keys jangled and the door opened. "Fulton, get washed and dressed, you've got a visit." A visit, wow, I staggered half blind because the forty-watt lights in the passageway seemed so bright but when I got out into the real sunlight, I had no chance. I couldn't even open my eyes for at least five minutes, but at last I was able to hobble out into the main courtyard where the prison Headquarters were. They led me into an office and there was a representative from the British High Commission.

I honestly can't remember what he came to see me about, but I asked him if he had a pen he could give me. "Of course," he said holding out the Bic he was using. "Under the table," I whispered without moving my lips. He drew it back and to give him his due, passed it to me surreptitiously. I then slid it up my shorts and further, before you could say "Abracadabra" I had my pen.

Within three days, I was able to write my own prescription for sixty tabs of Multivit, two months supply, and signed it Dr Mickey Mouse. My smuggled script reached the High Commission who then sent it back with the vitamins and thank God, they reached me.

Three weeks passed, which I was able to gauge only by the Sundays, the only time they allowed me out of my cell to attend "Church Service". Two of the pastors were able to tell me that the international community were outraged over what had happened to us. Sky news had broadcast the story worldwide, but the Dictator Jammeh was indifferent to anything but the advice of the Islamic Council and his witch doctors.

Another thing he told me was that we were being disowned by a number of Christian pastors who were afraid of being, and I quote "Tarred with the same brush" .Some said, "Me? I don't know the man." I was sad, but not in the least angry. After all if Peter could deny knowing the Lord, who was I to expect any better. Anyway, after Peter blew it, God used him greatly.

My diet was still a fish head and dry rice once a day, every day, with water to wash it down. Now as I look back on it I am surprised that after a few weeks I never felt hungry, the pounds were dropping off me, but I'd worked out that if I ate everything in my bowl I'd survive the few months I had left. Still occasionally, I'd refuse the food just to show that I had some control.


# TWISTING THE TRUTH

One night when I least expected it, they came. My body was no longer in pain; I was weak from malnutrition, but at least my boils and sores had healed thanks to lancing them and the vitamins I was able to take. It was the usual procedure, but this time I couldn't figure out why I'd be wanted, as we'd already been sentenced. It was Shades again, leaning himself against the wall, as usual saying nothing and for a change, I said nothing in return. There was nothing to say.

By the time I reached the pickup I was starting to get apprehensive, my thoughts were doing somersaults. Maybe they were going to release me. Maybe I was going to hospital. Maybe the British High Commissioner was here to see me, maybe, maybe, maybe. However, it didn't take long to realise that I was once again in the hands of the nasties; but why? Well I guess it wouldn't be long before I'd find out.

They took me out of the prison to the NIA headquarters, then herded me into a brightly lit interview room, Shades took station at the door and there was Smarmy, ensconced behind a Formica topped table. He motioned me to sit on a hard backed chair at the table. "How's prison?" was his opening remark. "You evil people will soon find out for yourself," I replied, "believe me this will turn round and bite you in the bum." What was I saying? Was I mad? It seemed that I was talking without considering or weighing up the consequences of my words, but my mouth went on; "The Bible says in the book of Mark, that if Satan opposes himself and is divided, he can't stand and his end has come." He laughed, "Are you suggesting that we are of Satan?" "Suggesting?" I replied, "Oh no, not suggesting, I'm telling you, as the Bible says, God, my God is a God of love, whereas the demon you worship spews out nothing but hate. You can see it every day worldwide and even here in this room just by looking at you." Well, I got something right, maybe at the wrong time though. Hate shone out of his dark eyes, it was almost palpable, causing a shiver down my spine.

He leaned back in his chair and reached into a black plastic bag at his side. Drawing out a number plate, he placed it face up on the table. I recognised it immediately; it was the red number plate that I made up after being given permission to do so by the Gambian Government in 2004, and had carried on my old Range Rover for the past six years. "Do you recognise this?"

he questioned. "Of course I recognise it," I said. He held up a uniform jacket bearing a cross on the shoulder epaulettes, and continued, "Do you recognise this?" "I should do," I replied. "As you well know, I've worn it most days of my life here." "Ah!" he exclaimed, "So you admit it" "Admit what?" I was somewhat confused, everyone in the Gambian services knew I wore the uniform of a Chaplain, everyone knows I've been driving around with the red TA Number plate GSC 1 TA for years. The GSC means Gambian Serviceman's Chaplain. "Where did you get this very number plate?" He went on. "What, that specific plate?" I questioned. "Yes this very one," he repeated, lifting it and waving it in the air. "Well," I went on calmly, "as I'm sure you know, there were no facilities to make number plates when I was given the authority to use that number. Instead of writing the number on the car as almost everyone else did, I sprayed the original plates red and stuck on the numbers and letters, which I made from white paper. I stuck them on, and then lacquered the plate to make it waterproof."

"So you admit to making this number plate with your own hands," he said thrusting the number plate in my face."I am charging you with defrauding the Gambian Government out of 500 dalais (£10) as you could have had one made up by the Government when we were able to do so, and that's been many months now. I am also going to charge you with impersonating a Gambian serviceman," he said with a serious face. I looked at him in silence, half expecting him to burst out laughing at the absurdity of it all, but his face was poker straight, not even a twitch at the corners of his mouth. However, I could feel my own mouth begin to grin, "Me, impersonating a Gambian security officer, which one? There are no white soldiers in the Gambian army or in any of the services. Next, you'll be producing a tin of black shoe polish to substantiate your nonsense charge. Oh, I can't wait till this gets to court; you'll be the laughing stock of the world."

"As for the number plate," I continued while my mouth was warm, "I have the paperwork in my safe at home which proves that the Government gave me the authority to bear that number."

He reached into the plastic bag and drew out an envelope from which he took a slip of paper. "Would this be the authority?" he queried. I took it and examined it. "Where did you get this?" I asked with growing apprehension. He said nothing, but just sat there smarming. "The police have the duplicate," I went on. He pulled out another slip identical to the first and waved it in my face. "I am the police, and the Islamic Council weren't happy with me for your light sentence, so either you suffer or I suffer and guess who I've nominated for that honour?" "No one will believe you," I protested. "No," he replied, "quite the contrary, you have lied before, so no one will believe you."

He nodded to Shades who came forward and took my arm. "Let's go," he said. I allowed him to usher me out of the building and into the pickup. I suppose I was in a state of shock, I was stunned, numb. Were these people so evil that they weren't satisfied with a year's sentence, and what about Fiona?

It was still dark when we got back in to prison and they took me quickly back to my cell. I was later to find that the NIA's nocturnal visits to the prison went unlogged in the movement book. Not only my regular outings, but also many others, in fact all the political prisoners who were tortured and many who disappeared were never logged out of Mile Two.

Come the morning when the prison stirred, a few of the men ignored the guard and when passing my cell shouted out encouragements. I couldn't help but think, wasn't God wonderful. Here I was, in prison to stop me preaching the Word of God and denouncing Islam as a false religion, and God was using Muslims to encourage me . . . awesome.

I prayed that God would show me what to do, where this was all going. Was it possible they could concoct a credible prosecution from such fabricated rubbish? I'd been driving with these plates on my car for years, many senior officers and even Government ministers had travelled in the car with me over these years. Everyone of importance knew me in my uniform, even to the extent that I was obliged to attend official functions in uniform when the President was present.

I'd taken services at police headquarters in uniform with my

Range Rover complete with red TA number plate on the front and back parked outside. How on earth, could they now say that was committing a fraud? I was asking God for some perspective on the situation, to help me fight it better. However, I guess that "position determines perspective" or put more simply, what you see and understand depends on where you're standing and I was standing at the bottom of the cliff looking up.

Some clarity did come once the numbness had worn off, I'd get a good lawyer and plead not guilty to both charges. I'd be able to get some witnesses who could back me up in refuting this fabricated nonsense. There were the policemen who issued the number plate paperwork, the Government minister who authorised the wearing of the Chaplaincy uniform, the Secretary of State and the Commander of the Defence Forces who asked me to be Chaplain to the armed forces. In a court of law they'd have to tell the truth, yes, by the grace of God I could beat this.

# MORE OF THE SAME

One week later, they took me back to the NIA again, and again it was early in the morning, probably about 1am. From the moment, I was unlocked until the moment they prodded me into the torture chamber, not one of the secret police spoke a word. I'd tried to speak, but my words were met with a stony silence. To me this was ominous, but then again maybe they just weren't in a chatty mood.

They removed my leg irons and handcuffs and made me undress, and then put them back on. What was going on? Obviously something new, but I hoped not too exciting. They fastened a rope around the cuffs, which were behind my back and then fed through the links in the leg irons. Beside me, there were two concrete block pillars about three and a half feet high with a groove cut along the top of both. They tried to make me kneel, but I resisted the temptation. The last time I'd done that I was shot. Zap! Zap! They hit me twice with a cattle prod, one behind my right knee and the other on the small of my back. I crumpled on to my knees where they pulled the rope tight, binding my hands and feet together.

I hadn't seen him, but Godzilla stepped into my line of sight holding the cattle prod and what looked like a car radio antenna. The old kind made of different diameters of chrome tubing that slide into each other and then into the wing of the car. Well this looked similar to that, but I found out later that it was solid. Accompanying him was another chap, who had a rusty steel bar, about one and a half inches in diameter. My apprehension was growing, it's that fear of the unknown, but it is nevertheless fear and I was disgusted at myself for feeling it. I thought of family, I thought of friends, I thought, not for the first time or the last "this is it." Then I remembered how Jesus died, I believed that these men were going to beat me to death. These people don't pray for their enemies, they bury them. Could I be like Jesus? I doubted it, but I'd try.

A Bible verse came to my mind and I started to say it out aloud.

> You are my servant.
> I have chosen you and have not rejected you,
> So, do not fear, for I am with you,
> Do not be dismayed, for I am your God
> I will strengthen you and help you,
> I will uphold you with my righteous right hand.
>
> Isaiah 41

It was then the two men slid the steel bar behind my knees and lifted me up in the air, I swung upside down on the bar which was then cradled in the grooves on top of the two concrete pillars. The bar slipped from behind my knees to the cuffs and leg irons and I was left hanging upside down, with my head about six inches from the ground and my feet in the air. "God," I prayed again, "may I live this night well."

I heard a swishing sound, then pain like an electric shock that

110

wouldn't go away erupted from the soles of both feet at the same time, up my legs and dissipated at my genitals. Another shot of electricity, and then another. On and on it went. They poured water over my feet and it ran down my body, into my nose and mouth almost choking me. I was determined not to scream, but above the swishing and cracking of the thin rod, I could hear myself moaning. It never stopped . . . that beating. Physically it did, it had to, but when I walk, even now two years later, I catch myself limping and remembering. That time, up until now is one of my most frequent of my flashbacks.

At some point, I passed out and when I came to, I was still hanging upside down, gently rocking and still moaning. I could feel that my face was suffused in blood, but only internally from hanging there. Even though the beatings had stopped, the pain was unending and terrible. Spikes of agony stabbed up my legs from my feet. "Oh God," was all I could say. "Oh God" . . . over and over again.

They didn't take me back to the prison that day, or for a few after that, but threw me into the blackness of "Bamba Dinka" with others who were undergoing interrogation. Some of these men were known to me as they were also housed in the confinement wing at Mile Two when not here, so we were able to talk. "There is only one way to help your feet sir," a former Major told me, "the skin must be cut and the blood must escape." One thing was for sure, the soles of my feet were one massive blood blister and bruise. "Where can we get a razor?" I asked him, "we're all naked and wounded." Some discussion went on with people I couldn't see in the darkness, and then it was obvious, by the triumphant conclusion of the conversation that a solution had been found.

It was passed from hand to hand, carefully in the darkness till it reached me. A piece of broken glass and a plastic bottle full to overflowing with urine. The former Major said, "You must cut the skin Sir, squeeze the blood out and then clean it with the piss." By the sound of his voice, I could tell he was serious and call me Mr Sceptical if you like, but I have to admit to a little reluctance. However, then I remembered reading from a book written by Wilbur Smith, that in the days of sailing ships urine helped to heal wounds and keep away infection. Now, I knew that Wilbur Smith was meticulous in getting his facts right, so? OK I didn't mind giving it a try, but I wish it had been my own urine.

It had to do this to myself, as I needed to feel my way through the process. I spat on the sliver of glass to sterilise it (we're not talking clinical procedures here) then cut into the sole of my right foot. The pain in my feet was far greater than any cut and I had to feel blood to be assured that I'd managed an incision. Blood was coming out so I followed the same procedure on the left foot, then doused them in the communal urine. When they took me back to prison, what must have been two or so days later, the skin on the soles of my feet was dead and hanging off, but it didn't seem to be infected.

# NEW CHARGES AND THREATS

It was two weeks before they took me to court to charge me with the two new counts, but I was still unable to walk properly, which delighted the reporters and TV people. Some of the time I crawled, going up the stairs to the courtroom, but I also managed to walk a little if I had some support. None of my acquaintances knew I was in court, so when I stood in front of the magistrate I pleaded not guilty to both charges and because I had no lawyer, they allowed me a two-week adjournment to find one. I was able through a prison officer to contact a lawyer called Lamin Camera. He'd come recommended, and had a reputation for being good and fair. He said he'd come to see me in prison before my next appearance. On the way back to prison one of the senior prison officers said, "You've been in solitary for one hundred and twenty days. I'll speak to the director so you can get some exercise." "Thank you," I replied, "but I won't hold my breath."

The next day I had a visit from a woman from the British High

Commission. They'd read about my court appearance in the papers and it was also on local radio and TV. I filled her in on what had happened and she was shocked, indeed, she wanted to make a formal complaint on behalf of the British Government. I explained that it wouldn't be a good idea. I said, "There is an old Arab saying, "The bird in the sleeping cat's mouth doesn't start whistling." I was in the clutches of a mad man and vindictive extremist Islamists, so far, I'd managed by God's grace to survive, but let's not make waves. She agreed and promised to be in court next time and to let my friends know the date. "Sorted," I thought.

About one week later my cell door opened and the guard told me to dress, I had a visit. Speculation soon ran wild in the confinement wing as to who it was. "Is it your Ambassador?" one would shout. "Maybe it's a lawyer's visit," said another. There was nothing to do there, nothing to talk about, so anything out of the ordinary was a talking point and reason for excitement. It was however the NIA. I was taken to an office and ordered to stand before two men I'd never seen before. Well, there were two other chairs against the wall, so I went over and sat down. "What are you doing?" shouted one of the men." I didn't answer. The other, a short thin man wearing a black suit two sizes too big for him said, "Mr Fulton." I looked at him. I had nothing to say to them so I said nothing. "You pleaded not guilty to the two new charges, why?" "I continued to stare at him and say nothing. "You will plead guilty next week when you go to court," he went on. I continued to stare at him. In the army, this would be called "dumb insolence" but this wasn't the army and I was in no mood to be bullied.

"OK," said the other man who was big and fat, but before he was able to go on I exclaimed, "You two are a comedy act, aren't you, you've been on telly, Little and Large, can I get your autograph?" They looked at each other perplexed. "What are you talking about?" Large said, and I went into my mute mode again. "As I was saying," He continued, "we've come to tell you that you will plead guilty to both charges next week or your wife will never leave this prison alive." That got my attention, "My wife?" I answered in a low threatening voice that made them start. "If you or any of the NIA ever lay a finger on my wife I'll hunt you down, all of you and I will kill you.

You'll never be able to sleep without having to keep one eye open for me. You'll never be able to eat without knowing if I've tampered with your food. You'll drive with your eyes peeled for me in a truck bearing down on you. You'll keep your eyes open in the Mosque when you pray to whatever demon you worship. If you touch my wife, you are dead," and with that I got up and limped forward to the desk. "I'm a Christian, but I'm also a man and I'm sure you know what kind of man. The Bible says over and over again that God will avenge me, but don't push it." I turned to the prison guard. "Take me back to my cell, these gentlemen are leaving," and I hobbled to the door and left the room, leaving them stunned and hopefully not a little frightened.

I can't say I was proud of myself but as I was led back to confinement, I felt a mixture of emotions. The way I had reacted embarrassed me, but I also felt "Yes!" While the officers were unchaining me, in confinement they were chatting excitedly in local language to anyone who would listen. It was obvious that what had happened was already being narrated, (and probably exaggerated) and I was congratulated and thumped on the back for my stand against the Nasties. Strangely enough, whether I'd done right or wrong, this was another pivotal point in my captivity and another step towards my eventual survival in prison.

That afternoon when the senior staff went home for the day, a junior officer opened me up and said, "Would you like to take exercise?" "Is the Pope a Catholic?" I replied. He frowned and said, "What's a Pope?" "Never mind," I quickly replied, "yes, I'd love to exercise." "Just inside in the passageway please," he went on, "we want you to live." Well what could I say, that made two of us. I'd been hobbling up and down the thirty metre passageway for about fifteen minutes, when a Sergeant and a corporal came strolling towards me carrying three chairs between them. "Join us in a seat Sir," the sergeant said as he lit a cigarette, "you did a brave thing today." "Foolish, might be a better word for it Sarg," I replied, sitting down. "We all hate the NIA, they are corrupt and we know that it's the President who's after you and most of us are against him, but what can we do?" "You don't get yourselves into trouble over me, that's what you do." I said. "I'm grateful for this exercise and for the time being that's enough." All too soon, I was back in my cell but feeling that I'd won a few more victories that day.

In the cell for twenty-four hours a day, for the lack of anything else to do, I was able to remember the times I had in The Gambia. I believed that evil existed in only a minority of Muslims, and Gambians. It wasn't the ordinary people; it was the extremist leaders of their false and hate-ridden religion. It was the President, a megalomaniac, a murderer and, as I said earlier, his belief in the power of witchcraft that was dragging The Gambia down.

I also got to thinking about predestination. I didn't really want to go there, especially in a tiny black cell with only myself for company. I thought about quirks of circumstance, in that I was born with a white skin in Scotland into a loving Christian family. I'd had all the advantages of a good education, that I didn't avail myself of it is neither here nor there. Money was never plentiful, but nether were we poor. Work was always available and I was able to choose my own path in life.

Whereas, take for example the kind Sergeant who'd let me have some exercise. He had been born black, nothing wrong with that, to an unloving (his words) Muslim family in a village in the interior of The Gambia where there was no chance of any education save the darra (Koranic school). He was working in the fields when he was five and never knew about electricity till he was ten. His family were so poor that they often boiled grass to make a soup in the dry season. The only job he could get was a prison guard and he educated himself by speaking to prisoners who were educated. So if I'd been born in the same circumstances as him where would I be, what would I be doing? Would I be a Christian or a Muslim? Sometimes it's better not to think too much.

The next day the Sergeant opened me up again at four o'clock, as indeed he did that whole week while he was on late duty. "Why are you doing this for me?" I asked. "Well sir," he said, "you made a good man out of my brother who was in the Immigration," "Your brother?" I queried. "Yes you made him a Christian in March 2007." "Ah! Yes I remember now," said I. "Ebrima Jallow, he's a good man. However Sarg, I can't 'make' anyone a good man and as for him becoming a Christian, well, all I can do is tell him about Christ." We sat in companionable silence for a while, a Christian and a Muslim with a brother in common. I remembered it well, that trip up river, and this is the email I sent as a report, although slightly expanded here to paint a fuller picture.

# EMAIL

*March 30ᵗʰ 2007*

Greetings from The Gambia. Well thank God things have settled down for a while and I was able to go up river this week. Someone has rightly described living in The Gambia as a roller coaster ride and that's proved so accurate yet again.

I set off up river into the interior with the tide at 3am while it was still dark. The moon was bright and the river was like a silver inland sea nine kilometres wide. As I passed St James Island the sun started to rise out of the eastern sky like a ball of fire. It was going to be a hot day, but so they all were. Lashing the wheel, I climbed down from the flying bridge to the galley to make a coffee, pausing only to check the tender, which was being towed behind on a ten-foot rope.

It was my intention to take the Alpha Course to six immigration outposts and break new ground with a "Marathon Alpha" on the South bank. When I got to the designated post, I was delighted to find that four other outposts joined for our starting time of 2pm. I'd decided to run the course till the last person dropped. Well, no one dropped, though I felt like it. That night I slept under the stars in a mosquito net (very David Livingstone I thought, except he didn't have the mossy net). We finished the course the following day and the great news is that at various stages during that day a total of six men and one woman made solid commitments to follow Christ.

As you can imagine I was on a high. The boat was going well, three of the four outposts trekked through the bush to come together for Alpha, for some a five-hour trek through serious bush. Seven people brought into the Kingdom, wow. If someone had jumped out of the bush and handed me ten thousand pounds I couldn't have been happier.

So, it was up anchor and off to the next outpost, this time two of them combining on the north bank. Dolphins were playing about the boat and the weather was hot and sunny. When is it not? This outpost is at the village where I delivered little David (into the world I mean, as opposed to, from demons). Well as usual, I anchored the boat in the main river and took the tender with the TV & Video to show the Alpha course. It's only about 7miles up the tributary into the interior and I was in high spirits.

From time to time, I'd see a face in the bush and then before I could shout a greeting it was gone. At about 4pm I rounded a bend in the bolong and the village bamboo jetty hove into view. However, I couldn't get near it, as the place was chock a block with native dugout canoes. I thought this was strange as they are normally pulled up on the bank. "No problem," I thought, I was in shorts and flip-flops, I'd beach on the mud bank.

Some village people were coming down toward the water, but I was too busy tilting the outboard to notice what they were doing, when I was hit by a small stone, then another and another. "Goodness me!" I thought and jumped into the water and ran at them. (Never was known for being the brightest bulb on the Christmas tree). Most of them started backing away (they obviously hadn't heard that I wasn't 40 anymore) except one. Yep! There's always one. This guy, whose nickname was probably Goliath (and there was a distinct resemblance it has to be said). Anyway, Goliath hurled this lump of rock at me, which hit my leg then my foot. "Ouch," was my expletive (and you can believe that if you like) then a few lesser ouches as smaller stones arrived thrown by the emboldened villagers.

I got back into the tender slipped and tore my shorts to bits on a rowlock. There are times when your mother's advice is a blessing, "Make sure you have clean underpants on, David," mum would say, "You never know when you'll be knocked down by a bus." Well, while there was a dearth of buses here, I was nevertheless thankful for my clean underpants.

Anyway, I digress. Before anything else could happen, the Immigration officers arrived like the seventh cavalry (LATE). Now it would seem that the Muslim community there hold me responsible for the fact that little David is being brought up in the Christian way and that the two women who tried to kidnap him back are still in prison after I foiled their less than cunning plan. The damage to me was negligible, I had to put two stitches in my leg and I have a broken big toe (both left leg so I can still kick).

As it happened, there was no power in that village anyway, as the genny has broken down (probably 25 years ago) and no one had noticed until I brought the TV & Video. However, we had a service and meaningful, question time, but the roller coaster had taken a dip and no one else was saved. (pity)

Well, there we are. You couldn't write the script, but sometimes I do ask why and in some ways that question was answered by an unbeliever yesterday. He said, "If a Moslem fundamentalist were to wheedle his way into the very heart of your security system, your immigration and prisons, preaching Islam, you (the British) would either deport or arrest him." I said to God (the true God, the only God) 7 years ago, "I'll tell it like it is for as long as you keep me here."

With much love, Dave

# AN ULTIMATUM

Well, it would seem that the roller coaster ride had taken another dip to a new low for me. The next day I was yet again, told to dress and when I had done, they put my shackles on, which meant that I was probably going out of the prison. Sure enough when I shuffled onto the main courtyard, there was the NIA pickup and two secret police. I can't underestimate the seriousness of the situation, but I couldn't help but laugh. The NIA were as always were dressed in the secret police uniform, adopted by secret police all over Africa. They wore; wraparound sunglasses day and night, the gaudy tourist shirt worn outside fake designer jeans with trainers, and to round it off, a baseball cap with the skip to the side.

This time they put me inside the cab of the pickup, and even though I knew, where I was going I still enjoyed the short trip to Banjul, especially the seat, which was soft and the first comfortable thing I'd sat on for months. It was surprising to find that life outside the gates of Mile Two was normal. Children were going to school; taxis were pushing their way through the traffic, horns blaring, market stalls selling everything new and well used at the side of the road. It made my situation seem even more unreal, even more desperate and even more unbelievable. Which I was to find out later to be true – people who had no idea what governments can and will do (any government, including the British) refused to believe the unbelievable.

When we arrived at the NIA headquarters, they took me to a large room with the usual Formica topped table and hard backed chairs. The whole place stank, but I couldn't figure out what of, then I had it, it was like an abattoir. Behind the desk was Smarmy, smarm plastered all over his face. "Good morning," he greeted me, "I hope you are enjoying our Gambian hospitality?" I think this was his attempt at humour, so I said nothing humour is something the Gambians don't do well. I knew he didn't like the dumb insolent look, so I sat there in silence and looked at him insolently. "You're in court on Monday. I trust you are going to plead guilty, it'll go better for your wife and yourself if you do," he said. I still said nothing and continued to stare at him as if I was examining something nasty.

"Very well then," he went on, "I've not brought you here for a discussion. I'm giving you an ultimatum." He paused and I waited. "On Monday you will be charged with two counts. The first is forgery, and that involves the making of a Technical Advisor number plate, which we have in our possession. Now, I know that you made it because there were no official plates available, but as you English say, "I couldn't give a shit." Have you anything to say?" I leaned forward, looked at him hard and said; "I'm Scottish, not English," then sat back again. After a moment to digest this, he continued, "The second and most damning is the impersonating of a Gambian soldier, to wit, this Gambian uniform jacket," and with a flourish worthy of a Spanish matador, showed me my Chaplain's jacket. I still said nothing; because I knew he was on a hiding to nothing. The jacket was a different shade of green, and different design than anything the Gambian army wore, indeed it was unique, not really a uniform *per se*. The shoulder epaulettes had a cross on each and so did the lapels.

"OK, now we know where we stand, I'm going to give you one last chance to get out of this alive, "Alive!" I thought, "Alive!" Now it seemed to me that things were spiralling downhill a bit too fast. "This has been sanctioned at the highest level," he continued. "Sign these, and you will be pardoned by the President himself." With that, he took out a sheaf of papers and pushed them across the table. I picked them up and read. It was the same thing that I'd refused to sign before, that I renounce Christianity as a false religion and embrace Islam as the one true religion, Allah as the one true god and Mohamed his prophet. As actions often speak louder than words, I tore it into little pieces and threw them at him. Maybe for me, God was blowing the full-time whistle.

"I see you are a very stubborn man," he said. "You refuse to talk to me and you refuse to sign these papers. Well, let me tell you what will happen if you don't plead guilty. We will have drugs planted on your wife in the prison. She will not get out, even if she doesn't get the death sentence."

"YOU BASTARD!" I shouted as I lunged across the table at him. However, he'd learned his lesson from the last time and had stationed two guards at either side of me who were ready for this reaction. They grabbed me pinned me down on the floor struggling, still trying to get at him. I felt the blow to the back of my head, and then everything went black.

I woke up with a lump on the back of my head the size of an egg. It was totally dark and people were all around me, one cradling my head, another gently slapping my cheeks. There was a sigh of relief when I spoke. "Where am I? What time is it? What's happened?" A voice I recognised as a former prison guard replied, "Babba Dinka, Sir."

Within an hour, the door opened and I was dragged out somewhat drowsily, told to dress as I was going back to Mile Two. There were three of us in the pickup and they handcuffed us together in the back, and then went for what I guessed was a cup of attaya (green tea). It wasn't often that I was given the opportunity to talk with the Gambian high ranking people and that half hour or so really opened my eyes.

"I'm sorry you are a Christian, Sir," said a former Government minister. "Why should you be sorry? Coz I'm not." "Well, your people are betraying you Sir; they are telling lies to the press to save their own miserable necks." "What things," I asked intrigued. "Church leaders and he went on to mention names, which I won't, though I really, really want to, "one called you and your wife cockroaches in the British press. One said you started a church taking people from other churches, just to make money."

"Some missionaries said that you are only interested in people becoming Christians and not in their welfare. The have said many bad things about you and your wife Sir, but we know you are a good man you are one of us. If you weren't a good man you wouldn't be the President's enemy, would you? Good point! You need to tell the press of the good things you did, fight back. Who are they to point the finger?"

"Thank you for telling me," I said, "I always want to know

where I stand." I have to say that I was somewhat taken aback and even distressed if the truth's to be told, but I wasn't allowed to contemplate on it further as the NIA guys came back and we were taken to Mile Two, and into what seemed eternal darkness with my own thoughts and they weren't very welcome, that was for sure.

# SHOCK AND HORROR
## June 2009

Monday came, as Mondays do, and a police pickup collected me and took me to court. I still hadn't made up my mind what to do. Should I slug it out with these people and risk Fiona being framed on a drugs wrap, (and I was under no illusion that they were quite capable of doing it), or plead guilty and after Fiona was free and back in UK I'd try to escape.

I was still mulling it over when I recognised the police driver. "Aren't you Modu Jatta?" I asked him. He looked at me quizzically in the interior mirror. "Yes Sir and I'm embarrassed to look at you, I can see what they've done, they're pigs." "Listen Modu," I quickly asked, "what is the sentence for making your own number plate and not buying a Government one?" The same as not having one," he replied, "I think it's a D500 fine." I made up my mind.

This time there were many people at the court, press, friends, well-wishers, enemies, the general public and my personal favourite Bin Ladin. Right in the middle of the courtroom in full view of the bench sat Mr Ladin, again dressed in his natty only slightly stained designer bottom sheet with matching tea towel covering his unwashed hair.

I was disappointed to find out that my lawyer, through no fault of his own, hadn't turned up and I was to appear without representation. In the dock, I stood watched by a hushed courtroom. The magistrate leaned forward and asked me in a very friendly manner how I pleaded to impersonating a Gambian Security Officer. "Not guilty," I replied, looking directly at Bin Ladin. "And how do you plead to the second charge of fraudulently making a number plate? "Guilty," I replied.

Prior to going into the dock, I told my friends there of my decision and the reasons why it would be thus, so that it wasn't a surprise. The big surprise came when the magistrate said, "Three years in prison." There was a communal gasp and some people shouted out "What!" and "Nonsense". The magistrate banged his gavel several times on the bench. "Silence!" he shouted, "This is contempt of court. Who's shouting?" When court quietened, he rose and left without looking in my direction. I looked over at the courtroom and saw Bin Ladin grinning from ear to ear, teeth looking like an old graveyard. "Bless you," I thought, or at least I think I did, what I thought certainly began with "B."

The policeman who had brought me to court was devastated, he thought I'd acted on what he told me. However, I was able to tell him that I'd made up my mind to plead guilty anyway. He took me to the courtyard at the back of the court where friends were gathered and let us have about two hours together. I was even able to speak on the mobile phone to some folks back in England, which was great. I told everyone that I'd be registering an appeal as soon as I saw the lawyer, but in my mind I'd worked out that in five months Fiona would be set free and I would then work on escaping.

Back in my cell in Mile Two, it was as if my hope and expectation of fairness and justice had been doused by a bucketful of cold dark Gambian reality. I realised that this was never going to be resolved in court, there was only one way out and God had to be the orchestrator of it. Peter walked out of prison (Acts 12,) and that must have caused a head or two to roll. God also did it for Paul and Silas, so I was ready for how God was going to do it for me. I decided on a strict training regime, when God said, "Go", I wasn't going to say, "Sorry I'm not ready," no way!

My new lawyer Lamin Camera came to see me a few days later

and he only confirmed that it didn't matter whether I'd pleaded guilty or not guilty, the President and the Islamic Council were determined that I'd go to prison for as long as possible. I told him of the torture and of course, it was no surprise to him. I told him that they tried to kill me and of the threats against us. He said something that has stuck in my mind. "If a man is not afraid to die, then it is of no avail to threaten him." For myself I'd agree, but when they threaten Fiona? I told Lamin that I was appealing against the judgement and that I had no intention of pleading guilty of impersonating anybody, I was quite happy being me and if they wanted to take it further I'd fight them tooth and nail. He agreed and said that maybe the total of four years would satisfy those who wished me ill. I knew that what he didn't say was more pertinent, that he thought I couldn't survive four years in Mile Two.

My life took on what felt like an eternity of pain, filth, darkness and discomfort. A time for reflection, a time where I was in almost constant touch with God, talking to him as if he was a physical presence in the cell. Once a guard banged on the cell door and shouted, "Who are you talking to in there?" I shouted back, "A friend, you don't know him." That brought the rattling of keys, I can tell you. I guess that during that time I thought a lot about the past and whether I could have done things better, but as the old song says, "If I knew then what I know now,'" and as an Irish friend of mine once said, "It's a great thing, the hindsight."

I knew what the President was like. I knew that I was walking on eggshells. I'd tried to warn the British High Commission about him, but I felt they didn't take my warnings seriously. Indeed, why should they? They must have thought, who was I to think I knew better than their analysts did? The diplomatic community only saw him on his best behaviour and even that was never good.

Since I've been back in UK I've kept abreast of what's going on in The Gambia, especially with regard to the friends I left behind, in prison and out and I know the danger they face at the whim of the mad dictator Jammeh. I came across an article in an online newspaper the other day.

"The Gambia Echo" dated 10/05/2011

# In Gambia, Alleged adultery and theft, crimes punishable by death?

**BY PROFESSOR ABDOULAYE SAINE,**
Miami University, Oxford, OH.

Oxford, Ohio—Amid the political chaos that currently engulfs The Gambia is Yahya Jammeh's sinister motive to remain in power at any cost. This is not difficult to see. Jammeh has orchestrated a state of siege to hold an entire population hostage, psychologically stressed, and paralyzed by fear. His objective is to keep the population, including civil servants, and even regime supporters constantly guessing. Always ahead of the game, Jammeh keeps the population in check with hoax coup attempts, always foiled at the eleventh hour, only to be followed by yet another wave of arrests, firings and detentions at Mile II.

Jammeh keeps the population hungry, sick and grovelling for crumbs, and revels in dishing out money to the sickly and hungry-looking crowds to construct an image of piety and magnanimity – slow to anger but swift to punish with vengeance those who dare double-cross him, real or imagined. The result is political instability, personal and professional insecurity and paranoia driven by Jammeh's own insecurities, demons and fear of being overthrown and possibly killed. Therefore, there is logic to the madness and the corrosive *fitna* that dwells in the hearts of most Gambians, spawned in Jammeh's mind that is deeply traumatized, and at the brink of madness.

# KNOW THINE ENEMY

That article confirmed what I'd known for some years; who my enemy was, who was out to get me and what he was capable of. I knew it was the extremists in the Gambian Islamic Council who wanted rid of me, and the President danced to their tune. What I hadn't known was that we'd been betrayed and maligned by Christians, whether wittingly or unwittingly and that people who should have known better, believed the misinformation and lies that the Islamic Council was feeding to a ravenous British press. To me it showed their lack of knowledge of the enemy, (when I say enemy I mean Satan and those who he uses) and their lack of discernment. I was at the centre of a concerted effort at character assassination – my character (which was far from being pristine in the first place). The secret police used their contacts in the media, much of which is under Jammeh's control anyway, as writing the truth about matters that concern the President could land you in prison as many honest journalists have found out or even murdered as newspaper editor Chief Maneh had been.

# MY OWN FAULT

Many things were to come out later and some of them, and I reiterate that "some of them", were lies or distortions of the truth, and were my own fault. There were also things that I had hidden, for whatever reason, and people used these, again to discredit me, and it worked. Christians listened to the gossip and believed it. Even now, there are some Christians who will have nothing to do with me, but I can't do anything about that, save write about it as it was and maybe there'll be closure, good for them, good for me.

However, I guess what hurt, and I admit angered me the most, was the lack of unity within the body of Christ in The Gambia. Back in UK where the newspapers were talking nonsense and the internet was gossiping it worldwide, for the most part, the Church stood behind us. Likewise, body's like Amnesty International, Christian Solidarity Worldwide and other Christian and human rights organizations who knew the Islamic, totalitarian regime of Jammeh, tried on our behalf.

The Church must stand up and be counted. We need to preach the gospel for the entire world to hear, even if that means arrest and/or imprisonment in some countries. If we don't, then we are like the Church in the book of Revelation 3:16 and God *will* "spit us out". If you are waiting for a perfect Christian to come along and do it for you, then don't hold your breath, coz it's not going to happen.

Two men there did have the courage of their convictions, but they were only two voices in the wilderness and those voices were silenced. The regime arrested both of these men, but never actually charged them with anything. One is, (at the time of writing this), still in Mile Two, and still not charged, so I won't mention his name. The other, James was the subject of the opening chapter of the book.

It really is difficult to say how I felt, how I feel, regret? Yes a little. Sadness? Some, but more than anything I suppose strangely a sense of acceptance, as a soldier who loses comrades in a skirmish, but knows he has to go on as there is still a war to be fought, a war to be won.

This sort of thinking was getting me nowhere, I could see that here in my cell there was a seed of bitterness beginning to germinate and that wasn't acceptable. If I was going to come out of this whole, sound in all my faculties, then I wasn't going to blame others, even if I could justify some of the stuff that I'd done. So maybe this was a good time to remember and a good time to pray as I'd never prayed before, because something had gone wrong. What was it? If I ever got out of this mess, I'd make sure it wouldn't happen again. What was I saying? 'If", there was going to be no 'if' about it, I would get out of here!

# SEEING AND BELIEVING

I don't envy people who seem to breeze through life on the crest of a wave with never a problem, never a doubt, seemingly having got it all and got it all right. I don't envy them because I don't believe them. That has not been my portion and to be honest with you I very much doubt if it ever will be. I remember a while ago, I was talking to a couple who seemed to have it all, wealth, health, good looks. They came to talk with me about their son who was in prison, and their daughter who was living in London as a prostitute to feed her drug habit. They were Christians and they were ashamed to tell anyone, but they felt that as I'd been on the "other side of the tracks" maybe I could help them. No, no one has the perfect life, but for some it does look that way.

For us it looked that way, it would seem that we were living a wonderful Christian life, indeed, for the most part we were. We helped many people give their lives to Christ, and we planted two churches. I had been, and was training chaplains for the army and immigration, we had some good friends and to top it all, the weather was nice. Yes, things seemed to be going well. But life is a roller coaster, and while we want folks to know the good stuff, we don't want to talk about the bad, its human nature, and I'm more human than anybody.

# A NIGHTMARE

My life in The Gambia was, as I've said before, hectic, exciting and often dangerous. When at home I'd be up before seven in the morning, working one way or the other straight through till six in the evening and more often than not, out again that evening doing Alpha courses or teaching chaplains. Most nights I'd come home exhausted and in pain from a neck injury that I'd sustained in a car crash some years previously. On average, I'd be working sixty-five to seventy hours a week and from about four in the afternoon I was in so much pain that I found it difficult to concentrate. In fact, in the evenings I was downright anti-social, (or so I was told.) I found that I was only able to sleep by deadening the pain with whisky and I don't mean dabbing it on my neck, I mean getting it down my neck.

When I went into the interior on the boat I was able to relax more, as skippering the boat for me was a pleasure and a joy, although there was extra danger, responsibility and pressure, as the elements often seemed to conspire against me as they do every sailor. I had deadlines to meet and many men and women who were depending on me. So even when I was up river doing what I loved doing, I was at it at least twelve hours a day and came back knackered.

There was no doubt I was putting my wife and family a very poor second to God's work, but that was alright wasn't it? This is what I'd been called to, wasn't it? Maybe I should have looked more closely at 1 Timothy 5:8. I was putting everyone else, indeed anyone else before my wife and family. That meant I wasn't giving us time to pray together, time to play together, time for the children, time for my wife, intimacy, sex. One thing that I can see now is that with the busy, exciting, fulfilling life I was leading, I had crippled my marriage and I was the only one still walking and still unaware.

I started to notice the change about July 2005 when Fiona's prayers in the morning became stilted, lacking her usual authority, almost as if she didn't want to pray, but did it because it was expected of her, I noticed it, but hadn't the time to question it, I was too busy, I was "about the Lord's business". What an important fellow I thought I was, Major Dave of God's army.

One morning in September 2005, the family were sitting at breakfast and I came home in uniform from some "good thing" I was doing instead of having breakfast with my family. So good that I can't even remember what it was. "Dave, I've got something to tell you," Fiona said. I turned and inclined my head. "I'm pregnant." There was a pause when the world seemed to stop: I believe it's called a pregnant pause. "Pregnant," I said, having done my sums, "pregnant? You can't be, it's been . . . ? WHO? Who was it?" She told me and I can tell you that I, to my shame, thought only of me. Not the children round the breakfast table, not how Fiona must have been feeling, not anything but blinding rage.

I barged into the bedroom where I kept my handgun, but it wasn't there. In a fit of fury, I turned everything over looking for it. It never crossed my mind that they might have hidden it. It never crossed my mind that God didn't want me to find it. It never crossed my mind that this was the last thing I should have been doing. Eventually, in frustration I took the shotgun and a handful of cartridges while the family were still sitting at the table in shock at what I was doing. "I'll kill the bastard," I shouted as I threw the shotgun in the Range Rover and went round to the driver's door, pausing only to shout at the gate boy to open the gates before I drove over them. Michael, who was the gate boy at the time, rushed to the gates and opened them just in the nick of time.

I drove to where the man who had been in our house to do some carpentry work had his workshop. The sand track was dry and bumpy and the old Range Rover was off it as much as it was on the ground and behind me, there was a great plume of dust that rose about fifteen feet into the air. I guess the journey to his place would normally take forty-five minutes. I did it in twenty. I don't know how many chickens I killed as I bombed through villages. I know I probably killed a donkey, coz I definitely hit one and I saw the blood, hair and stuff on the bull bar when I was *compos mentis* a few days later.

As I skidded to a halt in front of his workshop, I saw him running for the rear compound wall. I jumped out and grabbed the shotgun in one fluid motion. He was atop the wall about two hundred feet away when I fired and then he was gone. I ran to the wall hoping to find blood, but nothing. I'd missed, if anything I was angrier now, he'd been warned and it was only Fiona who could have done that on the mobile phone.

Back in the car I shoved the gun under the passenger seat and drove off before the police arrived. It might be the Wild West of Africa, but gunshots were always going to attract attention. Strangely enough even if I was arrested, I probably would have got away with it, as in Islamic law (and we were in an Islamic country) I would have been the aggrieved party, and in The Gambia as you'll have read earlier in that extract from the newspaper report, the penalty for adultery is death.

I was still angry and hurting; you name it, I felt it. I was a Christian, but to be honest, God took second place to my feelings at that time. I felt as though my insides had been ripped out, leaving me with an empty space, a void. It was the numbness of a bullet's strike before the pain hits. I really can't describe it adequately, not even close.

I drove in a daze back towards the house, but I never reached there. I couldn't go back, I had to plan, I had to think. I continued on this downward spiral, and went to a friend's house and asked him if he had any whisky. When he gave me a new bottle he asked me what was wrong and I couldn't answer for the shame I felt. Taking the Whisky I drove to a spot on the beach about one hundred yards from a locally owned beach bar where I stopped and took a swallow of the whisky, straight from the neck, then another and another.

So many thoughts went through my head and none of them were good. How could I cover this thing up? What would I say to people who looked up to my family and me? What would the folks back home think the people and the churches that prayed for and supported us? How would it affect my mother who was in her eighties? The shame of this could kill her. I couldn't pretend the baby was mine, as it would be mixed race. I'd divorce Fiona. I'd sell up and hide somewhere, no one would know what happened. I'd sell Nautilus, buy a sloop, sail to the Seychelles and live my life out chartering to the tourists. I'd run away one last time. My gaze kept returning to the gun, which had slid onto the floor between the seats; maybe that was the answer. Then as my thinking became more alcohol fuddled, I decided to lie about it.

One of the army officers Captain Jah had come to me only three weeks previously in a state. A gang of Rasta's had raped his wife. I went over the whole thing with them, prayed with them and while I'm not a counsellor, I believe it helped. What I did of course was to invite God into what had happened and that was what I wasn't doing here, I was effectively shutting God out. Another swallow and I headed further down that spiral.

There was a knock on the window and when I looked up there stood a beautiful woman, probably in her late twenties or early thirties, dark coffee coloured with long straight hair. She wasn't Gambian, I'd been in Africa long enough to differentiate between tribes and countries. She knocked again and I opened the window. "Are you all right," she asked in a very caring and sympathetic voice. "No," I replied, "I'm not." She stood for a moment looking at me and I was shocked to see tears in her eyes, then she reached in through the window and tried to take away the half-empty bottle of whisky. "This will solve nothing," she said, "whatever it is you can't hide from it in a bottle. Do you want to talk?" "Me," I thought, "I'm not a talker, I'm a doer."

# A WRONG IMPRESSION

I think that at this point I should let you know what the perception of me was like in The Gambia. Now, this is not reality as far as I or we were concerned, and it wasn't a perception that I fostered. Firstly, I was an "honorary" major in the Gambian army. The rank was real and given so that I would be equal in rank, or higher in rank than the OIC of the barracks in which I'd be working. When I wanted to do 'Church Service', (the expression used for all Christian activities in The Gambian armed services) in the barracks, and I wanted it held in the officer's mess, then I had the authority to do it. When men came to faith in Christ then I would be able, because of my rank, to some extent protect them from persecution and abuse within the army.

I was a man of rank, a man of importance and because I was

'white British', with the rank of major, there was an automatic respect far above the norm. The perception was that whites are a privileged class; a wealthy people, whites could do everything. To the rank and file, it seemed that I had influence and money. Rightly or wrongly, white British people were looked up to, and they were thought worth befriending at all costs. For example, a Gambian woman who had a white man would be the envy of her peers. She'd have the chance of a good life in "Tubabado" (white man's land) leaving behind poverty and the probability of an early death. She'd live in a manner that no other woman in The Gambia could ever hope to achieve, She'd have the chance to travel and be treated properly, not as a slave and she'd know that as she got older she wouldn't be pushed aside for a second and even a third wife.

We came to The Gambia and bought land on which I built a large house, well, large by Gambian standards. Now, it would never cross the mind of a Gambian that we had to sell our house in the UK to be able to have the money to build another. Oh no, they naturally assumed that we had pocketfuls of money and so just pulled out wads of it when required. There was a joke among the Tubabs that we clearly grew money-trees in our compounds.

I, being an engineer was able to make a 1980/81 Range Rover out of two scrap ones and when finished, repainted and looking like new, it was yet another perceived proof of the Tubab's wealth.

I was also, whether I wanted it or not, a high profile figure in The Gambia and when I was commanded by the President's office to attend some function or other where the President was present, I was often on the local television and being the only white man there attracted the cameramen. So every Gambian and their uncle knew me or of me. I couldn't travel anywhere in The Gambia without being recognised which wasn't something I enjoyed, but that was the way it was.

When I was in the Range Rover, out and about I'd be saluted by every policeman at every road junction and by every soldier at every check point. Every year when I went to renew my driving licence, they'd be a queue and as I walked in and was recognised I'd be ushered to the front to be dealt with immediately. The same with immigration ID cards, residential permits etc. I was also Chaplain to the airport and when friends or family came to visit, I'd go through the security and immigration to meet them while they were still on the wrong side of customs. Then when they had retrieved their bags, we'd be ushered through customs and formalities as VIPs.

Once when my mother came over with me and I was travelling in uniform, we were only halfway down the steps from the aircraft to the runway when two men in uniform, one army and one immigration came running up the steps against the flow of tourists, stood on the platform in the centre of the steps and saluted. "Welcome back Major," they said in unison. "Thank you," I replied "this is my mother." "Ah," they exclaimed, turning to my Mum, "welcome to you Mrs Major." Whereupon we were ushered to the VIP car and whisked to the terminal. I could see that mum was a little confused: she didn't know whether to be pleased or embarrassed.

When I rolled up in my car to the ferry terminal to cross the river, there would be a queue hours long. Instead of joining it, I'd go straight to the front which I felt was my right and with salutes and smiles I'd be directed onto the first ferry to leave.

A long time ago I did first aid classes then went on to do a paramedics course, the fruits of which I was able to utilize in The Gambia. In our village and others close by I was in great demand to give injections for malaria, stitch people up, remove splinters, treat burns and even deliver babies only in dire emergencies I quickly add.

We had our own compound with a large British style house in the best area. I had what was undoubtedly the best boat in The Gambia. However, people didn't know that it was bought largely with donated money. I drove a Range Rover that looked good despite it age, but to them this wasn't relevant. We kept two horses in our compound that my wife and daughter rode. We only looked after them for a white woman, but they'd never appreciate that.

Our children went to the international school; they didn't know that it almost crippled us financially to be able to afford it. It seemed to the average Gambian, that as a family and me in particular, (because women weren't counted as anything but chattels) we had it all. Like lords of the manor, they looked up to us, envied us and courted us. I was a church leader, and in our time in The Gambia, Fiona and I were involved in the planting of two vibrant churches. So, as Gambian serviceman's Chaplain, church leader, and white (sad, isn't it), I was, in the sights of other church leaders and Christians, male and female for different reasons, and when I say 'in their sights' I'm not joking.

Was it any wonder that I started to believe the things that other people, who didn't know any better believed? I was the one who went to rescue people in trouble with the police and negotiated their release from custody. There would be a telephone call in the evening and I'd leave the dinner table, climb into uniform and drive to whatever police station they were being held, lights flashing, siren blaring and demand to see the station CO. I'm talking about pastors and missionaries here as well as the ordinary people, both black and white who'd got themselves into a pickle.

Sadly, (and unwittingly towards the end,) I was sucked into believing that it was *me*, the big 'me' who had done all these things. That it was my efforts that had brought many service personnel to faith in Christ. I'm not making excuses, but I guess that it was partly due to having no-one to be accountable to, no spiritual mentor. However, it was also and mainly the human side of me that enjoyed being important, depended upon and looked up to.

# AN ANGEL IN DISGUISE

Anyway, that said, there was I with this beautiful woman who was so sympathetic that I actually talked. It's something I didn't do and still don't do easily. Somehow, she was inside the car sitting on the passenger seat. She told me quite matter-of-factly that her name was Elizabeth, and that she was from the Congo. She said that her mother and father were butchered before her eyes, and she had fled to The Gambia. She was now a refugee living in a one-room hut with no running water or electricity. She worked as a masseuse in a room behind the beach bar just up from where I had parked, so that she could survive. There was no self-pity in her words, she didn't complain. She went on to tell me to count my blessings, to be thankful to God for the good things and get over the bad.

What she could have said was to come back with her to her place, or to give her my mobile number. That would have been the norm, as hardly a day went by that I wasn't propositioned. Even in my fuddled state and despite her conciliatory manner I was half expecting it, maybe even half hoping. She told me that she was a Catholic and Born Again and that she understood. My shame seemed at that moment to quadruple and the tears started to flow. She gathered me in her arms and I cried on her shoulder, this stranger, this woman who rich men used, and this woman who God was using to help me. I cried in shame, shame for what had happened, for my way of trying to hide from the hurt in a bottle. Shame for letting my Lord down, shame that I'd looked longingly at the gun. Shame that I was so self-centred that I'd have passed this woman on the beach, and have known nothing about her and probably have cared even less, but she was interested in me and in mine.

Elizabeth gently took the bottle from my hand, opened the door and without another word left. I looked for the keys to start the car and go, but they were missing. I think I slept, and when I awoke I was in my bed in my house without knowing how I got there. It came out later that Elizabeth took my bottle and put it in her room. She then went to the nearest security post, told the OIC, that I was ill, and asked if anyone knew where I lived. The soldiers went with her, she gave the car keys to one of them who could drive and knew where my compound was, and he drove me home. However, finding the compound gates closed and locked, he left me in the car with the keys in the ignition.

The children had gone to school and on their return at about three thirty Luke, who was fourteen at the time, drove the car into the compound and with some help carried me to bed.

The next day I had to keep a clear head and work out what I should do. I couldn't pray. I couldn't read the Bible. I could make no pretence at normality. How I usually worked when things went wrong was firstly to consolidate, just stop and think. Damage limitation was the way forward I decided, so what would that involve . . . abortion? No, that was not an option though for the first time in my life I could understand how desperate people would consider it and persuade themselves that it was the only way out.

Well, it went without saying that in seven month's time the army and indeed all of The Gambia would know, and I would have to resign as Chaplain. So, I went to army headquarters and saw the CDS (Chief of Defence Staff). Explaining my predicament wasn't easy and he laughed when I handed over the resignation letter I'd written. "This happens all the time in The Gambia," he smiled, pushing the letter back. "Not to me it doesn't," I replied pushing it back to him, "please accept this, I can't continue as Chaplain." This conversation bounced back and forth and I was getting nowhere, but I'd tried.

Now, what to say to the people back home? How about, "We're going to have a baby, I hope it's not black," no I don't think so. I didn't know what to do, but one thing was for sure I was going to send Fiona back to her father in England and to that end I told her to phone her father and ask him to send money for air fares. I wasn't going to divorce her, (I was getting more African than the Africans), I was going to do as they do, "send her away". Did it matter that it didn't say anything about that in the Bible? No, not a bit of it, I was doing my own thing.

I'd tell people that Fiona was raped, that would solve this dilemma, and I'd use the circumstances surrounding Jah and his wife to make it sound convincing. Of course what I was in fact doing was digging a big hole for myself, which just got deeper and deeper, but at the time I felt it was the way out and I kidded myself it was to everyone's benefit. Wrong.

Again, as is my way, as soon as I decided on a course of action I implemented it. I phoned my family in England and Scotland and told them that Fiona had been a victim of rape and that she was pregnant. They were shocked and while I felt guilty about the lie, I still believed that was the only way out.

One day I went to the beach bar where the Congolese woman Elizabeth worked. She wasn't in but the barman said that if I came back that afternoon I'd find her there as she'd be covering for him because he was going to a funeral. That afternoon I returned and she was behind the bar and delighted to see me. "Tell me all that's been happening," she said as I sat on a barstool. I told her what I'd done to salvage the situation and when I was finished she left me sitting there without a word and went outside. Unsure whether I should follow or not I sat there sipping the bottle of beer she'd given me. Maybe about one minute later she returned with a tape in her hand and stuck it into the battery-powered player.

It was a song by Kris Kristofferson called 'Why me Lord' and as I listened, I cried again. What was it about this woman that did this to me?


Why me Lord?

What have I ever done, to deserve even one,
of the pleasures I've known.

Tell me lord,

What did I ever do, that was worth loving' You,
for the kindness You've shown

Lord help me Jesus, I've wasted it,
So help me Jesus, I know what I am,
but now that I know, that I needed you so,
help me Jesus, my souls in Your hands.

Try me Lord

If You think there's a way, I can try to repay
all I've taken' from you,

Maybe lord,

I can show someone else, what I've been through myself,
on my way back to You, Jesus, my soul's in Your hands

I didn't deserve anything that God had done for me, least of all forgiveness; all I deserved was death and eternal damnation. So why was I not able to forgive Fiona and deal with this in a godly way?

The die however was cast, the lie was told, and as is the case with lies, it had to be told and retold, expanded upon *ad infinitum* increasing in strength and depth with each retelling. Of course, several people knew the truth and this caused many a sleepless night. It went around and around in my head; what if someone who believed the lie spoke to another, who knew the truth? There were so many 'ifs'.

The time came to fly back to the UK. I had a return ticket and Fiona a single, for I was convinced that she wasn't coming back. I was still angry, but more than that, I was hurting as I've never hurt before or since.

Within two days of our, arrival, we chose to see our good friends Peter and Julia in Taunton. They are Christian counsellors, and I felt it was only right to put Fiona in their care. Me? I was fine; I'd deal with this my way. I was Major Dave after all wasn't I? The guy who fixes things, the guy who everyone and their uncle called on for help? Yes, as Frank Sinatra used to sing, 'I'd do it my way' . . . but my way was the wrong way.

# AND NOW, A SPY

My reverie shattered with the sound of countless keys being inserted into the padlock. Just for that while, how long I'd no idea of knowing, in my mind at least, I was outside the prison and I could empathise with those before me who could say, 'They can imprison my body but not my mind and spirit.'

Eventually, the cell door opened and Shades was standing against the passageway wall, arms folded and trying to look cool. "Out," the guard said, moving away from the door as quickly as he could. I blinked at the light, weak though it was, eased myself out and slowly managed to stand up. "Haven't you people had your pound of flesh yet?" I asked. "This way," the guard said and pointing to my clothes continued, "better take those. Sorry Sir but you're going out the prison." Shades snapped something at him in Jolla, which I couldn't understand, but by the tone of his voice he wasn't asking after the health of his granny.

The same routine, dressed, handcuffs, leg irons and shuffle out to the main courtyard where the same pickup was waiting. Again, it was pitch black, which meant that it was probably about 1am and I wasn't going to get anyone to give me a bet on where I was heading.

Sure enough, it was the NIA's secret headquarters. After driving through the gates they pushed me out of the cab of the pickup and I shuffled into the main building and up a flight of stairs. It was like another world, tiled floors and comfortable seats in a waiting room at the end of a tastefully painted corridor. A door opened and they shoved me into a carpeted office that had its air conditioning on at full blast. There was a padded seat in front of a large polished mahogany conference table, with a modern monitor and keyboard, behind which sat the ugly bloke with the face like a horseshoe turned upside-down, whom I'd met on a previous visit.

As he spoke, I had to concentrate on the clock on the wall over his head that proclaimed it was 12.35am. "I'm sure you're surprised to see me," he began. Countless retorts went through my head which would have done me no good at all, so I kept quiet. "You seem to have a knack of rubbing the President up the wrong way," he continued as he stared at me. Try as I might not to look, my eyes felt drawn to his face and the two large front teeth nibbling away at his bottom lip. "Secret Squirrel," I thought, "that's what I'll call him, "Secret Squirrel"

"Why did you plead not guilty on the impersonation charge and then lodge an appeal against your conviction?" he asked. I said nothing so he carried on this one-way conversation. "I think it's only fair to let you know what's ahead of you. Would you like that?"

I decided to break my silence and annoy him, as I got the feeling that he would divulge more information if he was angry. "What I'd like to know is this," I said in an innocent, but enquiring voice, "are you on night shift so that you don't scare the children going to school in the morning?" "You!" he shouted, "You will know what we Muslims do to infidels." "Ah! So now we're getting down to it," I replied, "it's all about Islam and Christianity, nothing to do with sedition or impersonation or whatever else you've conjured up." I was getting nicely warmed up so I went on, "At the end of World War II, some Japanese soldiers refused to believe that they had lost the war and kept on fighting. You Muslims are in the same position. Jesus is the son of God and he died to save us all, but you refuse to accept him as your Saviour."

Well that was a conversation stopper. It just came out and now I expected a backlash and wasn't disappointed. However, for the time being it wasn't violence, it was worse. "Look at this," he said, "this is your next charge: spying." He swung the monitor round and there on the screen was the map I used on my PowerPoint presentation when I spoke in Churches back in UK. It showed by bullet points the immigration posts and barracks I visited when I went up river into the interior, except this one had subtly altered. By one (a barracks), there was a caption "Can be taken by fifty men". Another caption by at an immigration post said "only fifteen men here and no coms". Every bullet point had a caption with recommendations, every word was damning, and every word spelt "SPY". It should have spelt "LIE". They knew it and I knew it.

"Furthermore," he said with what looked like an effort at a grin, "we plan not only to lock you up for life, but to bring embarrassment to the British Government. On your release after serving your present sentence, you will be deported. However, the plane you will be expecting to take you home to your spymasters won't take off, it will be stopped on the tarmac, in full view of our GRTS (Gambian Radio & Television Service). The world will know that we have outwitted a plot by our former colonial masters to gather intelligence and secret information through you."

"Right, let's talk," Secret Squirrel started to say, but I interrupted him. "I'm not a spy! And you know it!" I exclaimed, "I never made this," pointing to the screen. "Oh, we know that," he broke in with a hand raised to stop my protest, "but who's going to believe you? A former armed robber, a liar, oh yes, we know how you've tried to cover up your "adoptive" daughter's birth . . . adopted, hah! We know that you've become an embarrassment to your Government and you are on their 'Deniable' list for reasons that we haven't yet ascertained. You think because we're black we're stupid but it is you British who are stupid. I can make up something then have it printed in a Gambian newspaper and it will be copied almost verbatim in English newspapers, how stupid is that? No major, after what has been said about you, if you swear on a hundred bibles, you won't be believed. You see it's called 'disinformation'. "Actually," I countered, "what you are doing is called misinformation, you are trying to miss inform people." "And I've succeeded," he replied. "Oh no," I said, "Remember the Japanese soldiers? You're like them: you just don't know you've lost."

"Take him back to Mile Two!" he shouted, then to me, "I'll see you again when the gravity of your situation sinks in." With that, they pushed me out of the office and when the door shut, I looked back at it and there was a nameplate that said 'Director'. It seemed that my high profile status remained unchanged.

# MALARIA

Back in my cell, the gravity of the new situation was starting to dawn on me. Men, my friends from the army and immigration, gathered outside my door and tried to give me advice and comfort, but what came through was that I was in the same boat as them.

There was a bonding that day that's difficult to explain,

especially to women, because I suspect that it's a male thing to do with soldiers in battle and life and death situations. These people, these rough soldiers, dissidents, freedom fighters, we had a kinship that bordered on love. I guess the common denominator was that we were all strangers to this environment, refugees, and survivors, pitched upon the shores of this hellish island. If there was a bond between us, between Christian and Muslim, it was the bond of suffering, of survival, of the wrongfully dispossessed.

Three and a half months had passed and I still had no contact with the outside world and the Islamic chanting outside my cell was almost driving me mad. I was losing weight alarmingly to the extent that I could no longer lie on my back, as the knuckles of my spine would scrape on the rough concrete floor. My body was covered in sores, bites and boils and yet for all the physical afflictions, it was the mental and psychological torture that was the worst.

I had a visit from the police one day and they told me that my British citizenship had been withdrawn and could I sign a paper to enable them to hand over my passport to the High Commission. I said no and they went away, but of course, there was no paper to sign and the whole thing was just a lie, but I had no way of knowing that.

The next Sunday I began banging on the door shouting to attend church service, but when no one came, I realised that there was something else afoot. It was only the next day that I learned that David Collie the director had banned not only me, but also the other Christians from attending the service in the main yard. It was like another nail in the coffin and in the following weeks, I went into a depression, if not, then close to it. I still prayed, still sang hymns to lift my spirits. I was down and feeling that way didn't help my resistance to illness and sure enough one Friday evening I got malaria, cerebral malaria, and it doesn't get a lot worse than that.

Early on in our time in The Gambia, I got cerebral malaria and unconscious, was taken to the MRC where I remained on a drip for four days. During that time, a British friend of mine was in the same ward with the same thing. I lived and he died. After I got out, the doctor told me that I was unlikely get it again as I'd have immunity to it or at least a strong resistance.

What follows is an accurate account of what happened, given to me by Prison guards, medics, and inmates who were all rooting for me.

I was fitting and in a comatose state and after an outcry by prison officers and inmates they took me to the infirmary in the main yard and a vehicle was put on standby to take me to an outside hospital. SOP (Standard Operating Procedure), required the Director to be informed if anyone going to an outside hospital. By this time it was about eight at night, he was duly phoned and his response was that I shouldn't be moved and that no medication should be given to me.

They then left me on an iron bed with no mattress to die. 'I can imagine the report the prison would give, confirmed by an autopsy, 'patient died of malaria.' However, when all the officers has gone to sleep, one medic the fellow prisoner and a Muslim broke into the medicine cabinet and took out a canula and a bag of out of date Quinine and put me on a drip overnight. Before the shift started the following morning, he removed it and tidied up. This he did for three nights and on the fourth day a Tuesday I regained consciousness and was taken back to my cell, much to the surprise of everyone, as I wasn't expected to live.

I thanked God for my life, and yet I questioned 'Why?' I was in solitary confinement, unwell, weak, no light to read my bible, not allowed to speak English in a foreign land, why had God preserved my life yet again. It was all beyond me, but then again, weren't most things God did.

I knew that the Christian inmates in the confinement wing were up in arms about not being allowed to go the church in the main yard. So the officers said that they could meet in the confinement wing, in a passageway. "We don't have a Pastor," they complained. "Gather outside the Chaplain's cell," the guards told them, and that was how the Fellowship within the Confinement Wing started.

On a Sunday, there were no senior officers, so unless you

were like me, in a punishment cell, the junior officers gave the prisoners a chance to walk about and in our case to meet around my cell door. My hatch was jammed open while we read the Bible and I taught them stuff some of them had never heard before. No salvation without repentance, good works alone doesn't cut it with God; forgiveness is not an option, but a prerequisite for our own forgiveness and so on. It didn't take long before some of the nominal Christians were "born again" and soon there were Muslims added to the body of Christ as they too were born again. Maybe, just maybe, God still had a use for me.

# WOW

About two weeks after that first Fellowship meeting a prison officer came to my cell. He was one of the 'old guard' who Fiona and I knew well and helped when we worked in the prison. He opened the hatch and passed in a local newspaper. Keeping the hatch open he said, "You might want to read this major."

## David Fulton Discharged

_Africa_ » _Gambia_

Wednesday, June 17, 2009

David Fulton, a British national was on 16th June 2009 discharged by the Banjul Magistrates' Court presided over by Magistrate Lamin George for the offence of impersonation.

The alleged offence revealed that, the accused, David Fulton, sometime in the year 2007 and 2008 in the city of Banjul and diverse places in The Gambia, falsely represented himself as a military officer by wearing a military uniform.

Cpl Manga told the court that the accused could not appear in court due to circumstances beyond their control and therefore applied for an adjournment.

In response, the Defence Counsel Lamin Camara told the court that he was objecting to any further adjournment of the case. He said there was a court order on the last adjourned date that the accused should be brought to court for hearing on the case.

According to Defence Counsel Camara, apart from the order, the accused had not been brought to court since 25 March 2009, and the case had been repeatedly adjourned at the instance of the prosecution for one reason or the other. He submitted that "it is a violation of the accused's fair hearing and speeding trial."

He added that not a single witness had been called in this case since it was first mentioned. Lawyer Camara further applied under the CPC for the court to discharge the accused person in the interest of justice.

In his ruling, the presiding Magistrate Lamin George said "bearing in mind all what the defence stated in court and in accordance with the Criminal Procedure Code (CPC), I hereby discharge the accused person and the case struck out.

Wow! I wasn't even in court and God sort of did it behind my back. "Wow" again.

The Wow factor had also reached the Islamic Council, but they weren't happy bunnies. While I was thanking God for his goodness and for the encouragement that I derived from seeing Him at work, they were spitting nails and planning all sorts of skulduggery against me to try to win the end game.

# CELEBRATE

Sunday arrived and I was able to share with the men who gathered round the cell door how good was our God. It wasn't our habit to sing as I didn't know how the officers who allowed us to meet would feel about it. However, I started to sing and others who knew the words joined in.

> How great is our God,
> How great is His name,
> How great is his love,
> Forever the same.
> He rolled back the waters,
> Of the mighty Red sea,
> And He says "I'll never leave you,
> Put your trust in me."

"Don't you hate these people, Sir?" said an ex soldier, "Who?" I asked. "Those people who are trying to kill you, or keep you here for life." I thought about it for a moment. "No, in fact I forgive them." "What?" he exclaimed, "Forgive, how can you do that? I never could." "Maybe I'll start a teaching session in forgiveness," I said, "how'd you like that?" "Yeh, that'd be good," he replied and went his way.

It got me to thinking, to remembering again, when I'd taken Fiona back to UK with not an ounce of forgiveness in my heart.

# HEALING BEGINS
## July 2005

When we arrived at Peter and Julia's it was my intention to leave Fiona, turn round and exit stage left. However, they weren't the kind of people to let me off as lightly as that and before you could say Houdini, we were both having coffee with them and told that our bedrooms were ready for us upstairs. We took up days of their time and through the hours of counselling the Holy Spirit ministered healing and forgiveness to both of us.

It was decided that I'd take Fiona back with me to The Gambia and we'd continue the healing process there. When we arrived at Banjul airport Iona and Luke were very happy that we came back together to make a go of it, and as a family, we were determined to make things work. Gradually things improved and like scar tissue, started to form over our wounds, mine in particular.

I'm not saying that it was an easy time for us, but at least there was an 'us' and we were working this out together. Of course, there were setbacks, but there were also times where we had to show a united front as a family.

For example, I decided to tell the Pastor of the church we were going to, what had happened, and explain that after counselling we were on the way to recovery. As a Christian leader myself I'd have been delighted if it were told to me and I'd have asked how I could help in the healing process.

However, he said that we should attend a meeting of the church leaders after the morning service, who would interview us. I thought they would have been concerned, but happy that, though Fiona had fallen into sin, she had repented, before God and man, and I had forgiven her and we were moving forward.

Such was not the case. It turned out to be a witch-hunt with no compassion or love shown. They wanted Fiona to stand before the whole church and confess her sin. I felt I was blocking for Fiona and defending her for over an hour before I said, "Enough, this is totally unscriptural and well out of order, we're leaving," and with Fiona in tears we got to our feet and left.

What a lot of forgiving we had to do, there are times when what Jesus said in Matthew 18, that we must forgive seventy times seven, it's so real and so very difficult.

The following Sunday we went to 'that church', and sat at the front as a family to show that we were one as a family and with the Lord. The thing that was most difficult for me was to keep my mouth shut, as I knew a lot of stuff about most of the church leaders and their wives. It's not often I do the right thing, but sometimes I get it right, just sometimes.

I continued with my work in the barracks and immigration posts and to me it was a little surprising that there still seemed to be a regular stream of men and woman coming to faith in Christ. I often shared what had happened, sometimes to answer the question "where have you been Sir." or as an illustration of forgiveness. More often than not, I shared because one of my people had "blown it as a Christian" and couldn't understand how they could have done such a thing. Anyway, it was good that people knew, as they'd know soon enough when the baby was born.

# SEPTEMBER 2005

We decided that Fiona would deliver in England as she was over forty and "just in case". In The Gambia, many mothers and babies die in childbirth so we weren't taking any chances. Unfortunately, Fiona started to feel a little unwell in September 2005 so we thought that we'd get over to UK as soon as possible. When we were there, we also continued the counselling with Peter and Julia.

As it turned out, that was a good decision because within a week of arriving Fiona was back and forward to the hospital with pre-eclampsia and other complications that its best we men don't know about. I flew back to The Gambia to look after Iona and Luke, though they, young as they were, were more than capable. The next few months were a nightmare for us all: Fiona was taken into hospital where she was given the best care that she could have been given anywhere.

Looking back on it, this care was only available to us because of my work. In fact, our contributions had been paid by . . . whom, I wonder. You see an ex-pat isn't entitled to NHS when they come home, unless they resume residency, so how come we got it? I mention this, because when I eventually came back home I discovered I had been disowned by the British High Commission to the Gambian Government and castigated by the British press. I should have raised that point and the fact that my contributions stopped the day the regime took us into captivity. It's called 'deniability': the British wouldn't do that, would they? Anyway, there is more on this later.

Fiona became seriously ill and I was on one occasion phoned in The Gambia at four in the morning by the SNO in charge of the prenatal stuff to say that Fiona was seriously ill and I'd best come over. "Yeh, right," I told her, "I'll just jump on a number nine bus, will I?" "You should make it as quick as you can," she replied. It dawned on me that she didn't know where I was as I was on a mobile the country code looked all part of the long number. "I'm in West Africa," I said down the phone. "Oh!" she answered. Before she could say any more I said, "I'll be there as soon as I can."

Thanks to a legacy left to us from Fiona's mother in her will, we had some money in our account and during the next six months, I was back and forth from The Gambia to England like a yo-yo. In fact, I spent over £7,000 on transport during that time, but God had already seen to the finance.

# ELIZABETH
## 11<sup>th</sup> February 2006

I had a phone call to say that Elizabeth had come two months early and both mother and daughter were in intensive care after surgery and complication upon complication. Again, it was about four in the morning could I get over as soon as possible as they'd had to de-fib Fiona twice while on the operating table, and couldn't manage to stop her bleeding. She was getting blood transfusions and losing blood just as fast as it was going in.

I phoned a friend at Gambian Experience the travel company that flew in and out of The Gambia. Explaining the latest circumstances to her, (she already knew the whole story), and she pulled a few strings to get me on the afternoon flight to East Midlands Airport in England, which is just over two hundred miles from Exeter where Fiona and Elizabeth were.

A phone call secured a car from another friend, which would be waiting for me in the airport car park with the keys on the rear tyre and the tank full. I used the time to get plenty of food in for the kids, and make sure that they'd be looked in on even though there was someone in the compound at all times. Filled the car with fuel as they both drove well, Luke was fifteen and Iona seventeen. Finally, I spoke to Ali, a Lebanese man we were friendly with, and who owned a local restaurant. "When the kids come to eat, put it on a tab and I'll sort it out when I get back." "No problem," he replied, "Give our love to Fiona and the new baby." "Thanks," I replied waving at him and went home to pack.

The plane took off at 15.45 Gambian time, and the six hour journey plus the hour's time difference meant I landed at East Midlands airport at 22.45 GMT. Only carrying a holdall, I cleared customs and immigration in no time and was soon on the motorway heading south.

Keeping to the speed limit was never an option, as I needed to get to the hospital a.s.a.p. looking at my watch as I swung into the car park at Wanford Maternity Hospital in Exeter I saw it was 03.52. I'd made it from our home in The Gambia, West Africa to the hospital in Exeter, England, in less than twenty four hours from the phone call, not bad going.

As it happened Fiona was out of danger but still very ill. Elizabeth was 2lbs something and so tiny that when I put my hand in the incubator she measured the length of it. Something wonderful happened when I held Elizabeth. Firstly, the forgiveness that I'd been working on clicked into place. Instead of being a head thing, it was a heart thing, wonderful. Secondly, I just loved that little thing in my hand to bits, and anyone that had anything to say against her or Fiona would have their tongue ripped out and stuffed down their throat. I know, I know, not very Christian like, but let them try.

I was only able to stay a week as Iona and Luke were still in The Gambia and as sure as apples are apples, the Christian gossip factory would be talking about me leaving them to their own devices. 'What would these children be up to when their mother and father were away' was indeed the order of the day. Christians! What was it Gandhi said? "I like your Christ, I do not like your Christians. Your Christians are so unlike your Christ". Shame on us.

Fiona and Elizabeth were a further nine weeks in hospital and then another three convalescing before I was able to bring them home. All told, in four months I was back and forward from The Gambia to the UK eight times and Fiona twice and Elizabeth one single. Sadly, no air miles, just dog tired

# HERMANN BORING
## June 2009

It was the following Friday and I was laying in the darkness of my cell when footsteps going along the passageway stopped outside and the keys started to jingle. Minutes later the door opened and a stranger stood peering in. "Fulton?" he enquired. "Depends on who's asking," I replied, "My name is Hermann, with two N's, Jobateh, I'm a senior officer in the NIA."

Well you could have knocked me down with a feather; he looked anything but a secret police operative. He stood at the cell door seemingly unaffected by the stench from which even the guards recoiled. He sported a small scraggly beard that was half way between an artistic statement and a lazy approach to shaving. When he spoke, it was in a monotone pronouncing every word as if he was going to be marked out of ten. "You will come with me," he continued. "If it's all the same to you, I think I'll stay where I am," I replied. "If it was up to me, I would have you shot," he said quite matter-of-factly, and shouted, "Come now!" Some people you instinctively know not to mess with, and this cold, boring, unemotional man was one of those. Therefore, I argued no further and stumbled out into the passageway.

This time it wasn't the pickup that had come to collect me, it was a new 4x4 Nissan Patrol. I assumed that this nice car hadn't been laid on especially for me, but was either his personal car or a badge of rank and importance in the NIA. Either way, it showed me this guy was a cut above the ordinary NIA operatives, maybe even close to the President.

There were two other men to escort me plus the driver. The sun was shining and people were going about their normal business. I really enjoyed the drive in the air-conditioned car, "luxury." Bob Marley was playing from the CD player "Don't worry about a thing, every little things gonna be all right" and the clock said ten o'clock, which probably meant no torturing. Maybe every little thing was gonna be alright.

Arriving at the NIA headquarters, they took me to a bare office with a table and six chairs. Hermann with two N's and three other NIA men sat down and he gestured me to do the same. I sat, still in handcuffs and leg irons, (not an easy thing to since my buttocks were covered in boils,) it's not something that crops up in civilized conversation. "Can you take these manacles off," I asked. Herman nodded to one of the men with him, "Take off the handcuffs, he'll need his hands free for later." With that they took the handcuffs off from behind my back and I was able to lean on the table with my elbows and take the weight off my backside, but he fastened the hand cuffs to the chain of the leg irons and then to the chair.

"You've been very foolish;" he began "pleading not guilty to the impersonation charge has angered the Head of State. Why did you do that?" "Hmm, let me guess," I replied, stroking my unshaven chin. "Could it be that it was because I wasn't guilty?" He ignored that and went on, "And appealing against your additional three year sentence? Very foolish indeed, but we must get on, today is prayer day."

The questions they asked me were in relation to my supposed involvement in two attempted coups. They showed me printouts of over twenty phone calls made over a twelve-month period. On the printouts were highlighted lines. "Do you recognise these numbers?" Hermann asked. "Of course I do," I replied, "they're mine." "Why would you be in touch with these coup plotters?" he went on. "I can't remember the specific conversation," I said, "just as you are unlikely to remember a conversation you had three years ago, but at the time I had no idea that they were involved in anything except their legitimate employment." "In what way were the British involved in these coup plots?" another man asked. "Were they?" I said in feigned astonishment, "I wish I'd known, I'd have helped them"

This line of questioning went on for hours: they were getting nowhere but tried their utmost to wear me down so that I'd make a mistake. However, I didn't have anything to do with any coup plots and so there was no mistake to make and I was Mr Cool.

We had been closeted in that stifling room for so long that the place was starting to smell of sweat and frustration. It didn't bother me as I was used to far worse in the prison, but when the call for prayer came at two o'clock the NIA men couldn't get out of there quick enough. "We'll leave you to consider the consequences of spying and being a mercenary for the British," Hermann said in his boring monotone, "We are going to pray," and with that, they all left.

# MY FILE

I sat back for a moment, these guys were seriously trying to get me on coup plotting and spying. It was difficult to take Hermann seriously. Hermann, yes I know what his nickname will be "Reich Marshall Hermann Boring." As I was chuckling to myself, I noticed an open briefcase on the floor where the Reich Marshall had been sitting. I shuffled the chair along the floor to as near as I could get and fell on my knees to retrieve it. It was already open so I didn't need to use any plastic explosives to access the paperwork therein.

I wasn't looking for anything specific, to be honest I was nosey and as I said before 'knowledge is power.' In hindsight, I believe that this opportunity was God given. Anyway, the briefcase was full of papers and when I drew out a folder that had David Fulton printed on it in magic marker pen, I had to have a peek.

Now, what would you do? Actually, I don't care what you'd have done, I opened it and got the shock of my life. My file was there, mapping out the sequence of events that led to our capture and subsequent imprisonment and I will try to relate it as best as I can remember.

There was an email from a British subject residing in England to one Pastor Momodu Daffeh, Victory Gospel Church, The Gambia. The email came from an English Christian asking for verification about one of my emails to a friend in UK about an incident, which happened to me in the barracks. Momodu Daffeh then sent the email on to the NIA, the Islamic Council, the President's office and the police, with directions to my compound. After a hurried meeting, these four parties consulted the President who ordered them to take direct action against me.

At this stage, I should point out that this Daffeh and I had had a run in concerning a business that he was operating in The Gambia. He was travelling to the UK to raise funds for his church (which if it weren't for him was good). When he was speaking, he also asked the churches to send quality second hand goods from house clearances etc, via him to The Gambia to help the poor. He said that he would give of his time to distribute them to the poor and needy. Containers of stuff came in and letters accompanied them from the churches that they were Aid for The Gambia, Daffeh managed to get duty waivers for them despite the duty already effectively paid by the UK churches, he got the stuff in free.

Now I knew nothing about this until one of our church attendees came up to me after the service one Sunday. "Why don't you start a shop selling second-hand British furniture?" he asked. "Victory Gospel Church is." "I haven't got the time," I replied, "but maybe I'll go along and see what they've got. Where is it?" He told me and a few days later, I went along, as we needed a European mattress to replace an old foam one. I found a small warehouse that was relatively busy. I slipped in the door and had a nose about, (as is my wont) and to my surprise, there were boxes labelled "Aid for The Gambia." I snooped around some more and found other boxes labelled "Support for Sierra Leone Orphanage, from and the donor church name." Many other items were stacked up. Three piece suites, beds, wardrobes, boxes with computers, tools, fridges, all sorts. Every one with the name of a UK church and either Aid or Support written on them. "Can I help you?" said a girl. "Yes" I replied, "I'm looking for a British style mattress." "Oh, all our goods are from England," she continued, "we get a container in regularly."

That was when I decided to enquire further and found out that this was a swindle and the churches in England were being conned. I didn't know what to do as he was the head man in his "ministry" so I decided to see him. On confronting him about it and telling him it had to stop, he was abusive and told me to get out of his office.

Anyway, I digress, but returning to my file, you had to know the connection.

I wasn't able to read any more as the Muslim prayers had finished, so I put things back the way I'd found them and got back to where I'd been left, looking helpless and dejected.

In those few minutes before they returned I believe I went into a state of shock, mixed with anger, but also with a sense of relief.

At least I now knew the events leading up to our arrest and that it was not any mistake on my part that caused it. I had always suspected that we had been betrayed, but could never prove it, and couldn't work out who would do that. However now I knew.

The door opened, in they trouped and the interrogation started again, but there was a lacking in intensity this time. On the other hand, maybe it was just how I felt within myself; I didn't believe that finding my file was a 'stroke of luck', I don't believe in luck. I suspected that God directed me to it and now I had more knowledge and knowledge is power. Power to pray specifically, power to overcome self-doubts and to sort things out in my mind and to draw some of the lose threads together.

"So who's going to replace you now your cover's been blown as a spy?" Hermann said as the interrogation drew to a close. "What are you talking about?" I replied irritably: I hadn't eaten for over twenty four hours and was a little tired. "I'm not a spy and no one will be taking over my role as chaplain as far as I know." He leaned over and lifted his briefcase onto the table and rummaged around inside. At last, he found what he was looking for and put an email printout in front of me, and said, "But you've advertised!" I read it and laughed.

## MISSION VACANCY IN THE GAMBIA
### JOB DESCRIPTION

*A vacancy may soon be opening for the right person to work in The Gambia (Just a small corner of God's vineyard)*

1.  The suitable applicant must be of unsound mind and be able to multi task, preferably twenty tasks per minute.

2.  He (and we are using the biblical gender here) will have to have a high rank in the armed forces, preferably the army, as he will be working with extremist Muslims (the rank may just save his life).

3.  The suitable and lucky (I mean "Blessed") applicant must also be an evangelist and basic Bible teacher. He must be

able to understand the mind of the Gambians, a gift given to only a few, "e.g." The incumbent, the Archangel Gabriel and God Himself.

4. This person, "(God have mercy on him")", must be a paramedic, able and willing to stitch the local people up (I do mean in the medical sense), deliver babies and give injections.

5. He must be qualified in martial arts and small arms, (It has to be noted that this is not normally taught in Bible College). This discipline has been known to keep missionaries in Muslim countries alive to kick another day.

6. Multi linguistics would be an advantage, as the incumbent is able to communicate, and is fluent in many languages "e.g." English, American, New Zealandish, Canadian and Australian.

7. The very blessed person to get the chance to work in this part of God's vineyard must also have at the very least an inshore skipper's certificate, but preferably a deep sea Cert. This is because he must be able to skipper and navigate up river in the course of his mission and be using the boat (Which comes with the calling) must be able to evacuate at least 15 people (including his own family) if the smelly stuff were ever to hit the whirly thing in this unstable part of the vineyard.

8. The exceptionally fortunately applicant must be a marksman in all type of small arms. While his main work in the vineyard is to win souls to the Lord, he must also be able to defend his family and himself against ne'er-do-wells who are about the work of the Devil.

9. A general working knowledge of car mechanics and fabricating cars out of other scrap vehicles would also be useful. However, the Spiritual gift of discernment is also needed, to be able to tell the scrap cars from the ones that have only broken down or run out of fuel.

10. Our hero "God bless him" must be keen to try Church planting. This involves recognising other people's gifts as opposed to them recognising you as a white man and wanting gifts from you.

11. The successful spiritual giant will be required to manage teams of men, as they say "Many hands make light work" and that's all the electricity he'll get.

12. This man of God needs to be proficient with an instrument of some kind. The incumbent is proficient in the guitar, the scalpel, forceps and clamps.

13. A liking for hot climes is a must, as the weather gets to a comfortable 43$^c$ with a nice humidity of 83%. Think of the advantages of being able to wash without the need of a tap. A must for all energy saving environmentalists.

## Inducements

The position comes with a 1976 Range Rover with many 1981 bits and some Peugeot add ons. This vehicle will keep the Saint who takes over from the incumbent busy in the evenings, happily tinkering about it in order that it will start the next day in the vineyard.

We are happy to inform the hundreds of applicants that there is a boat provided, with which he will be able to take many leisurely mission trips into the interior. Crocs, hippos, poisonous river snakes and pirates add a little spice to the enjoyment.

## Remuneration

This absolute gem of a Godly and brave man will get nothing by way of wages. This paragon, this incredible human being, will be "LIVING BY FAITH." Tempting, Huh! "Living by faith is one of the most exciting and rewarding things a Missionary can do." At least that's what I'm told by many Christians who don't do it. "It's such a privilege," said a company director. "Wow!" said his wife through layers of makeup "I wish I was you." Well now's your chance.

All applications should be sent to me by jungle drum in Morse code.

Good luck, I mean blessing. Dave Fulton.

*Footnote*: Things do look iffy here. It's a difficult time, everyone's on edge and the net seems to be closing on us. Please pray for our safety, the nasties are on my case. However, no complaints, no worries, God's in control. Dave.

I laughed until my sides were sore and it was really ticking off the NIA guys, but I couldn't stop. (I believe, looking back that it was almost hysterical laughter). "Enough, if you can't be serious, then you'll have to take the consequences," Reich Marshall Boring shouted. "Take him away," he said to the others, then pointing at me said, "I'll be seeing you again."

For them it had been a waste of a day, but for me, I was elated and even as they drove me back to prison, I was thanking God for this visit to the NIA. However, it was to be the last time I'd do that, as things were about to get worse. It was only the next day that I was told that I was going to court for judgement on the number plate appeal.

# THEIR CUNNING PLAN

They followed the same procedure of allowing me to wash and shave, which made it worthwhile going, even though I knew that nothing was going to happen. You see, it was a public holiday and they'd be no sitting at court, this was a "not so cunning" trick to ensure that I went to court, but that nothing would happen.

The two prison officers who escorted me were glad to have a

light duty and the sergeant said, "Sir, when we get there we can take our time getting back. If you promise not to try to escape we'll have a relaxing day." "Sounds good to me," I replied, and with that, he unshackled me and offered me a cigarette. It was twenty-five years since I'd given up smoking, but the temptation to take it was almost overwhelming. However, I held my hand up and said, "Thanks, but no thanks."

We drove from the courthouse which was, as predicted, shut up to Bund Road, which was one way back to the prison and which passed the place where the fishermen had their pirogues and to me was a taste of one of the things I was missing . . . the sea.

Pulling off the road next to the water, the driver got out and deflated the near side rear tyre. "We can relax now," said the Sergeant, "there's no mobile reception in this area, so we can't report the puncture." I wasn't going to complain, especially as he produced the ubiquitous black plastic bag and withdrew two large Tapalapa, (very heavy baguette-looking local bread), filled with spicy beans in chilli sauce. We sat on the ground with our backs against the vehicle in companionable silence and after I prayed over my portion of food, I devoured it. For almost an hour, we stared out to sea, watching the local fishing pirogues come and go and I was almost content.

All good things must come to an end, and the Sergeant flagged down a passing pickup and after a moment's discussion the driver pulled off the road in front of our vehicle and we climbed into the back. We were only a few miles from the prison and en route, they put me back in cuffs and leg irons before we arrived back.

We disembarked from the pickup outside the main gate and I shuffled through. As soon as I was recognised and logged in there was a flurry of guards and the gate man ran to the headquarters building. "What's the problem?" the sergeant asked loudly to anyone who might give him an answer. As if in reply, there was a roar from two senior prison officers. They were also on the run, but towards us. "Where have you been," they shouted at the Sergeant, "what took you so long?" "We had a puncture," he lied, "we've just been able to get a lift." "Take him to his cell," the SO-called Jimbo said, pointing at me. "What's the problem?" The

Sarg persisted. Still pointing to me Jimbo said, "He's in serious shit, do as I say!"

As the saying goes, "My feet never touched the ground." Gone was the good natured 'we're all pals together' attitude of fifteen minutes ago, as I was half pushed, half dragged back to my cell wondering what this was all about. Unchained, undressed and thrown into darkness was such a contrast to sitting beside the sea in the sunshine that I was somewhat confused and more than a little concerned.

# REPORTER WITH NO SCRUPLES

It was probably about an hour later that the door opened and I was dragged out into the passageway where there was six guards standing about in various aggressive postures. There, in the middle was David Collie the director of prisons. "He didn't say anything, but one man, a superintendant spoke for him. "You've been sending letters out to the British Newspapers," he accused. "That would be a great trick," I replied holding up my still swollen hands with two grotesquely bent fingers, "were they done on my in-cell computer, or did I dictate them to my personal secretary?" "You sent them," he shouted. "Was it by Royal Mail, or email?" I asked.

Just when I thought I was starting to understand that something had ruffled the Director's feathers badly, two NIA men came into the passageway from the far side. "What are you doing here?" the director shouted at them in local language, "This is my prison!" The NIA guys looked at each other and shrugged, "He's our prisoner," they said, "we are taking him to headquarters, our boss is an angry man." "Who's your boss?" shouted David Collie. "The President," they replied in unison. Oops! That was a show-stopper.

They took me in a pickup to the NIA Headquarters and into

an interrogation room where five men with clubs surrounded me. They used them to push me around but they didn't hurt me. Then, in came Reich Marshall Hermann Boring and in his precise methodical way of talking he said, "The British newspapers have published a letter from you saying that you cannot say much to them now, but when you get out you will tell all. I will find out from you what it is that you know. I need you to believe me that you will tell me what you know and that you will never get out of prison alive."

With that, he nodded to one of the men and they started to hit me with their clubs. The man directly in front of me tried to hit me on the head and I raised my left arm to block it. "Crack" the pain shot through my arm and I dropped it, I held it by the elbow cradling it and protecting it in my right. I knew it was broken. I've had so many broken bones in my lifetime that I've become a bit of an expert, this one is called a "nightstick fracture". I had no option but to curl up as I went down under the weight of blows and try to protect my vital organs. Kicks started as the clubs were not so effective with me on the ground. These guys were really getting the hang of this. For some reason they got angrier and angrier and at some point, thank God, I lost consciousness.

When I came too, it was with a certain amount of wonder that I was alive. My body was sore from top to toe, my face was cut up and my nose was bleeding. My broken arm was hurting like hell, but I was alone in the room and could give a whimper or two without them hearing me. My right hand seemed to be unharmed and unhurt and as it felt the length and breadth of my body, not that there seemed to be much breadth left, and it seemed, apart from the arm I was in reasonable condition.

I felt my face; one cut above my left eye going up to the hairline that ought to have been stitched. In the assault, they had knocked out and lost one of my back teeth, so no tooth fairy for me. A few minor cuts and abrasions, but overall it was roughly the same face I'd been shaving for the last forty odd years. No one came for me for about an hour, which gave me plenty of time to stiffen up, but when they did come, they were still angry. They gave me a few more kicks before hauling me away by the ankles, down the concrete steps to Babba Dinka.

Thrown into that darkness I was asked by those already there who I was, but as soon as I spoke everyone knew it was me. They tried to help as best as they could, but I just wanted to be left alone, and the place settled down to a quiet contented peace. I remember thinking how strange that was, but in retrospect I guess it was for the time being a place of safety. As long as the door remained shut, there would be no beatings; it was a place of false security.

I was there for four days and while it wasn't good at least there was company, the food was reasonable, and there was plenty of it. Yet to my surprise, I wasn't able to eat much at one time: I guess my stomach had shrunk, so I ate little and often.

When I was taken back to Mile Two there was a real change in atmosphere, not only among the officers, but in the inmates' attitude towards me. Because I was in solitary and wasn't affected I didn't know that there was a now harsher regime in place. Some of the privileges that others had enjoyed had been taken away and it was perceived by everyone to be my fault, but I couldn't think for the life of me how.

The hatch slid open and Sanneh's face appeared, "How are you?" he asked in a rather brusque manner. "I think my arm is broken," I replied. "Maybe you deserve it," he answered. "What?" I said, "Maybe you deserve it, you should think before you put everyone's life in danger," was his parting shot before shutting the hatch.

What was going on? Was this another way of getting to me? Was someone trying and succeeding, to turn even my fellow prisoners against me? "Lord, help me. You know I've done nothing against these men, please reveal whatever it is so that it can be sorted, Amen."

Nothing happened for days, (or was it weeks) except my food being put through the hatch every afternoon. I wasn't allowed to empty my 'chamber pot' and had to designate a corner of the cell to be a toilet. The place stank and I could hardly move without kneeling in my own faeces and the floor was running with urine. I was developing more boils and but I didn't think it was a good idea to lance them in these deteriorating conditions. Depression came upon me like a blanket: it was smothering, debilitating, not only physically, but also mentally and spiritually.

I was no longer hungry, I ate the food that they gave me, but it was more for something to do than to keep me alive. While by nature I am a loner, I have to say that in these days, I felt acute loneliness and I thought of the thousands of people in towns and cities, surrounded by people but lonely, even terminally lonely. I got to thinking about the millions of people who were hungry and would have been glad of what I ate and gradually I started to take the focus off myself and started to pray for others. It was then that I remembered that I had made up my mind that I wouldn't be beaten and that my belief in God would see me through this. I wasn't afraid of dying but "I'M NOT GOING TO DIE IN HERE!"

The door opened, I must have been sleeping, as I never heard the keys. There stood the medic next to a prison guard and without a greeting said, "Sanneh tells me you think you've got a broken arm." I didn't say anything, but held out my left arm which was quite swollen. He gestured me outside and when he smelt and saw the state of my cell spoke sharply to the guard in local language. "Get someone to clean this place up or he'll die in there." Much to my surprise the guard left us and the inmate medic told me what had happened.

"A prominent British newspaper printed a letter which was said to have come from you, but we've been making some enquiries and it's obvious to everyone that it wasn't possible, so we found out what happened."

As he talked he was also working and in the way of doctors and nurses wasn't as gentle as I'd have liked. "Hmm, no question, a broken ulna, feel it? Just there." "I know where it is," I replied through gritted teeth, "it's me that's got it, just get on with the story will you?" "Ah, yes," he went on, "we discovered that a white female reporter approached a prison officer and offered him money, in fact it was D3,000 if he could get you to write a statement for the British press." I interrupted him there, "Wow, yes, it was P.O. Jatta, he came to my cell and asked me for a statement, but I told him an emphatic NO." "Well," he continued, "it seems he was able to write a statement himself which the journalist believed came from you and collected his money."

The officer returned before we were able to carry on our conversation and the medic carried on with my arm. He produced several bits of long twigs that people tie together to make local brooms (not unlike the brooms that witches traditionally fly about on). "Do you have any cloth or string we can use to tie these on to your arm as a splint?" he asked. "No," I replied, "but if you need to, you could tear a strip off my blanket." "Where did you get a blanket," he exclaimed. "Ah" said I, "them that asks no questions isn't told a lie, so watch the wall my darling while the gentlemen go by." "What?" he said frowning; I think he thought I'd lost it, "it's part of a poem by an Englishman called Rudyard Kipling." He found the blanket, it was covered in excreta and urine, as I'd rolled it up and used it to try and dam off my 'toilet' area.

**At this point maybe I should remind you that the floor area of the cell is six feet by four feet (6x4). Now if you look at your lounge door and imagine it lying flat on the ground, add one foot to the width and you've got my floor space.**

Anyway, before anything else happened three inmates came along the passageway with cloths, buckets and mops. The medic went to wash the strip he'd torn off the width of the blanket and the men got to work on my cell. "Sorry for ignoring you, Sir," said one, "we know now that it wasn't your doing, that paper article, sorry eh!"

For once, there was plenty of water, and they poured it into the cell by the bucketful and the other men mopped up. They emptied my 'chamber pot', and cleaned and filled my water container. While all this was going on the inmate medic splinted my arm, and they gave me a 'concoction' for the pain. "Thanks guys," I said gratefully, "may God bless you all." The officer said he was sorry that a prison officer was responsible for all this nonsense, but would let me stay in the passageway till my cell floor dried.

"Can I take a shower?" I asked hopefully and as he turned to go he said, "You've got half an hour till the end of my shift," and he left. From being down at rock bottom, only a few hours ago here I was in the lap of luxury well, everything is relative, an answer to prayer I believe.

# NAUTILUS 1

I love boats and the sea, there is something living about a boat, even when she is at anchor. She bobs and swings with the waves and tide. When you get into your bunk on a boat, you are rocked to sleep. However, in bad weather she will work with you to keep you both alive. When a car stops it's inert, dead, but a boat is always alive.

I thought of my boat "Nautilus 1" 46ft and 17 tons she could sleep seven in reasonable comfort, and she was a great workhorse. I guess I went up and down the river about forty times and it was about one thousand km round trip. So, with all the other small trips I did, I would imagine it wouldn't be far off fifty thousand kilometres I travelled in her. Wow, put like that it's staggering, that's about twice round the earth, (in my old boat?). Wow again.

Then I thought about the circumstances surrounding how I came to buy her. I was asked by the S.O.S. for the Interior in 2005 if I'd be responsible for the Chaplaincy of the Christian Immigration service men and women. I explained that this would be difficult for many reasons. Firstly that I didn't have a boat that would be suitable for the job, as the Immigration posts were scattered far and wide and mostly accessible only by the river. Secondly was the fact that I had a neck injury and it was going to prove physically too difficult.

He asked me to think about it and I said I would, though I couldn't see how it would be possible. What I had done yet again was to leave God out of the equation; it's what I often did. Anyway, to cut a long story short, two couples from UK, friends of ours, were over in The Gambia, Jim and Audrey, and Martin and Eddy. Christian leaders in England, people whom we respected and knew that they believed that God could and does heal today and they were coming to our house one Saturday evening for a meal.

That afternoon I was preparing for preaching and teaching from James 5 and verses 14 & 15 jumped out at me, specifically where it says that the prayer of faith will heal. My neck had already been prayed for repeatedly, and I have to confess that I was prayed out. Nevertheless, if I was reading this right then it was the faith of those praying for me that would heal.

I started to pray, "Lord I don't believe it's a coincidence that these people are here at this time, so if you want me to take up this Immigration post then I need good health and a fixed neck. I'm tired of asking for prayer, but I'll do it once again. If it's your will that I'm to be healed, then let it be for the sole purpose of leading people to Christ, Amen."

It was at dinner when I casually dropped the subject of the Chaplaincy of the Immigration and my inability to do it because of my neck. "Do you guys have faith for my healing?" I subtly dropped in to the conversation. There was a unanimous 'yes' as dessert was served followed by coffee.

Well, there was no getting away from it, the moment of truth had come. I stood in our lounge surrounded by six people; Jim, Audrey, Martin, Eddy, Fiona, and our son Luke. Iona had gone to her room as she'd seen me prayed for so often she didn't want to be disappointed again. Anyway, they prayed for me for some time and I felt myself falling to the floor, it was as if I had fallen asleep on my feet. I woke up to see them all watching me and as I stood up, I realised that the pain was gone. We were all elated and thanking God when Iona came in and she burst into tears at my healing. (She takes after her dad; emotional).

There was only one obstacle now to my taking on the Immigration as Chaplain . . . the boat. I had a twenty-one foot fibreglass boat, which was open save for a small day cabin forward. The river Gambia is wide, long and as it wends its way into the interior, it can be as tempestuous as any sea. Hippos, crocs and poisonous river snakes populate it. One bite from a Hippo would take a lump out of the boat and the crocs would finish us off. In the evening, after dark mosquitoes would plague anyone close to the riverbank and in the day the tsetse fly was waiting to put you to sleep. No, I was going to need another boat if I was going to accept this post.

At that time, there was a boat on the market the Nautilus 1. She was ideal for the job, but costly. She was the only boat of European construction in The Gambia, but I felt she was right and fit for purpose. At 45 feet long and with a beam of 12.5 feet, built in Holland from steel and weighed 17 ton. Pushing her along at a max speed of 8 knots was a single screw 125 hp Ford diesel.

There was a saloon/wheelhouse amidships accessed by a sliding door on either side of the boat. On the starboard side of the saloon, was a corner-folding table that when lowered could be used as a large double bunk. Forward of the saloon was a two bunk cabin which doubled as a galley. Astern of the saloon was a passageway, in which the head was sited, on the starboard side, and the shower on the port. Continuing past the head was the stern cabin, which had a three quarter bunk to starboard and a single to port.

Then there was the flying bridge accessed from the stern. All the controls and steering were duplicated there and there was a cushioned bench with seating for eight people and the captain's chair. There was also the advantage of a small tender and a permanent mooring on the river at Denton Bridge.

I mentioned it in an email to my cousin Al and he said that I should ask the churches in UK if they would support the buying of a boat I had sourced. I was going to sell my smaller boat and use that as a deposit. I managed to get £6,000 for it and then all I had to raise was a further £19,000. Well, I believed if God really wanted me to take this on, then the money would come in. I put down the £6,000 deposit and was told that if the balance were not forthcoming within ninety days then I'd lose it. Ninety days later, the boat was paid for in full. The day after that, I accepted the job as Chaplain to the Immigration.

# THE CHIMNEY

Days later, they came for me at midnight. Nothing much was said. The NIA man, Shades, threw me my clothes and put on the leg irons, only this time because of my broken arm they didn't put on the handcuffs. As usual, the destination was the NIA Headquarters but they pushed me into a room I'd never been in before.

I can't say it was a nice surprise to see Hermann Boring again, but there he was, sitting behind an important looking desk, sitting in an important looking revolving leather chair, looking anything but important. "I said I'd see you again," he intoned. "Are you going to sign this document or not, though I suspect not."

"Isn't it great to get something right?" I said to him as I looked up at the clock, "It's first thing in the morning? And the answer is no." He said nothing, only raised his right hand and pointed to the door.

He prodded me outside to the back courtyard and into the torture chamber. I have to say that I was frightened, not for my life, but for my arm. If they strung me up again, it would probably have made it irreparable. They stripped me and took me to the chimney, threw me into that confined space with the thundering silence and the blinding darkness. I knew the pain that was coming and so I determined to think of something else, maybe mind over matter would help.

It could have been hours or days later when there banging on the door. "I don't hear you Major, you should be screaming by now." It was the Reich Marshall. I said nothing. I made no sound. I did appreciate my sorry condition, but with no idea how long I'd been there I looked up, and the sky shone blue, so many hours must have passed. My body had an all-enveloping pain that was duller than the acute pain of the other occasion I was in the chimney. He banged again, "No one can stand the tunnel more than twenty four hours and you've been there thirty eight, speak to me, are you dead, like your God Jesus?"

I couldn't let that one go, could I? "Thank you for your concern, but Jesus and I are very much alive as you'll find out one day asshole." I know, I know, I shouldn't have said asshole, but I did. Anyway, it seemed as if my speaking satisfied him and he wouldn't have to explain away my death to the British Government. A final bang on the door and he shouted, "There's a little surprise for you later that will maybe make you think again," and with that I heard the jackboots retreat (metaphorically speaking of course).

By the light from the top of what they called the tunnel, (because they don't know about chimneys), I could see that my legs had swollen up as had my left arm. The pain just went on and on, but again I stopped thinking of myself, and realised there were probably millions of people suffering much worse. Gradually a blanket of night covered the top of the chimney and with the darkness came the mosquitoes and cockroaches. I had almost given up hope of getting out of there, when suddenly the door opened and I fell out. The NIA guard didn't seem an unkindly man, and said, "Forty-four hours Tubab, that's a long time," and with that he turned on his heel and walked out, leaving me alone, but I wasn't alone.

It was difficult to know what time it was, my guess would have been between one and four in the morning. I lay on the concrete floor, with my feet still in the tiny cell, covered in excreta and urine, feeling nothing but humiliation. There was an oil lamp burning on the desk at the far end of the room, which cast a pale glow over the place. I wanted to get water as I hadn't drunk anything in two days, but I couldn't move with only one serviceable arm.

Lying there, I was aware of something not being right, a strange thing to say but I felt something in my spirit, which was sending shivers down my spine, even to some extent over-riding the pain. Now, I'm not someone who hears God very well, he speaks to me through the Bible and through my thoughts. However, it was as if God said to me, "Death is here," The ambience of the place, the smell that left a coppery taste in the back of my throat, what was it; Evil? No, I was used to that. Then a memory was triggered in my subconscious, it was of being with my mother when she went shopping, I'd probably be about four years old. We went into the local butcher's and while she was waiting at the counter, I wandered off into the back of the shop. All the hanging carcasses, fascinated me by their size I guessed cows, sheep and rabbits, but it was the smell, the smell I recognised now as, 'death'.

I scanned the place as best as I could, and gradually as my eyes got used to what light there was I could see a bundle, a lump, about fifteen feet away in a corner. I pulled myself up on my good arm and looked over, I saw it was a body and as I peered into the gloom the head moved and it made a groaning noise.

How could I get over there, and why was I left alone? First things first, I managed to roll onto my right hip and using my right arm, drag my, by now lightweight body over to the man. He was a big fellow and like me naked, but unlike me he was in a physical mess. I could see the white of his bones as they stuck out of various parts of his body and as I dragged myself to his head, I was horrified to recognise him though they'd left him almost unrecognisable. "James! James," I managed in a husky whisper, "James its Dave." He watched me as I dragged myself closer; his eyes were wide and staring, never blinking only staring, pleading.

I came to the top of his head, he was a big man, about six four and his head was like a cannonball, always shaved and shining. I put my good hand under his head to lift it onto my swollen lap when he moaned and coughed. Seeing that he was starting to choke I lay it back down and tried to check his airways. Putting my finger in his mouth I was shocked to discover there was something stuffed in his mouth and I drew it out. It was one of his testicles and his tongue was missing. At least that's what I realised when I looked down and saw he'd been castrated.

I felt as if my life had stopped as I seemed to watch the whole scene from above, this wasn't real; nothing that was happening was true. How could it be? God would never allow this. His eyes followed mine as I looked at what they had done to him and still kept him alive. Those eyes I realised had no eyelids, they'd cut them off! Both his legs had been broken many times over and his arms were broken too. I counted six ribs protruding through the skin. It goes without saying that I can only recount what I was able to see in that dimly lit evil place, in the presence of death.

I believe he was beyond pain, (it does happen) but he knew he was going to die. He tried to say something that I can't describe; part gurgle, part words, but I knew very well what it was. It was what I'd have said if I were him, 'Finish it.'

How could I? How could I not?

As I write this next, what, five hundred words? I will be crossing a line that I never wanted to see or reach, never mind cross. It's possible I will be thrown out of the church, maybe people who have befriended me of late will disown any knowledge of me, and that's OK. At the beginning of this book, I said I'd tell it like it is and by God's grace I will.

I looked about me and there was nothing but my prison shorts and t-shirt by the door of the cell and a tap, which had been reaffixed on the wall (with the handle on it) plus an iron bucket by the tap. I pulled myself over to my clothes and draping them over my shoulder headed to the tap. My mind was as clear as a bell. I realised that if I succeeded in what I was going to do that it would be tantamount to committing suicide. I didn't know how much time I had, or indeed why I wasn't already on my way back to Mile Two. All I could do was focus on the job at hand.

I managed to reach the tap and to my relief the bucket was full of water in which I soaked the clothes. Again, I draped the clothes over my shoulders and started dragging my body towards James. Looking behind me, I could see a trail of blood mixed with water. While I could feel nothing at the time over the pain in my limbs, I realised that I was scraping the skin off my hip as it was dragged across the rough concrete floor.

"So what Dave," I thought, "you'll be dead soon anyway, what's a little blood?"

Reaching James I told him what I thought he wanted me to do. And said that if I'd got it right he should look right with his eyes and if not then he should turn his eyes left.

Maybe again there should be a word of explanation. This, as I write it sounds so clinical, but it was anything but. I was in floods of tears; this was the last thing in the world I wanted to do. I was angry at myself for putting James in this situation, I was angry at James for not keeping his head down, I was angry at the extremist Muslims who had done this to him and to me. I have to say that I was also angry with God who could have stopped it and still could, but I knew he wouldn't.

James was one of my chaplains who I brought to faith in Christ some years previously. He was one of my spiritual children and this was breaking my heart.

He looked right, then to the centre and right again. It was time, and for me time stopped. I started to recite the 23$^{rd}$ Psalm as a prayer for both of us, and covered his mouth and nose with the wet clothes. Looking into his eyes, which were full of gratitude as well as regret, for he believed as I did, that we'd both be dead within the hour and nobody but God would know what had happened in this place, this day.

The Lord is *our* shepherd, *we* shall not want.
He makes *us* to lie in green pastures,
He leads *us* beside still waters, He restores *our* souls
He guides *us* in paths of righteousness for his name sake.
Even though *we* walk through the valley of the shadow
    of death,
*We* will fear no evil, for You are with *us*,
Your rod and Your staff, they comfort *us*.
You prepare a table before *us* in the presence of *our*
    enemies.
You anoint *our heads* with oil, and *our* cup overflows.
Surely goodness and mercy will follow *us* all the days
    of *our lives*
And *we* will dwell in the house of the Lord forever.


Amen


James died in late March, or maybe early April, I don't know which. May God forgive me for what I have done, for I doubt if I ever will.

Not a word was said about what had transpired in that dark

dungeon. I had dragged my body over to the bucket and washed myself as best as I could and removed any blood that was on my clothes. They came in without so much as a glance at James and two men gripped my upper arms and dragged me out. I must have felt pain, especially in my broken arm, but I can't recall it.

Still naked I was thrown into the back of the pickup and taken to Mile Two where after being dumped unceremoniously in the courtyard I was carried in by prison guards. I felt as if I wasn't wholly there, like things were happening to me while I was wandering about in slow motion as if in a mist. The guards were as kind as they could be and I remember thanking them and telling them that I forgave them. When the cell door clanged shut I started to pray. I believed that I had lost my salvation because of what I had done, but I still believed God was there and listening.

# NO CONDEMNATION

The next day the guards unlocked my cell. I thought it was because of my injuries that they left the door open, but it was because it was Sunday and brothers in the fellowship had spoken to them. They all came around and it goes without saying that we were really pleased to see each other, as each time I was taken away by the NIA, I wasn't expected to return, which was the norm.

I couldn't say much because as I've said I believed I had thrown away my salvation, so who was I to teach these new Christians? One man (we'll call him John) a former Captain in the army and a coup plotter, came into my cell and sat with me while the others sat cross-legged outside praying. Putting his arm round my shoulder (which I wasn't at all comfortable with, remember we were all naked) he said, "I don't know what's wrong, but it was you that told me that there is nothing to difficult for God." Hmm! John had been a nominal Roman Catholic, but had come to a solid relationship with Christ a few weeks earlier and had a powerful ministry in saying the right thing at the right time (unlike me).

I broke down and cried. Me? I can hardly believe it, me? I don't really want to write about it, crying's not what I do. Picture the scene if you can. Sixteen black naked men in a stinking dimly lit prison passageway, sitting or kneeling round the door of a naked white man who was bawling his eyes out. My black brothers, Gambian, Ghanaian, Senegalese and Nigerian, were praying with arms outstretched towards me and all this, in the confinement wing of the notorious Mile Two Prison, where the rest of the prisoners (about one hundred and seventy) were Muslim.

God really ministered to me through them that day, I cried it all out, I cried for James, I cried for my family, for my attitude towards those who abused me. I cried for the fact that when Jesus said, "Father, forgive them, for they know not what they do," He was talking not only about those who were nailing Him to the cross, but also about those who were torturing me and other Christians.

I wasn't quite there yet and I knew it, but I started to forgive them in my head and by God's grace it would someday drop those twelve inches to my heart. Again, I started to believe, I knew that God's grace was sufficient.

I told them what had happened over the previous three days and nobody condemned me, even those ex soldiers who knew James. We prayed and the men all said Amen together with one voice. Tears rolling down our faces, these hard ex soldiers, these outcasts, we from five countries shed tears, not of self-pity or pain, but of sadness mixed with joy. Any one of us could be next, but our eternal future was secure. I wished those torturers could see us now.

I still wasn't able to walk properly, as it took the best part of two weeks for the swelling to go down and during that time whenever possible the guards would open the cell door for a few hours in the evening. That also allowed me to receive a little food that had been smuggled from the kitchen. Maybe a few ground nuts or a bit of intestine that nobody wanted. God was keeping me alive and Dictator Jammeh was getting annoyed about it.

# I'M GETTING BETTER

The weather started to get very warm and the cell was like an oven. It had been weeks since I had my kicking and two since James passed away. I was pretty well healed up, my arm was still sore at the break, but it was now out of the homemade splints and sling and I was careful not to knock it. Also in that time I had my first visit, half an hour with friends from whom I learned all the news about how Fiona was, and that Luke had passed his driving test and Iona given birth to a baby boy and, quite incredibly, called him James.

Even after what I'd experienced I was still able to be optimistic, I'd seen so many give in, some who had taken their own lives, some who had totally lost the plot and were as mad as a hatter. Of course, there were those who cracked under the torture and gave the NIA information and names of people who they said were against the President, most of which was lies.

At that time, I could see that God had gone before and that he was with me. For example, I had started this sentence in a very fit condition, physically, mentally and spiritually. I became aware that the God who knows the end from the beginning, Wow, had prepared me for this! That's awesome.

To keep some sense of balance I'd often deliberately cast my mind back to the good times, the fun times in The Gambia, and there were many. We'd made quite a few friends here, it was so easy to major on these bad times, but I was determined to look at the bright side. Just then, there was the rumble of thunder that must have been close as I was able to hear it over the Islamic chanting.

# LET IT RAIN

Unlike most of the ex-pat white people in The Gambia, I loved the monsoon season. When the rains come, the temperature dropped and just for a while, it was quite cool. I never minded being out in the rain either. Remembering a time when I took the boat up river in the rains made me sit in the darkness and smile.

# AUGUST 2006

There is some dispute about the origin of the saying "Time and tide waits for no man." However, I believe it was to do with the departure of sailing vessels in the days before steam or diesel. In those days, ships were helped on their way out to sea by an outgoing tide. The tide in the harbour would be high, thereby giving them enough water under their keels to navigate more safely and the tide going out from high to low was to their benefit.

However, in my case I used the tide the other way round, which was helpful only in as far as when I left at low tide, the incoming tide was astern of me as I made my way up the river. The River Gambia is tidal most of its length. This made it difficult to navigate the bolongs where I moored the Nautilus, because in the bolong to the main river there were many shallow places and hazards, the unseen deep channel was only about fifteen feet wide.

The day that was on my mind was in the rainy season and low tide was at four in the morning, which meant leaving home at three in order to cast off just after four. It doesn't matter where you are or what the weather is like, getting out of bed at three for a four-ish start is never a joy.

I'd fuelled and provisioned the boat the previous day so that I'd have a flying start, but as the famous Scottish poet Robert

Burns once wrote, "The best laid schemes o' mice an' men, gang aft agley."

This day especially was a bummer; the tropical rain sounded like a herd of wild stallions stampeding across the tin roof of the house. I knew that I was going to get soaked to the skin before I'd even crossed the fifteen paces from the veranda to the Range Rover and yes I could see it from where I stood, I'd left the window open.

I went back into the house and took off my uniform and put it in a plastic bag along with a towel, then made a dash for the car. I laid the towel on the seat and sat on it with only my underpants on. You really have to imagine the scene: I was sitting there on a soggy seat, only wearing my underpants, cap with a shiny badge on it and uniform jacket, at three o'clock in the morning. The lightning was illuminating the sky and from time to time, it was so close that the air fizzled and I felt as if my skin was going to fry. The thunderclap came almost immediately and it was so loud that the Range Rover shook. The windscreen wipers, even at full speed, struggled to clear the deluge.

The old Range Rover was resolutely ploughing through water and mud about twelve to eighteen inches deep and from time to time; I had to put it into diff lock to enable me to get through.

The reason for me putting on the jacket and cap was that the army, to discourage nocturnal coup attempts, had checkpoints all along the roads, especially at Denton Bridge where the boat my boat was moored. I drove to the first checkpoint and as soon as my vehicle was recognised, the three soldiers saluted and re-moved the barrier. I slowed down and commiserated with them on their duty in this weather, a little bullshit never goes wrong. This happened four times before I managed to reach the boat.

Anyway, before getting out of the car I took off my uniform jacket and cap again, and put them in the plastic bag. The tender was tied up to a small jetty I jumped in and bailed the rain water out before anything else The little Yamaha Enduro 15 outboard started first pull. It only took a few minutes to reach the Nautilus and while steering the tender I used a half bucket to bail out the rest of the rainwater.

Because of the weather and driving conditions, it had taken me much longer than normal to get to Denton Bridge and the Nautilus was swinging round on the mooring to face the strong incoming tide. Not an auspicious start, but that's the way it goes sometimes.

Every time prior to casting off I'd spend time in prayer, as indeed I know many men who go to sea in small boats do. This morning, despite being later that I'd have wished I made no exception and read a passage from the Bible and prayed.

As I've mentioned, the Nautilus had two steering and control positions, below (inside) in the wheelhouse/saloon and on the flying bridge but for some reason the ignition was situated only in the wheelhouse. I connected the battery and turned the key and as was the usual way with the old diesel, she ground over for a few turns then fired into life.

Running to the stern where I could access the flying bridge, I got to the wheel. It was exhilarating on the open bridge with the rain coming down in curtains of water. Looking at the speed log, I saw that although still tied to the mooring, the tide was rushing under Denton Bridge and us at about five knots. In order to slip the moorings I had to put her ahead into the current with enough revs to make five and a half knots.

Then I went quickly forward grabbing the boathook before she over ran the mooring buoy at the end of the twenty foot rope. Leaning over the bow in the pitch darkness, I located the bright yellow buoy, hauled it on board and untied the rope before throwing it back in.

Back on the bridge I throttled down, as the engine slowed we were pushed astern by the current, and as soon as I knew I was clear of the buoy and tackle I spun the wheel hard to port. She swung round and we were off. Before switching on the running lights I covered them with cowls that I had made to make sure there was no glow in my eyes. I couldn't afford to lose my night sight and especially now as the rain was still thundering down. Thankfully the lightning was now many miles away, as that can also ruin your night vision.

With the tide coming in at five knots, I had to have revs for seven on the GPS in order to maintain steerageway of two knots. Now for a boat on the open sea or even on a wide river, seven knots is not fast, but in the narrow bolong, it was like slalom course which often turned back on itself. Not long after I bought her I fitted two powerful flood lights on her, but the rain was so heavy that if I'd switched them on the light would have reflected back on me making things ten times worse.

I loved it, every adrenalin packed minute of it. I remembered standing at the wheel fifteen feet above the water level, whooping and laughing. Slowly, just as I was coming out of the bolong, the darkness started to weaken and the shapes of fishing pirogues could be seen in the distance on the main river.

Avoiding the sandbank, I turned east into the River Gambia proper and set the revs to continue at seven knots. This required more revs as in the main river because of its width of approximately 6km at that point the current wasn't so strong, only about three knots.

With the coming of the light, the rain seemed to decrease to a downpour as opposed to a deluge. I lashed the wheel and went below to make a strong coffee and breakfast. The galley was in the forward cabin so I was able, through the forward cabin windows, to keep an eye on the direction and drift of the boat. I wasn't too worried about other river traffic as it would be only be a very few fishermen on the river. Not only that, but it was still raining hard and Gambians don't go out in the rain if possible, even fishermen.

I often joked with Gambians who asked me if I could help them to acquire a visa to England. I'd ask them what they'd do when it rained and the reply would inevitably be "shelter". "Where would you like to live in England?" I'd say. "Manchester," would be the usual reply, as 90% of them supported Man United. I could just envisage it, all the Gambians heading to the wettest place on the UK.

Yes, it was good to reminisce about the good times, The Gambia was a challenge twenty-four hours a day, but I loved the people and the country. Reminding myself of this stopped me becoming resentful towards all Gambians.

# A PROMISE

I used the blanket as a pillow and despite my bones being cushioned only by thin skin I slept. I was becoming used to the discomfort.

I have said often that I'm far from being a super spiritual person and I will reiterate it now. However, something extraordinary happened that night. I woke up with a scripture reference in my mind and I had no idea where it came from. It was Zephaniah 3:15, Zephaniah. I didn't know where Zephaniah was in the Old Testament, so it couldn't have been a thought provoked by something I'd read or heard earlier. It was pitch black and so I groped to the wall and taking out the nail I scratched it on the wall as best as I could and went back to sleep.

The next day some of the brothers came to the cell door for the impromptu Bible study that happened almost every morning. "Hey guys," I said, "I believe that God gave me a scripture last night can someone look it up for me?" I slid my Bible through the food hatch and one of the Nigerians who was good with English read.

> The Lord has taken away thy judgements; he has cast
>    out thine enemy.
> The king of Israel, even the Lord is in the midst of thee.
> Thou wilt not see evil any more. King James Bible.

There were whoops and shouts so loud that not only did it turn the heads of the other prisoners, but also it brought the guards running and stopped bible study for a week.

Could this be true? All the other Christians believed it to be so, but me, I hoped it was. No I believed it was but when was I going home, how was it going to be worked out? However, fundamentally it's God against the President: no contest. I guess I was on a high, it was only a matter of time, one count had been overturned already and the last one was heading that way.

When I managed to sleep my dreams would be good. I'd be out and back with the family. We'd have a big Silver Wedding celebration, lots of people there It would be a multi celebration, our anniversary, a belated eighteenth for Luke, a belated twenty first for Iona, a wetting of the baby's head for James and a freedom party for Fiona and me. Yep, it would be a storm of a party.

Strangely though, time seemed to drag for a while. What was keeping them, why wasn't I rushed to court where justice would be done? It's a strange thing time, it weighs most on those who have least of it and I wasn't getting any younger. I believed God had done it, but when was he going to bring it about.

It was two days later that a guard came to the cell door. "Fulton," he said in the famous loud prison whisper, "My brother, but not the same mother and father is Jobateh the judge, and he told me that your judgement is "Acquit and Discharge". That's good for you. As soon as you get to court you'll be a free man." I was delighted, all I needed to do was get to court and I had a date for next week. "Yes!"

The only fly in the ointment was that nobody seemed to have told the NIA the judgement had been overturned and a few nights later, they came for me with the usual rattling of keys and Shades trying, but failing to look cool.

My arm had all but healed and apart from sores and my skeletal appearance, I felt that I was in not bad condition. However, what I'd failed to take into consideration was that I was comparing my appearance with that of those around me, who were thinner, but that was their general build even before Mile Two so they had head start in me anyway.

They took me straight to the torture chamber, and again strung up by the wrists. This time however, Godzilla came and stood before me and as he looked up into my face, a shiver went up and down my spine. If ever I have looked into the eyes of sheer evil that was it. There was blood on his hands and upper arms and splashes on his face. "We've got a treat for you tonight," he said and with that, he sent a punch into my stomach.

Now, I'd like to say that because of my intensive training he broke his knuckles on my stomach muscles, but despite realising what was coming and tensing them every breath was driven out of my body. I suffered a rain of punches to my ribs and abdomen. Sometimes when I swung past him like a punch bag, he'd punch me in the ribs at the side.

I think it only lasted a few minutes, maybe shorter, but it seemed an eternity to me. I never lost consciousness and when he was done, I was left swinging like a carcass in an abattoir and that isn't a bad analogy. In the spread-eagle position, it's hard to breathe, but after having had the shit beaten out of me quite literally, I thought I was going to suffocate to death. I couldn't even adjust my posture as both my thumbs had dislocated again. It wasn't good. I remember thinking, "God, why did you overturn my judgement just for me to die like this?"

Struggling, each breath was like a knife stabbing my side, and yet my mind was as sharp as a razor. I assessed my situation and condition and realised that the NIA did know of the judge's decision to acquit and discharge me and if my guess was right, then they would try to extract their pound of flesh before I went to court on Monday. That was reinforced when I realisation that despite my beating there would be no visible marks when I was fully clothed.

When a judge makes a decision on an appeal, his judgement has then to go to the Chief Justice for rubber-stamping. The Chief Justice is appointed by the President, and of course is his man. He'd report what the judgement was to the President, the President would tell the NIA, and they in turn would be instructed to do something. What was that saying? "If the only tool you can use is a hammer, you see everything and everyone else as a nail." Well I hoped that this was it, that they'd feel that I'd had enough, but somehow I doubted that.

I was still in this reverie when I felt my feet touching the ground as they lowered me down. I buckled up in pain and started to feel my body for damage. The place giving me the greatest pain was my lower back at the right side and as I reached around with my left arm, my hand caught on a rib that was protruding out, but not breaking the skin. Overall I had four broken ribs but what to do about it? I guess nothing for the time being, as I didn't want to ruffle any feathers so close to my release which would surely come on Monday. Yes, that was it; I'd manage till Monday, then, when I got back to UK, like Humpty Dumpty I could be put back together again . . . Sorted.

It was a painful trip back to Mile Two, and the NIA guys weren't as gentle as they might be. However, when I got to prison at three in the morning, the night shift of guards couldn't have been better. "Can you walk Sir?" they asked me. "I think so if I get a hand," I replied and with that I was gently helped back into confinement, where I lay in the passageway outside my cell. One guard went into the main yard and brought the prisoner medic who immediately started to issue instructions to the guards, which included hot water, the presence of two mess boys and some sort of bandages.

After hearing what had happened the assembled group of prisoners and guards were horrified. Not just that, they were incredulous that the British Government was allowing Fiona and I remain in captivity. They told me news of an American prisoner who had been brought out of North Korea by ex-President Carter, and of a French man released from Iran and other people released when their government intervened. "Has the British bulldog lost its teeth Sir?" they asked, "Why don't they come and get you and your wife?"

Me, I'm proud to be British, but I have to say that I couldn't come up with an answer that would satisfy them. In fact, the more I thought about it; the more it seemed that the British Government was doing nothing.

It was that 'deniability' thing again, what could I expect. They didn't want anyone delving into my past; something embarrassing for them might turn up. No, better to let me rot, maybe even die of malaria or malnutrition: that could solve their problem.

I was starting to get negative again. Someone brought a bowl of hot fish soup and that went down well and all the while, I was being strapped up with more strips torn off my blanket, soon there'd be none left but, "thank you God that I'm still alive."

A painkilling concoction appeared and this time there was

no hesitation in getting it down my neck. After a few minutes, it started to work, "What's in this guys?" I asked "we could market it in Europe and make our fortune." "You don't want to know Sir," they laughed, and they were probably right.

# A SHAFT OF LIGHT

The guard took the prisoners back to their cells where they could continue their disturbed night's sleep. They left me alone until about 7am, which is just before the end of the night shift and the senior officers came in. During that time, I used my engineering knowledge to examine the hatch in the door beside me. It was a simple affair, two 5mm pieces of cheap angle iron welded onto the door in the upright position with the outer pieces facing each other making two U shapes. A solid piece of 4mm plate with a handle welded to it, which slid up and down. There was a groove in the concrete floor into which the hatch slotted, so with the weight of the hatch and no purchase it couldn't be opened from the inside.

Simple, but effective, so how could I deal with it, I was tired of total darkness. You could take out the sheet of steel as the stoppers, (which had been welded to the door to prevent its removal), had long since broken off. Wincing with pain, I slid it up and out, but it was quite a hefty piece of stuff. There was no way I could bend it to prevent it sliding, especially in my present condition. I couldn't hide it as it would soon be found and the guard would be in serious trouble.

I angled it against the wall and floor and slowly stood up and hurt my foot trying to bend it. Hmm! There was a way, as the advertisement for a washing machine says, 'The appliance of science.' I struggled onto my knees and put it in the door just between the hinges, then slammed the door shut. Looking at it, I couldn't see any change, so as the Scottish King Robert the

Bruce once said, "If at first ye don't succeed, try, try, try again." As I always do what I'm told, I put the plate in again at as near as I could judge the same place and slammed the door on it even harder.

Again, it didn't look to have bent, but hold on, maybe just a tad. So I did it one more time and this time I thought I detected a slight bend where a line marked the place I'd put it in the door. Rubbing dirt on the metal hatch to hide the mark, I reinserted it into the slot. It went in but didn't slide down, there was only ever 1mm of leeway for it to slide and with a little rust even that was reduced.

"Sorry to lock you up," the night guard said, "but I would be in a problem if my boss found you out here." "That's alright," I replied, "I'm grateful for all that you've done, God bless you." The door was slammed shut and the guard tried to push the hatch down but it wouldn't budge. He jumped on it with his boots on and managed to wedge it more firmly in place.

For the rest of my time in Mile Two that hatch stayed open and I had some light on the floor, if I lay down facing the door I was able to read. A victory and no one but me knew, or cared. Sunday night came and a guard came to the cell and shouted through the door, "Court tomorrow Fulton."

# COURT AGAIN
## July 2009

Monday morning came and I was opened up early so that I could have a wash and shave. I also took this opportunity to go round the other cells and distribute the stuff I had accumulated in the almost six months I'd been in Mile Two. Toothpaste and brush, a sliver of soap, a rusty razor blade as well as the one I'd just used. What was left of my blanket was a prize for John along with the pen I'd got from the High Commission. The men from the Fellowship who were out and the mess boys all wished me well.

Fiona and I still had the balance of the Sedition sentence of one year to finish, but when this number plate charge was quashed I wouldn't be back in confinement, I'd go into the main yard to finish off the remaining two months weeks.

There was a real change in attitude among the guards, I wasn't put in shackles and it was a police pickup that came for me. Smiles and good wishes seemed to be the norm as the Gambians were now trying to get in my good books so they might have something to their advantage on my release.

I was able to smile again, not necessarily at my position, but at what was happening. Nothing had really changed. If a Gambian could see a better future for himself then he'd be nice, but who could blame them if they could gain an advantage and help themselves out of this country and have a new life.

However, if nothing good happened to me then I'd be treated like the white former colonial master that they really thought I was (generally speaking that is). When I wasn't expected to live through this, for the most part I was ignored, but now I was to be set free in a short while it was a whole different ball game

I got to court and there were the usual reporters and TV cameras, the world and its uncle looking for a story, true or not. To my delight, there were friends there and we were able to have time together. They showed me photos of my family in England and my first glimpse of my grandson James. However I could see that everyone was shocked at my appearance, which I have to say was a surprise to me as I truly thought I was in quite good condition.

It was while we were talking and planning about what was going to happen when Fiona and I were free, that a policeman came and told us that the judge had been sent up country and there would be no sitting, it was adjourned for one week. I can well remember the feeling of disappointment and even anger just for a moment. I believe It was Patricia that said, "Oh well, next time eh!"

She was right of course, a week or two wasn't going to make

much of a difference to my going out with Fiona, but I still felt down. The police gave me another hour with friends and I was able to eat a chicken sandwich and have a cold Fanta, wonderful!

Of course, they took me back to the confinement wing where the news of what had happened was already common knowledge. In the first five minutes of being locked in my cell, all the things I'd given away came back to me. I will say this again, "The Gambia is full of good men and women, Muslims, but not fanatics, people who only want freedom from oppression and God bless them, are prepared to die to get it for others."

# KEEPING SANE

In the female wing, there was an old TV, which showed mostly religious Islamic programmes. They also showed the news, international and local. It was all in local language, but Fiona did try to see the news and imagine her shock when she saw me, star of stage and screen, struggling to climb the stairs to the courthouse. Some of the women said, "Who is that white man? He is too old to be treated like that." Fiona replied, "He's not old, that's my husband." The medic passed on this information to me and being considered old upset me more than the court not sitting, but as the life expectancy of a Gambian is fifty-six, I guess in their eyes I was old. I know there will come a time when I'd rather sit on the mountain than move it, but that won't be for a while yet.

John came to the cell and as we talked, he said something that was niggling at the back of my mind also. "I think that this was a set up. I have no doubt that Justice Jobateh was sent to the provinces so that he couldn't pass his judgement on your appeal." As I say, I wondered about that too.

Things seemed to get slightly better now I could see, albeit dimly, in the cell. I was even given soap that had been handed in over the six months I'd been in captivity. I had twenty-three bars of mixed soap, twelve of which were Cussons Imperial Leather, pure white, and I knew exactly what I was going to do with them.

Keeping one bar of the other soap and the white stuff separate, I halved each bar of the ten remaining and distributed them among various people, especially foreigners who got nothing sent in. The reaction was incredible, people were so grateful for such a small thing, but to me it meant that I was able in some small way to bless and thank people who had accepted me as one of themselves, comrades in suffering.

Another thing that this did was to bring Muslims along to the morning's Bible study. Staggering, God used just half a bar of soap to break down the remaining barriers between some of the Muslim men and myself. Three of these men came to faith in Christ later.

I was expecting to leave in a week or so, but in the meantime, I was going to do two things. One was to make a place where I could hide things and that was going to be a challenge in a 6x4 ft cell. The second was to make a chess set out of soap, I had the white, but how was I going to get black soap? Indeed, was there such a thing?

# MAN'S INHUMANITY TO MAN

A few days later the NIA came for me again. When I asked the guard what time it was he told me it was 1am. There was a new NIA guy this time. He put the shackles on again and I noticed absent-mindedly, that they tightened the handcuffs an extra notch each time. It caused me to look at my arms and wrists and they did look a little on the thin side.

This time I wasn't alone, two other men Ebo, who I had led to faith in Christ three weeks previously and Modu, both from the confinement wing were already standing in the passageway. I was surprised to see that they also had handcuffs and leg irons on, but they were linked to each other. Another set of leg irons joined on to the chains of those on their ankles. I NIA guy pushed me, shuffling along towards them and yet another set of leg irons were attached from mine to the back of theirs.

The length of the chain on the leg irons was about one foot and so we were hardly able to shuffle along, but shuffle we did and eventually got out to the pickup. If it wasn't so serious it would have been funny as we tried to get onto the back of the pickup. Ebo was crying, it was his first time to experience the nocturnal excursion as it was known, and he was terrified. "Remember Ebo," I told him, "anticipation is usually worse than the event, and don't give them the pleasure of them seeing you weak. I've been there lots of times and look at me." That got a laugh.

We were split up, Modu was taken to the chimney and I don't know what happened to Ebo. They took me into another room about eighteen feet square. The walls were rough concrete blocks and in the centre of the room two ropes hung down from the ceiling. They were about six feet apart and each had a hook dangling about two feet from the floor. I stared at them wondering what was coming next. Having seen the film about Edi Amin "The Last King of Scotland" I was concerned that they were going to stick them in my ribs and string me up that way. Thankfully, as I looked closer I could see that the hooks weren't sharp enough for that.

Three men came towards me and I was pushed to the ground face first, my hands still in handcuffs behind my back. They attached the hooks to the handcuffs, and they lifted me off the ground by my wrists. It felt as though my shoulders would part company with their sockets and I thought I must surely pass out. I tried to pray, but couldn't, I heard screaming and somewhere in my mind I knew it was me, and I was ashamed.

Gritting my teeth, I stopped screaming and tried to tense my shoulder muscles when two of the men, one at my head and the other at my feet, started to wind me around and around. Slowly they walked round and round and I could see that I was getting further away from the floor as the two ropes intertwined. I don't know exactly how long it took to wind me up till I was about five feet above the ground, it seemed like an eternity.

One of the men stepped back and the other span me round to undo the twisted rope. I started spinning faster and faster and vomited what little there was in my stomach. There were shouts, laughter and jeering from the men and to this day, I find it difficult to believe that they were enjoying themselves, but they were. What did these men see in me, was I someone to hate, someone who posed a threat? Were they jealous, racist, what, why???

I wished that I had died earlier but as soon as the thought entered my head, I banished it. God knew all about this and for some reason he was allowing it to happen: a curious thought while hanging by my wrists with my arms behind my back.

I was unceremoniously dumped back on the ground and left in pain, but everything is relative, being on the deck was a big improvement, believe me.

Again, I haven't a clue how long I was there, but at some point I was uncuffed and thrown into Babba Dinka. As usual, there were others there and as soon as the cell door shut, many hands groped about my body trying to help.

Looking back on it, I was inadvertently touched all over by men and there was no sense of revulsion only gratefulness that at last someone was massaging my poor shoulders and arms. I honestly felt that I'd lost the use of my arms forever, but these guys were no stranger to the NIA's torture and knew what to do.

I guess twenty-four hours passed before we were dumped in the pickup and taken back to Mile Two. Modu and Ebo were with me. While Modu was in a reasonable state, Ebo was unconscious and when they lifted him out there was a pool of blood where he lay. The guards carried him into the prison and as Modu and I were able to walk, we gathered up all the clothes and took them in with us. In my cell, I was relieved to be back alive and thanked God again for preserving my life.

I went over it all in my mind, not just the events of the past twenty-four hours, but the whole thing. It was so hard to believe that this was happening to me. It was harder still to believe that I was surviving this. Many others in the confinement wing who were much younger and fitter than I was didn't make it. It could only be God. There was no other explanation and that was so encouraging for me, it meant that I still had a rank in God's army, even if it was only a private.

I slept, for how long I haven't a clue, but I didn't hear the keys, so it must have been a deep sleep and I was startled when the door flew open banging against the wall. "It's Ebo," the guard shouted, "you've got to make him well." With that, he turned and headed to Ebo's cell, which was five cells down from mine. I groggily followed him to where the door of Ebo's cell was wide to the wall.

When I arrived, the guard was dragging Ebo out leaving a trail of blood behind him. I knelt beside him; he was bleeding from every orifice, eyes, mouth, nose, anus and ears. I checked his pulse and it was very weak but he was conscious, looked up at me, and said, "Am I dying?" There was no use lying, "Yes," I replied softly "I think so".

After a minute he said, "I'm I going to heaven?" "Yes," I assured him.

"Can you pray?" "Of course" and I prayed.

"Remember the song that I taught all you guys Ebo?" I asked him after I finished praying.

No more sorrow there, we are going to see the King.
No more suffering there, we are going to see the King.
No more dying there, we are going to see the King.
No more illness there, we are going to see the King.
No more Mile Two there we are going to see the King
Hallelujah, hallelujah, we're going to see the King.

"Tell my wife I'll see her in heaven." I nodded, unable to speak, with tears running down my cheeks Ebo died, and something in me died too.

I came to realise that night that every time I saw someone I'd led to the Lord, (who I guess were my spiritual children) die, then I'd left a part of me with them, soon there would be nothing to leave behind.

I just wanted to get back to my cell before all the hullaba-loo broke loose. I turned to the guard and was shocked to see his shoulders heaving as he cried in quiet heaving sobs. "He was my brother," he managed to say, "a good and kind man. He put my children through school, a good, good man. I'll give charity for him, for his soul."

I put my arm round his shoulders and said, "He's in heaven now, no need to pray to your god, he's with Jesus."

I walked back to my cell, all pain in my back and shoulders forgotten and I grieved for the men and women who had become martyrs in The Gambia. People who wouldn't consider them-selves anything special, but who, I believe, will have a special place in heaven. I'd like to say that I was happy that Ebo was in heaven, but what happened was that I went into a sort of minor depression. I started to question many of the things I'd done in The Gambia, and I probably thought too much, even questioned my motives for being here in the first place.

# MIND GAMES

The next day the men in the Fellowship gathered round my cell door. "Where is Ebo?" they asked. "He's dead," I replied, "they killed him." John took out his Bible and read Psalm 23, then Psalm 70. "That's my prayer," he said, then closed his Bible and walked away.

The others hung around and I read out to them my prayer, "I don't know if I can say that," said Samba Njie a former Navy commander. "Take it and say it every day," I told him, "one day God will grant your prayer, it'll save you from becoming bitter." I hoped it would do the same for me.

They split up, leaving me alone with my thoughts, and for me that's always a dangerous thing. I know I'm not the sharpest tool in the box, but I was coming to the conclusion that for whatever reason the President and the Islamic Council were out to get me and it seems it had become an obsession with them. If that were the case then there wouldn't be any court appearances, or a release date for that matter.

Another pack with a dozen bars of Imperial Leather Soap came my way and I was determined to get a hold of some local black soap. I had made up my mind a while ago to make a chess set. Getting the black soap proved easy as a few days later the medic came to see me and said he'd get something for my skin infections and boils and when it came it was black medicated soap.

I started to make the chess men using a blunt razor: they were intricate and I was quite proud of my work. Then more soap came and I decided to make two sets, maybe I could sell one set for food.

Across the passageway was a former Colonel, the head of the Military Police who I had known outside this hellhole. I managed to get him to make a chess board on the floor as I had done and we numbered and lettered both boards the same. With my extra chess set, we spent endless hours playing against each other, shouting moves through the doors.

# PRISON POST

I had by this time also developed quite a good system of communication with the High Commission about various things I'd been told about the President by the killer teams he had employed, and who were now languishing in Mile Two. I never got any feedback, so whether it was ever acted upon, I don't know but I felt it was worth the risk. I was also able to send a letter or two through the prison underground to Fiona. What I didn't know was that when she did receive them, but I'd given her a problem.

Firstly, she was in a communal cell and to have any privacy to read was virtually impossible. Secondly, I wrote in such tiny writing that she had great difficulty in reading it anyway. However, the main reason for her problem was that Fiona's survival strategy; the way she dealt with her captivity was very different from mine, certainly no worse, no better, just different. We faced different environments and potentially a different outcome.

Apparently, Fiona was a model prisoner. She knew a few of the long-term prisoners and the female senior prison officers, because she used to work in the female wing. She'd help clean up without complaint and it would be, "Yes ma'am, no ma'am, three bags full ma'am," and it worked for her.

The odd time when I was in the main courtyard in transit somewhere, a senior female officer would pass by and say, "Your wife is fine; she's a good woman, no trouble." Funnily enough, this was the opposite of what my escort said about me. I heard him mutter "Not like you then," under his breath

# MIND BENDING BROKE
## June 2009

I think it was around June 2009 I had finally had enough of the Islamic chanting. I felt if I heard another day of it I'd either go mad, or start chanting along. I had to hatch a 'cunning plan.' I'd already pulled the wires out as they hung from the ceiling, but they were soon mended. The problem was that the ceiling was about ten feet high and the speaker was attached to it behind a half-inch wire grill directly above my door and I couldn't reach it.

There was a Nigerian Christian who had been a doorman in a nightclub in the tourist area. He was a big lad and as strong as an ox, I solicited his help. It took a day or two to sharpen my toothbrush on the concrete floor to a long thin point, but when it was finished, it was a joy to behold.

The next day I banged on the door and said to the guard it had been two days since I'd emptied my "chamber pot." He opened me up and left me to get on with it and I called Usefer the Nigerian. He'd been primed and was waiting for me when I came back.

I quickly dumped the paint tin in the cell and came out with the sharpened toothbrush. He lifted me as if I was a feather and I reached up with the toothbrush and plunged it through the cage without damaging the mesh. There was a distortion in the chanting, and I plunged at it again and again until it stopped altogether. The silence was deafening and I was back in my cell before you could say 'bulls' eye' and the cheer that went up wasn't only from the Christians.

There were no repercussions since they couldn't work out how the speaker had failed, after all it couldn't have been sabotage as the wire mesh was intact. I could hear, 'Inshallah,' (God's will) being mumbled by the guards as my padlock was closed and with it ended the chapter of me being subjected to that mind-bending chanting.

# POSTPONED

A few days later, in the evening they told me that I had court the next day. That night I prayed and prayed that this would be the one when I would get a judgement. Despite my former scepticism, I refused to step on the downhill path signposted "Negative" and started to climb the hard one.

This time the police came for me this time. I never did understand the criteria for my transport to the court. The police were much better than the prison authorities were, they were happy to give me time with those who come to see me at court, and this time was no exception.

Various people came to the court and even before we went in to the police station, (which adjoined the courthouse in Banjul), I could see my people. As we went in via the side entrance I shouted at P and J (they still live there), but they never heard me. The man that had transported me from the prison, put me into a cell at the police station, and I asked him, "Can you tell the two 'Tubabs' who are outside, that I'm in the cells please." He said he would and I sat down with many guys, some of whom had been there for weeks and smelled even worse than me. "Got a smoke Tubab?" was the greeting that I got as soon as the door shut. "Sorry fella," I replied, "don't use them."

I guess about twenty men, mostly Rastas, gathered round. "Where you from man?" was the main question. "UK," I'd reply, I didn't really want to get into a deep and meaningful relationship with any of them. "Got an email number Tubab?" "I think you mean an email address," I corrected. "Whatever man, you got one?"

Thankfully, the cell door swung open and a policewoman gestured me to come out. "Sorry guys, got to go," I said over my shoulder and realised that despite all I'd gone through I hadn't changed a great deal, I still wasn't a people person.

My friends were there and the policeman who had been my escort was with them. They led us to a courtyard behind the court building where we chatted. It was great to have a conversation in English that wasn't pidgin. There was however some not so good news, the judge was still up country and there would be no sitting. This only reinforced our belief that if I was ever to be allowed to get my judgement read out, it would have to be through a miracle.

After about an hour, a prosecutor came up to us and told us that the new date was the end of June. There was such a mixture of emotions: I was so glad to be with my people that I was on a high and sort of took it in my stride. Everyone else, seeing how my body and mind had deteriorated were shocked as privately they were sure I wouldn't survive till the end of the month.

I was given a chicken sandwich and a can of ice cold Orange Fanta by my friends, but half way through eating it the policeman told us that the pickup was waiting to take me back to Mile Two. After our goodbyes my friends waved me off and I found out later that they were sure that was it for me, and that I'd die in prison.

It wasn't till I was put back in my cell that I truly realized the gravity of what had just happened. It was the intention of the President and the Islamic Council that I should rot in prison, indeed die there. Not a comforting thought, but there was also something inside of me, a spark, a belief, call it what you will, but I knew somewhere deep inside me, that I wasn't going to die at the hands of these people.

# SUSTAINED

What I didn't know at the time was there were thousands of Christians around the world praying for Fiona and me. Word was getting out of the torture I was being subjected to, and I now know of three large churches, two in the USA and one in England, which had a rolling 24hr hour prayer rota for us . . . Amazing! I didn't realise it then, but it was the prayers of the saints that sustained me through that time and gave me the determination to fight on.

I recalled the time Fiona and I came over with Elizabeth back to UK for a holiday. Holiday it was not. We flew on the Friday and returned four weeks later, which made a total of thirty days between flights. I had a three day conference that has been denied by the authorities, (but more about that later) which brought our time 'on holiday' together to twenty-seven days. In those twenty-seven days, I spoke at churches from the North of Scotland to the South of England thirty seven times. Fiona and I shared the driving, thank goodness, but in the words of the immortal Cockney rhyming slang, I was 'cream crackered.'

Incredibly, the prayers of the people that we met on that trip, and others that were holding us before God. In James, 5:16 we read, "The effectual fervent prayer of a righteous man availeth much" and I know the truth of it.

# THEIR ON MY CASE

A guard called Tamba awoke me from my reverie by unlocking the door. A little confused at why I'd be opened up so soon I asked him, "Where are we going now?" He replied, "Visit." Putting on my clothes, he led me to the main yard without my usual chain, so I knew that this was an important one.

We went out of confinement towards the headquarter buildings and into the conference room. Inside there were two black men, well dressed in light coloured European suits, and one woman in African dress. They rose when I entered and shook my hand. The smaller of the two men took a photo from a briefcase, which was on the floor by his seat. "Mr Fulton?" he began, with a quizzical look on his face. "Yes," I answered, "that's me." He looked at the photo in his hand and shook his head from side to side. "Please sit down," he went on. We all sat and he put the photo of me face up on the table. It had been taken about four years ago when I had been attending a function at the British High Commission, wearing full Scottish Highland dress. "If I met you in the street I wouldn't have recognised you from this photograph." "Well, they won't allow me to wear the kilt here," I quipped.

He took the photo back and passed it to the others and while they glanced from the photo to me then back again he said, "We are from the African Human Rights Commission and we have been inundated with enquiries regarding your welfare. How are you?" "Well as you can see I'm not so bad, mustn't grumble, I'm alive" "Only just by the look of you," said the woman in an emotional outburst, "you look like death warmed up" "I can't comment on that," I said, "I haven't seen myself for a long time, but as I say I'm alive." "Mr Fulton," the other man said gently, "This lady is a doctor specializing in malnourishment and malnutrition, if she's concerned then so should you be." "Oh don't think that I'm not concerned," I countered, "it's just that I am doing all I can to keep from dying, and believe me, sometimes just to slip into death would be the easy way out."

I felt embarrassed to see the woman quietly crying; the tears rolling down her cheeks and with her clenched fists thumping the table. "Bastard, bastard, bastard," she repeated until one of the men put his hand on her shoulder. "Be careful," he whispered to her and gestured with a nod to the guard who stood by the door.

"Mr Fulton is there anything you want to tell us about your treatment in here, or at the hands of any government employees?" the smaller man said. "No," I replied, "I am trying to survive in here so that I will live to be an old man with my children and grandchildren. You, while good intentioned could be the death of me." "Sorry?" he said furrowing his brows. "There is a saying," I told them (similar to the one I had told the lady from the British High Commission, I'm a dab hand at inventing old sayings) "The bird in the sleeping cat's mouth sits quietly and waits till it yawns." Nodding towards the guard I said, "You work it out, he can't."

The men made to rise, but the woman said, "Hold on" and produced a large hand mirror from her shoulder bag, which looked big enough to be a flight bag. "You might want to see yourself," she said to me as she turned the glass towards me. "My God", I exclaimed as I saw how thin my face was. She stood there with the mirror about eight feet away. I whipped off my t-shirt, "My God!" I said again.

My body was just turning a fetching deep blue and my ribs stood out like those I'd seen on films of people coming out of Nazi concentration camps, similar to the horror pictures of children in famine-torn countries in other parts of Africa. I was shocked and rocked. I hadn't realised just how far I'd gone downhill. I turned sideways and the protruding rib seemed to move beneath the skin.

The guard was looking over at us and I knew it was his job to report as much as he could hear and see. "Did they do that to you in here," the woman asked, incredulous at the sight of me. "No," I replied, "I'm on a diet."

The guard was getting stressed and, wanted the visit to finish so he could report to David Collie the Director. I called him over and pointing to the woman said, "This woman is a doctor and she's pleased that you let me show her my injuries." I could see that this fazed him because I knew he would face discipline if it was discovered that he allowed this.

"Yes Sir," he mumbled, "I didn't know she was a doctor. If I had I'd have had the medical S.O. present." "Oh dear," I said in s voice that showed nothing but concern for his own welfare. "I think the best thing we can do is to say nothing, that way you'll keep your job and the NIA won't know anything, how's that?" "Thank you Sir," he said, "that would be good."

Everyone stood up as we all realised that this was a good time to finish. I held out my hand "So mum's the word eh!" Shaking it, the smaller man said, "All in confidence," and they left. As Tamba and I walked back to the confinement wing, I said, "Weren't they nice people? They were happy with everything they saw and heard." As he turned to me he said, "Were they?" "Oh yes, very happy," I assured him, and that was what David Collie heard. Again back in the cell I was quietly satisfied that someone in the international community was on my case. Not that I expected a regiment of African Union troops to assault the prison and rescue me, but it was a small victory that had turned out well, thanks to a spot of fast talking.

# SOMETHING TO DO
## July 2009

Fiona and I were on our eighth month and for me things were looking grim. However, there were things that happened that were, if not life changing, then *'lifestyle'* changing.

There was a young charismatic Lebanese man I had gotten to know reasonably well, Ahmed. He seemed to be able to get some things smuggled in through friends outside bribing guards. One day he came to my cell and passed in a plastic pill pot with coffee in it. The coffee was thick, black and unsweetened. When I drank it, wow, my mind sort of went, ping! Eyes flew open and I was full of energy with nothing to do. From that day, I have taken my coffee black.

A sat for a moment and thought; "I know, I'll make my hidey-hole' so that day I looked for the joins in the concrete blocks and set to with a nail to scrape away the cement around one. Phase 1 took me about a week, only working in the daytime when there was noise outside to cover my scrapings. I rubbed the nail along the joint, gradually wearing away the cement, gathering the dust and wetting it with urine at the end of my daily efforts. I pressed it back into the grooves I'd made to disguise my work.

One major problem was that my nail was only four inches long and I guessed the block would be at least six inches in width. I managed to scrape a 4" groove round the block, but it remained unmoveable. The only thing to do was to cut a 'V' in it that would enable my fingers to get in-between the blocks. Easier said than done, as I wasn't cutting cement this time, but concrete.

This phase took longer than the first, in fact, it took the best part of two weeks and wore out the original nail, but I had the other one. A further few days on the cement and I felt the nail scraping against concrete again, another block behind the one I was working on. Yes!

What I needed now was some sort of heavy hammer to loosen it from anything holding at the back where I wasn't able to get to. I was going to need help here, but who to trust? Sanneh, the "mess boy" (I hate thinking of him that way as he was a former military commander). Anyway, Sanneh and I had a good rapport and I thought he might be able to help me. Without telling him what it was for, I asked him if there was anything heavy around I could use for a few minutes. "Heavy," he said, "there's only the guard's bench in the store, but that can't get through the hatch." "Ok," I replied, "don't worry I'll think of something," but I couldn't.

For days I braced my bony back against the wall and hit the block with my heels, but the only thing that happened was I managed to bruise my heals.

Having the food hatch jammed open not only gave me some light but because of the daily routine going on in the passageway

I knew roughly what time of day it was, morning or afternoon. It was one afternoon that a guard opened up my cell and told to put my clothes on.

# THE UNION JACK

No shackles this time, so I knew that I wasn't on my way to the NIA, anyway it was daytime and they were nocturnal animals. As I limped along, I asked the guard, "Who's come to see me?" "Your ambassador," he replied. It wasn't worth the bother trying to explain to him that we had a High Commission in The Gambia not an embassy.

As we walked through the gate to the headquarters building there was a new Land Rover Discovery 4 sitting there with the Union Jack flapping in the wind, a bright splash of colour against the concrete grey of the prison.

The High Commissioner himself was there and I was touched that he had come. They assured me that the British Government were doing everything in their power to get us out and I should let him know if there was anything, he should know.

They told me that the family were well and that a few publishers had expressed interest in a book. In fact, just a nice visit that wouldn't help me out of the situation. He turned to the guard and asked, "Can Mr Fulton have this book?", and held out a paperback copy of 'The Constant Gardener' by John Le Carre. "Of course," said the guard to my surprise. Holding out his hand for the obligatory handshake, he handed me the book and left. I was so underwhelmed I was tempted to march on the spot singing God Save the Queen, but like the good Christian that I am, resisted the temptation.

Back in confinement, a senior officer inspected the book. "You don't need no gardening book." he said. I smiled, "You're having a laugh, right?" and with that, he threw it on the mud outside the wing. I was taken back to my cell and to this day, I've never read *'The Constant Gardener.'*

# DIGGING FOR VICTORY

When I returned to my cell, I found a lump of hardwood on the floor in the shadow cast by the outside light when the door was open; it was about 10" long and 2" square. I suspected Sanneh had worked his magic, but I would have to be careful doing any hammering in the now quiet prison.

When one of the guys came outside my cell to talk to me I said, "Can you do me a favour? I need a bit of noise in the corridor but not directly outside my cell. Can you organize that?" "No problem," he replied, "Give me about half an hour." That's the thing I like about soldiers, no questions, no ifs or buts, just a 'no problem'.

I had to be ready and there I was kneeling in the semi-darkness, wood in my hand, waiting for the diversion. It started with one shout then another; someone started banging on a door, and then more banging followed. Perfect, using the wood like a battering ram I thumped the block over and over again until it started to vibrate. Then I knocked the sides to loosen it more and it was free.

The cheering and door thumping intensified outside, so I thought I'd join in. Yes! I shouted and whistled. My own door was banging from the outside. "Good news Tubab," the officer shouted, "The Gambia has qualified for the world cup." "What?" I shouted back over the din, "you must be joking." "No it's true," he replied, "Sanneh told us"

The Gambia, like most third world countries was football mad and it seemed to me that Sanneh had managed what the Gambian national team never could: earn a place in the world cup . . . good one Sanneh.

I removed the block whole and saw it was made the same way as the cement blocks that I'd made to build my house. There is a tin box 6" x18" with an inset, which moist cement is mixed and pushed into and then you pull the inset out. This is so the block wouldn't be solid concrete; it keeps down the cost, reduces the weight and makes for better insulation. So now, I had a hollow block the inside measurements of which were ten by eight by four, success!

I finished just in time and as the racket gradually died down, all I could hear were individual voices shouting at Sanneh. "Talk of the devil," I thought as Sanneh's face appeared at the hatch by the floor, "What happened" Sanneh?" I asked, "Ah, well I got it wrong, a mistake you understand, we were beaten seven nil," and he laughed." Pass me the wood; I hope you were able to do what you wanted." "Yes I did. Thank you, I'll tell you what I was doing later," and passed the wood through to him.

I'd kept all the dust and grit which, mixed with urine, made great paste to hide the excavation. Sliding the block back in and filling the cracks was the work of a moment and I was able to chalk up another victory.

# WHAT GOES AROUND

I began to hear horror stories from most of the new guys who were coming into the confinement wing, stories about the President and the illegal arms that he was buying from his friend and fellow lunatic Muammar Gaddafi, the President of Libya, stories and genuine information about his, (the President's) drug deals. This from top men who used to be close to the President and I could see there was an anomaly there which I had noticed before I was taken into captivity.

In the years I had spent with people close to the top of military and political life, I was conscious of many disappearing either totally off the face of the planet or into Mile Two for some obscure reason. I was able to observe only at arm's length, but observe I did. It seemed to me that the President got people to do his dirty work and if anything went wrong then, so that no blame could be traced through them to him, he'd dispose of them in some way or another, Mile Two's confinement wing being one.

As I mentioned earlier, my Christian brother John's prayer was Psalm 70, a great prayer, especially in our circumstances. However, there were some of the guys who I'd led to The Lord from Islam who were more into the Exodus 21:24 "eye for an eye" kind of prayers, as befits their past. I suppose a little teaching wouldn't go amiss there, and yet their prayers were most certainly being answered. Many of the soldiers who had betrayed my friends before their attempted coup were themselves put in Mile Two for an attempted coup plot of their own.

The incredible thing was that I knew them all well, the former and the present coup plotters. The only difference between them was tribal, in my opinion the bane of Africa, that and the extended family. Anyway, in came those who had put many others in prison, which was interesting to watch, not that I could do a lot of that, but I could see and hear how former soldiers who were now Christians were dealing with those who they had prayed against.

It goes without saying that when they came to me looking for guidance, I spoke of forgiveness, of the new covenant teaching and as Jesus taught on the Sermon on the Mount in Matthew, where He said, "You were taught this, but I say . . ." However, a few weeks later I found myself tested. After the arrest of the Inspector General of Police, (for all kind of nastiness), I shouted out, "Yes!" and punched the air. Maybe I needed some of that teaching too.

His name is Essa Badjie and he was the one who gave the order to arrest my wife Fiona. He and others were of the opinion that I was capable of escaping from captivity and even escape from The Gambia, so if Fiona was also held captive separate from me, then I wouldn't be tempted to go and leave her behind. It wasn't often they were right, but this time they were spot on.

# THE CARROT

It was July 2009 and expectations were high that on 22$^{nd}$ July, there would be an armistice announced by the President and a pardoning of political prisoners. This was the anniversary of the coup by the military, which had brought Jammeh to power.

I doubted very much whether it would happen. Other countries in West Africa did it, but I didn't believe that the President had an ounce of compassion in him. This rumour of pardons had been on the go during my time as chaplain there and I was surprised that anybody still fell for it. On every notable occasion throughout the year, there was a sense of expectancy: New Years day, Independence Day, Jammeh's birthday, Revolution day, Koriteh, (the end of Ramadan), Tobaski, Eid and Christmas. To me the carrot was as plain as the nose on my face.

I managed to write on a scrap of paper what I have written in the last paragraph. Then I passed the word for as many of the most senior officers to come to my cell as was physically possible. Eight men came that afternoon. Two former Chief of Defence Staff, one former General, two former Lieut. Colonels, one former Major, an Army Captain, a Rear Admiral and a Navy Captain. In normal circumstances, there'd be enough brass to start a scrap yard.

"What's wrong Sir," they asked. "You," I replied, "that's what's wrong, I know you can't see it but if you look at the dates from the start of this list to the end, you'll see that Jammeh is feeding you guys rumours of releases on such a regular basis that you don't think about getting out of this place by yourselves." They took the paper and suddenly as if a light switched on in their heads, they exclaimed, "You're right"; "he's been giving us hope without delivering, the bastard!"

"He's been dangling a carrot in front of you so you'll not think it worth breaking out for only a few months." "What should we do?" they asked. "That's not for me to decide," Said I, "but after Fiona's released, count me in with your plans."

It was no surprise when the July 22nd celebrations came and went with no court appearance for me and no releases for my friends and fellow prisoners. However, being left alone for all of three weeks by the NIA, that had to be a plus. Those around me reckoned that it was because of the preparations leading up to the July 22nd shindig, (and probably the hangovers following it), that they spared me.

# A STITCH UP

"How does the saying go?" "All good things come to an end" and one night they came. I'd almost persuaded myself that they'd got their pound of flesh and I'd been forgotten. Alas, again such was not my portion. Again, it was well after midnight when the keys rattled in the door. I didn't think it was a Pizza delivery, and I was right it was Shades, the talkative NIA man.

"Get dressed," he barked. "Me?" I replied pointing at myself. "Me? Are you sure you've come to the right address?" It was no use; I just couldn't prise another word out of him.

Dressed and shackled I shuffled down the passageway to the good wishes of everyone in the cells I passed en route. Now that the 24-hour Islamic chanting had mysteriously stopped, every sound reverberated around the concrete wing, the keys, padlock, and my cell door banging had awakened the men. "Good luck Major, All the best Sir, tell them nothing Dave. Remember Pastor you're heaven bound," and many other words of encouragement from Christian and Muslim alike. I won't write what they shouted at the NIA man but it wasn't very complimentary.

Out in the main yard it was torrential but warm rain, the lightning was a pyrotechnic display that humans could never come close to equalling and accompanied by the loudest thunder of music imaginable. I turned to Shades, "My God's doing all this for me, to remind me of His power and to tell you that you're on a hiding to nothing."

We were standing in the rain and it poured off us as he shrugged and said, "On." I am sure that he actually knew how to put a sentence together, but his vocabulary seemed to be getting less every time I saw him. The tailgate was down so I sat on it and swung my legs in, but before I could move my body properly into the back he grabbed my legs by the leg irons and handcuffed them to the chain holding the tailboard up.

I lay down in the back luxuriating in the rain that threatened to flail the skin off my skinny frame. Shades then climbed into the cab and drove off. This was the first time I'd been collected by only one person and I wondered if there was any significance . . . probably not.

Arriving at NIA headquarters, they took me into one of the offices. This one had white walls, and on a table in the centre of the room, a projector was beaming white light on the far wall. Shades pointed to one of several seats against the rear wall. It looked as if we were going to watch a film.

In came Hermann Boring. "Good morning Reich Marshall," I said. Frowning, he replied, "I doubt if you'll find it good," and with that he nodded to a man standing by the light switch. The lights went out and the first picture came up on the wall. It was of me in uniform loading the Range Rover prior to heading for Denton Bridge and the boat. I remembered the photo because as well as carrying other equipment, I was cradling a Remington repeater shotgun under my arm, and a sidearm was obvious in the holster on my webbing belt. I didn't use this photo on the PowerPoint as some churches might have taken exception to my carrying arms, but it had still been on the computer. Under the photo was the caption "Make my day". Then another picture flickered up on the wall. This was of my boat underway. The caption they'd added was. "She can hide thirty or more fully armed soldiers below decks with arms and ammunition."

The picture changed, this time, again to the map I'd used on the PowerPoint to show where I went on my trips into the interior. They had put bullet points on all the immigration outposts and barracks that I visited. Oddly, they had added their own captions; for example, at one it said "Only twenty metres from the border, no coms" Another said "Can be taken by ten good men" While at the Farafenni barracks there was a note "OIC is Jammeh's man, take him out or he'll gather resistance" .

This is how it went on without a word being spoken. I could see my life disappearing in front of my very eyes, but strangely enough, I wasn't despondent, indeed I found myself quietly singing an old Country Gospel song by Randy Travis.

All our days are numbered
Some live on borrowed time
But life is what you make it
Thank God I was so inclined
To accept my Lord and Saviour
When the Good News sunk in
He paid the price by giving His life
Can't wait to go home to him.

I'm ready to go the distance
God knows when that might be
But Oh what joy waits me up yonder
Once this world has set me free

"Shut up!" It was Hermann, every syllable accentuated. "Shut up," he shouted again, thumping his fists on the table. "You've got nothing to sing about." I didn't say a word, though it was hard not to, and I almost burst out with three verses and the chorus of "This world is not my home; I'm just a passin' through".

The show went on and although it was all fabrication as far as the captions were concerned, the photos were all mine. There was no doubt in my mind that in a court they would be damning, it was a prosecutor's dream. "We also have some letters from you to your bosses at MI5 which we have written in your own idiom." I so very nearly told him that it was MI6 that dealt with foreign problems such as him, not MI5, but checked myself; I couldn't see any reason to help him.

Leaning forward towards me in a fatherly way he said, "Now Major (strange that he should call me Major), I know, that you know, that we have you, by? How do you say it: the short and curries". It was all I could do to stop myself from falling off the chair laughing, "The short and what?" I said, "Do me a favour, stick to your Gambian sayings, you might get one right."

Well that outburst went down like a lead balloon. "Take him away," he shouted, "I'll be dawn soon.

They pushed me out of the office and I stumbled and shuffled along the corridor. The torture chamber was prepped and ready for me so I gathered that my reaction was predictable.

Godzilla was using the hose that he normally used to soak me down prior to beatings to wash the floor of excreta. It was then I noticed another person there and by the look of him and because of the task Godzilla was involved in, I guessed he had just been given the treatment that I was about to get. He was on the floor and crying like a baby.

No one seemed particularly interested in me so I shuffled over to him. He looked up at me. "Help me," he cried, "they are killing me." I actually staggered back in shock; it was the former Inspector General of Police. This man had put Fiona in prison to disable me. I just looked at him. "Help me," he pleaded again. Of course, there was nothing I could do, but I'm not proud of the fact that I just shuffled away with loathing in my heart.

It was my turn again. I won't go through what happened as you already know, save to say that it doesn't get any better and this time the skin where the broken rib was pushing, broke and I bled. This was obviously not what a well-trained torturer like him should have done to a prisoner that wasn't meant to be marked. I learned later that he trained in Libya. I think that was the reason my session with them was cut short and I was taken back to Mile Two. Interestingly, the medic inmate was up at 4am to treat my wounds. Can't have Fulton bleeding everywhere, can we?

Later that morning at shift change when some of the men were out, I was able to let people know that I'd seen IGP Badjie with the NIA and of his condition. I have to say there was not one sympathetic voice, either from the inmates or from the officers who gathered round to hear the news. It seemed he wasn't going to win any popularity contests any time soon in Mile Two, even if they were all looking forward to seeing him there.

The medic came with an old-fashioned instrument to take my blood pressure, which he was surprised to find normal. In fact, he took mine three times and his own once, to make sure it was calibrated properly before he was satisfied.

This all took place in the passageway so that he would have light to read his instrument. He also brought a scales and I was duly weighed, 105lbs he announced, which I divided by fourteen to convert to stones, 7.5 stone. Wow! That's not a lot. I am 5ft 9ins and when I came in, I was 198lbs or 14.2 stone, a bit overweight. 7.5 was not good, I could see why my people were concerned.

My hair was crawling with lice and I decided to shave it off. One of the officers let me have three of my own Bic razors to do the job. It wasn't till I started to shave that I realised that the blades were blunt, in fact they'd been used by the officers before I got them. I didn't even get annoyed I was by a tap shaving my itchy scalp and it was bliss.

# MY FIRST MAIL
## September 2009

Not long after this, I received a half hour visit. This would be my second in nine months and I was excited. My hair had grown back to resemble a buzz cut and I had a shave to look my best. It was three of our 'ladies' from church, good friends all, and I was delighted to see them. They brought toothpaste, soap, razors, underpants, but more importantly news. They had been able to visited Fiona and so could tell me how she was. One of the women 'P' had been back to UK and was able to give me news of family and friends. You have no idea how quickly half an hour goes and when the guard who sat in on the visit said, "Time's up" we were surprised. The 'ladies' insisted on praying and of course the guard being a good Muslim would never refuse a prayer.

Back in my cell, I had a real down time. It was the normal reaction for everyone after visits. It's the excitement and the anticipation of the visit followed by seeing family and friends leaving without you; normal, but what a downer. I got my prayer out, especially the last bit. Lord be my comfort, my strength, my victory.

Hardly had I prayed that when an officer came with a load of post. I could not believe it. Letters from family, friends and Christians all over the world, most of whom I'd never even met or heard of. I was so encouraged by the news that people were praying for us all the time, there is no way I could ever thank them. A card came from a brother in the Czech Republic; a letter from St Andrews University in Scotland, indeed from all over the world. Switzerland, India, Holland, New Zealand, Slovenia, Southern Ireland, Ecuador, England, Australia, Nepal, Finland, Singapore, Wales, Germany, St Croix In the Caribbean, Hong Kong, The Gambia, USA, Belgium, Canada, South Africa, France, Puerto Rico, Kuwait, Tenerife, Seychelles, Spain, Rwanda, China, The Falklands, Japan, Northern Ireland. (You get the picture).

I wasn't allowed to keep them. If I got ten in one day I had to hand ten out the next day in order to receive more when they arrived. I loved the colour of the cards and to keep them I'd take a letter with two pages and separate it. Then I'd give back an empty envelope and two sheets of paper and instead of one, they'd count it as three. So that way I'd have a surplus of cards and then I took out my block where I'd hide them in the wall.

As ever with good things, they come to an end, and Mile Two was no exception. Firstly, the mail stopped and that was a disappointment and the cause of many arguments with the authorities and complaints to the British High Commission when they came in or I got a letter smuggled out to them.

Secondly, through my sources I found out that Fiona's name wasn't on the release list which is put up in the main yard at the beginning of every month. According to my calculations,

9th September should be her release date, which would have been eight months ten days from the date of conviction. I couldn't understand it and I was getting quite angry. I sent an 'underground letter" to the BHC and to the lawyer. I informed anyone who would listen, that if Fiona spent one day more than she was sentenced to then they'd have me to answer to one day . . . And that still holds true.

A senior prison officer whom both Fiona and I knew came one day and told me that David Collie had revoked her remission. He also told me that it was illegal. Remission could only be revoked on the grounds of bad behaviour, or if the person is a risk to national security. Because of her exemplary record, he said she was a risk to Gambian national security. I was so angry that I told the officer, "If you ever see David Collie, please tell him that he's a dead man walking," and believe me at that moment I meant it from the bottom of my very being.

Well, how many husbands could say that their wives were a risk to a nation's security? It certainly makes me think twice before saying "no" to such a powerful and threatening woman! The medic who was our go-between managed to get a message to me that she was all right about it and was just worried about me. What a woman.

So now, Fiona's date was the 29th December 2009, just over two and a half months. Compared to what we'd done it didn't seem long, but I knew that neither of us had the physical strength we had at the start, so it was a worry.

In the meantime, life for me went on normally, well, normally as far as Mile Two was concerned. More senior servicemen were arrested and it was noticeable that about 40% of them were Christian. Please note that I said 'Christian' as opposed to 'Christians'. This wasn't lost on the more intelligent people there, but they saw it a different way from me. "A lot of the men in confinement are Christian," said a Muslim officer, "that's a high percentage of men compared to the general population." I could see where he was coming from, but I argued, "That's because the Christians are trying to stand up for truth and justice." He didn't say any more and I let it hang.

# DELAYING TACTICS

Various fantasy court dates came and went, the ones scheduled for public holidays. It was becoming a joke in the prison. If anyone wanted to know when the next public holiday was, they'd come and ask me when my next court appearance was. However, despite the fact that it was known that the court wasn't sitting on these dates, the S.I.P. (System In Place) in the prison dictated that I was taken to court, left in the custody of the police, then brought back when the police were ready.

Everyone in the prison thought I would be annoyed, but I looked on these days as a nice change, a day out. The officers were also of the same mind and I have gotten to know many of them better. They told me their salary was about D1, 200 per month (£24) before deductions so they wouldn't be able to afford to buy me anything. "No problem," I used to say, "Being out of the cell is wonderful in itself."

# ELECTRIFYING EXPERIENCE

One night in mid-December, the NIA came for me and again manacled hand and foot, took me to their headquarters. The Reich Marshall was sitting immaculately dressed behind his desk. "Sit," he commanded, "It's almost your Christmas," he began, without as much as a "Hello Mr Fulton". Anyway, he went on, "so I've decided to offer you an early Christmas present." "That's nice," I said a trifle sarcastically. "Yes isn't it," he replied, not picking up the subtle nuance.

"You," he said, pointing at me, "you could go home with your wife if you play your cards right. I think you have made your point, the world knows you've not given in. I'm sure your Government is proud of you and your stubbornness." "Hold on," I interrupted, "I've got nothing to do with the British Government." "Please major," he went on, "don't take us for fools. Since your arrest, they and everyone else has been distancing themselves from you and your work here. If you were nothing to do with them, they would have said nothing. You know, we play this game with our people abroad, if they are nothing to do with us we do and say nothing, let them rot because we don't care. If, however, (he was using my word!) he was one of our "people" then we disown him, we discredit him in the gullible British press."

I was at a loss as to what to say. The press had castigated me, but I guess they had their job to do. What was that exactly? Well at the end of the day, I suppose that they exist to sell newspapers, to make a profit, and to do that some newspapers pandered only to the prejudices of small-minded people regardless of the consequences, regardless of the truth. Makes you think, doesn't it? How often have I read their lies, indeed how often have I believed them?

"So," the Reich Marshall continued, (shaking me out of my reverie), "This is your last chance, I am presenting you with the carrot and the stick." "I don't like carrots," I replied, "but thanks to a window of about thirty minutes in my busy schedule I'm prepared to hear you out"

"You will be able to go home to England with your wife on the 29th December if you sign this letter and if you don't then, as you have no fear dying, we'll cripple you for life."

Well he had struck a chord there: my greatest fear was not dying but being crippled. I had said it to folks often enough, "I'd rather be dead than crippled." Some people have told me that's a cowardly thing to say. Who knows they might be right, but it's the way I feel.

There was a momentary hesitation that I'm sure he noticed. "This is the deal," he said, "you sign only one letter and you and your wife will be on Friday's plane bound for England. If not then you will never leave The Gambia alive and while here you will wish with all your heart that you were dead."

"Can you put it any more clearly?" I asked. "Read it and sign it," he said shoving the paper across the table. I write this accurately from a copy of the document:

> I David Fulton do this day 16th Dec 2009 renounce everything
> to do with the very false religion of Christianity.
> I have this day delightedly embraced Islam and the one true
> god Allah and His Prophet Mohamed as my god and mentor.
> I am very sorryfull at having deceived many true believers into
> that false religion of christianity.
> I have been treated well by my Muslim brothers and this letter
> has by any means not been extracted from me.
>
> Signed . . . . . . . . . . . . . . . . . . . . . . . . . . . . . . . . . . . . . . . . . . . . . . . . . .

I was tempted to sign Mickey Mouse as I had with my prescription, as they would probably be none the wiser and no one would believe I'd written that badly worded and grammatically incorrect, misspelt statement anyway. Instead I simply said, "Let me have it and I'll think about what you say."

He pondered this for a moment, eyebrows coming together in concentration. "I think you need some more persuasion, some illumination to your brain cells, take him away," he said laughing, I took it there was a joke in there somewhere, but for the life of me I couldn't see it. As I stood up, I palmed the paper and crumpled it in my hand.

Monotonously, they pushed me shuffling down the corridor towards the outer courtyard and the torture chamber. If the shouts and screams were anything to go by I'd have to wait in line to be beaten tonight. Not that I was in a hurry, but in some perverse way it's better to get it over and done with.

Inside there was one man bent over what looked like a vaulting horse. They had cuffed his hands and tied them to rings set into the floor. His feet, they had tied by ropes to rings in the floor on the opposite side of the horse about six feet apart. There was a hose stuck up his anus and the tap was on. He was screaming, shouting and crying to his god Allah in Jolla, but Allah didn't hear and he was left with only tears and pain.

I was pushed passed him, passed the rack I'd often hung on towards the chimneys. "Oh no," I mumbled to myself. I really hated the chimneys, it seemed never-ending in there. I felt it was the most debilitating of all the things they did to me, not just physically, but psychologically. It was where I felt most alone, most vulnerable.

However, this was not to be my portion today, there was a loud scraping noise and two NIA men dragged a heavy table out from a room I hadn't noticed before. They managed to get it through the door and only about another six feet or so before they stopped and I could see they did not intend to move it further.

It was constructed of hardwood planks on what looked like 3x3 timber legs. The tabletop would be 8'x4', no wonder they were struggling. Bolted onto the top round the edges were 'U' bolts probably about 18" apart.

I was still at a loss to know what this had to do with me, when they went back into the room and emerged with various pieces of equipment and what looked like a mile of tangled electric cable. I also recognised something that sent my blood cold, a rheostat.

Now, a rheostat is a piece of electrical equipment that gradually adjusts voltage. It's most common domestic usage is on dimmer lights in your home. Now I didn't think they were going to over-haul the lighting in the torture chamber, no, I knew what people like these do with that sort of stuff and I hoped it wasn't going to be used on me. Wrong again.

I watched with growing horror as two men started to get out a hose and run it to the tap. Another guy started to unlock my leg irons first and then my handcuffs. I started to assess my situation. Looking about me, I saw that there were five NIA men in the room, all of them busy. Taking the man who was with me down would be easy, but the only way out was past the others and it was plain that it wasn't going to happen.

The fellow who had undone my cuffs became aware that I was looking about, was poised to do something, and started shouting at his colleagues. I knew then that the moment had passed and not wanting to make matters worse, relaxed and let them hold me. "Easy guys," I said as soothingly as I could, "no problems eh."

They ripped off my clothes and I knew it 'was' going to be a problem.

And so it began . . . something that I'd never heard of happening in The Gambia, even from all the men tortured in the confinement. It was only later that I found out that was because they didn't survive.

They grabbed me and put separate handcuffs on both wrists and they dragged to the table. I wasn't going to do this quietly and so I struggled with them. Some of the other men left what they were doing and bodily lifted me and threw me onto the table on my back, where they pinned me down. They put more cuffs on my ankles and attached all four to the "U" bolts. Three of them grabbed my head and forced it on the table with me looking straight up and a leather strap was pulled through a slot in the table behind my right ear across my forehead and through a slot behind my left ear and tightened so that I couldn't move my head.

What went on then I didn't see, but there was a lot of activity and eventually they turned the hose on me and I was saturated in water. Then one man grabbed my face and with his fingers, pushing my cheeks in forced my mouth open, while another put a three-inch crocodile clip on my bottom lip inside and outside my mouth. That was sore enough, but they then put another crocodile clip on my testicles, now what? Well I guess you'll work it out for yourself. Again, I was drenched with water and I started to feel a tingling sensation where both clips were.

I tried to push the clip off my lip with my tongue, but only succeeded in making it cut in deeper. I was struck with a pain that made me scream out involuntarily. As quickly as it started, so it stopped and when it did my body crashed to the table. I hadn't realised that my back had arched so much that the only bits of me that were touching the table was what was affixed there.

Bam! It happened again. I felt the crocodile clips burning into my testicles and lip and I thought my body was going to explode. They hit it up to twenty, or it could have been two hundred times, there came a point when there was only pain and more pain. I concentrated on not dying then wishing I were dead. Not the best thing to try to describe, but I felt as if my brain was frazzled.

At some point, I heard a cultured voice saying in a boring monotone. "Are you ready to stop playing silly buggers now Major?" I couldn't formulate any reply, my mouth was swollen and burnt and my brain felt as if it was fried to a crisp.

I couldn't even shake my head, but he took my silence as a negative response and as he left he said over his shoulder, "Carry on." The words were hardly out of his mouth when they pulled the switch and I was up in the air again.

# A BABBA-DINKA MEETING

As was the case all too often, I found myself waking up somewhere else, but this time it was in Babba Dinka again. Someone was trickling water down my throat and what was most disconcerting was that there was someone massaging my "private parts". Instinctively, but maybe a little too quickly, I lashed out in the dark and caught the guy on the head with my knee. That caused a bit of commotion as in the pitch darkness he didn't know where the blow came from and I certainly didn't know what was going on.

When things settled down and I was sitting with my back to the wall, they bombarded me with questions as to why I was going through this and when I told them they were, to a man, disgusted. "Sir," said one, "this isn't the Islam we follow, these people are fanatics, the President is a fanatic as is his Government"

"Who are you?" I asked into the darkness. "I'm Musa Sallah (not his real name) minister of finance, or rather former minister of finance." "Ah yes!" I exclaimed, "I believe we've met."

"2006," he confirmed, "the July 22nd celebrations at the State House. I had an interesting conversation with you about the President's state of mental health."

"Correct," said I. "I remember when questioned by you, that I thought Jammeh was as mad as a hatter."

"Well I can now take this opportunity to apologise. You were right, he's totally mad and no one is prepared to stand up to him."

I was just about to continue the conversation when another of Babba Dinka's guests interrupted us. "Sir, four of us were commandeered to carry you back to this cell and when I picked up your clothes this paper drooped out so I hid it from them and brought it here. With that, he groped about until he found my hand and pressed a paper into it. I couldn't see it but I hoped it was the letter they wanted me to sign. "Does anyone have a plastic bag or any paper," I asked.

"I have a piece of plastic bag," somebody said, and we passed it from hand to hand to me. "Thanks, if this is what I hope it is, one day it'll be important." I carefully wrapped the paper in the piece of plastic bag, making sure there were no sharp corners and . . . Well, guess.

It was maybe two days later that they showed me into the Reich Marshall's office. "Have you considered my offer of a Christmas present yet?" he asked with a grin on his face. "I stopped believing in Santa Claus two years ago when I didn't get the Porsche I asked him for" I replied. The grin slipped a little. "You'll be sorry," he said, "Not as sorry as you'll be mate," I interrupted, "one day you'll be in hell and believe me the worst you can do to me doesn't even begin to compare to hell."

Yep, I know, you don't need to tell me. It wasn't a good witness, but I didn't feel like a good witness at the time.

I was taken from there back to Mile Two and again greeted with an enthusiastic welcome by my fellow prisoners. They had heard through the grapevine that I'd been electrocuted and they were sure I was dead. I wasn't, but I was experiencing severe pain in my testicles, my bottom lip was burnt and swollen and my joints ached as if I had arthritis.

It may sound strange to you, but I was glad to get into my cell and for the door to close. I had peace and quiet, a time to think, to pray and to heal. When Sanneh came round with some food the men had scrounged for me, I asked him the date. "It's 20th December," he replied, "five days to Christmas." "Five days," I thought, and to end this episode, I extracted the paper in the piece of plastic bag to find it *'was'* the letter they wanted me to sign; I took out the block and hid it.

"Thank you God that I am still alive when I should be dead, that I can still reason with a brain that is still functioning. Amen"

# A CUNNING PLAN
## 2010

Christmas and New Year came and went, and with it the hope of an amnesty. Once again, the servicemen who were political prisoners were disappointed, only this time their eyes had been opened.

I heard that at the end of December, they finally released Fiona. Words could not express the joy and relief I felt. Together with the other Christians, we thanked God.

I guess it would have been early February that I was told by an officer that I would be out of the cell for the day and that I was going to block number one. "Why?" I asked. "I was told to," was the reply. Well as far as I was concerned, it was a change and that's "as good as a rest".

They led me to block number one, which had eleven cells round three of the walls and a toilet and shower and a place to wash out bowls, and it was clean. In the area as we went in, someone had placed three benches and milling about were eleven men. Each of them were former senior officers in the armed service.

An electric kettle was boiling in the corner and one of them was making coffee. I couldn't believe it, the smell of coffee was almost overpowering, making me salivate. They asked me to sit and did I like sugar in my coffee? I can clearly remember thinking, "How surreal." The surroundings, while obviously harsh, were clean, and there was a sense of order. In the violence, shouting and chaos of prison life here was an oasis of quiet and order.

As I reflected on it I was also amused by the incongruity of it, in as far as we were all naked. The most recent among us still sporting some body fat, but mostly we were thin and emaciated. Maybe it was because I was the only white man in the gathering, but despite that we were all naked, I felt uncomfortable. Everyone sat down except one man I didn't know and as I continued to speculate about what this was all about he came round to us all with bits of blanket, probably several whole blankets torn into four pieces. Watching the others, I followed their example. I stood up wrapped it round myself like a towel and sat down again. I don't know about anyone else, but I felt just a tad more comfortable.

"Welcome Major," the former CDS began, "I suppose you'll be wondering what this is all about eh?" "Well the thought did cross my mind," I replied as I accepted a plastic mug of steaming hot sweet coffee and half a Tapalapa. I tried my best to show restraint with this feast in my hands, but lost miserably and stuffed my mouth with bread and softened it with the best coffee I'd ever drunk.

"We need your help and advice," he continued. "As you know we are the individual leaders of four failed coup attempts. I don't think we need to be told why we failed, but we need to know what we can do now." He stopped there and everyone turned their eyes from him to me.

I deliberately let the silence hang for about a minute while I sipped appreciatively at the coffee before speaking. "Well gentlemen, since I've known most of you before coming in here, and of course while here. I have given much thought to what went wrong. I know that you know the people who sank the coup attempts, because you grassed each other up. Let us start at the beginning.

"I think I have to go back to the failed attempts. There were four main reasons for the failures.

"Number one and I held up my index finger, "Tribalism. The attempt in 2006 was thwarted by General Tamba," and I pointed at the former CDS, "Because you believed that the Jolla's, the President's tribe and yours would be excluded from a new government. And the same with subsequent attempts, you all wanted your own tribes to be the kingpins in the new government."

Ignoring the hubbub that ensued I held up another finger.

"Two, you all had different agendas. You major," I spoke to one of the men whose name but not his rank had escaped me, "and your group wanted The Gambia to unite with Senegal, which didn't go down well with the others and so your group were betrayed to the President, and so I could go on, you all had different agendas.

"Three," I said raising a third finger, "jealousy", the curse of Africa. Neither of you wanted to see one of your peers getting a better position than you do.

"Fourth," I went on, holding out my right hand with only my thumb tucked in, "the extended family. You all wanted family members with you in the coup attempt and they just weren't up to the job."

The noise had quietened down and was replaced by an embarrassing mumble. These men weren't used to being talked to like this, but they recognised the truth of it. "So there we have it gentlemen," I ploughed on, "Tribalism, Nepotism, Jealousy and Personal Ambition brought us all together in this hellhole."

"Thank you Sir," said one of the men, "but where do we go from here?"

"Good point and I have thought long and hard about it," I said, "however, I am concerned that something of what I say will get back to the NIA and the President and as you know they are looking for a reason to do me harm. What guarantee do I have that it won't?"

"Sir," said the former CDS, "we can't give you anything but our word, but I know if you were to give us good advice and one of our number betrayed you then the rest of us would take an oath to kill that individual, it's all I can say."

The other men nodded and mumbled their agreement in the silence that followed.

I picked up my coffee which I hadn't realised I'd put on the floor and was now almost cold. "OK, but before we talk about any plan, I must ask you something that if you are unable to answer in the affirmative then there's no use in going on to the next stage.

"Are you men willing to put nationality before tribalism? In other words, are you Gambians before you are Jollas, Wallofs, and Mandinkoes? Ah! "I said pointing rudely "even a Seri and a Manjako."

There was a resounding "Yes". "Now, I am willing to continue and say that you must believe that the only way forward for the country is that government ministers are chosen for their qualifications and abilities, not their family connections or tribe.

After a complete row of nods I continued with what I believed would be a bombshell. "Everyone in this room except me has either been sentenced to death or natural life for treason. So I put it to you gentlemen, that none of you has anything to lose by breaking out of Mile Two and taking over the State House."

Unexpectedly there was a burst of applause and the man who had made the coffee, given out the bread and was now the lookout rushed in, "Shh!" he whispered wildly gesticulating, "they'll hear you."

"Sorry Major," said the CDS, "but that was what we'd hoped to hear."

"Someone's coming," the lookout said as he grabbed my arm, "in here quickly." He led me to the shower and closed the door while I heard scraping as they replaced the heavy benches. There were raised voices for about a minute and then the door opened. "Come with me Sir," it was the officer who had brought me, "you'll be back another time," and with that, he returned me back to my dark reality.

I was fully aware that I was taking a risk even talking to these guys, but I am of the opinion that Christians should be involved in good things. Not necessarily the overthrowing of governments, although in my opinion, many evil regimes need toppling. However, when injustice and evil is the norm as it is in The Gambia, I felt to help the oppressed was the right thing to do, even if it was only by giving sound advice.

Fiona was gone now and I felt a freedom to try to change things. I believe that if Christians were more involved in things then the people would listen to them about Jesus more readily. What is that Scripture? "Faith without works is dead." On the other hand, was I just trying to justify my actions, maybe even looking for a way out of my situation and to be well in with the next government? Was that a subconscious motive . . . Possibly?

I didn't think I was going to get involved in dodging the bullets, though I'd have given a lot to feel that I could legally and morally join them in a coup attempt. However, thanks to the interruption I'd have time to think. Food came so it was about 15.30hrs and I knew that lockdown for everyone except the mess boy was 16.00, so the day was gone. I lay back against the wall and reminisced about the times I'd put myself in harm's way.

# CONCUSSION
# 2007

There was the time that two brothers who had same mother and father came to faith in Christ on the same day. One was a sergeant in the army and his brother worked in the immigration. As their father was the part-time village Imam and a hunter, they were understandably reluctant to tell him of their commitment to Christ.

As time went on and other servicemen and women became believers and told their families, these two became determined to bite the bullet and tell their father.

They asked me if I would go with them to the compound to explain what Christianity was all about and of course, I agreed. I picked them up in Banjul and took them to their compound, which was just outside the village of Old Busimballa, about one and a half hours from Banjul. We passed Kerrsering, the village I lived in and went on a further twenty or so kilometres on bush tracks.

The compound was big, much bigger than mine was; it was probably three acres in total. It had a boundary of palm leaf strips woven into mats which were then joined together to form an impenetrable fence, cheap, but effective fence. The only concrete I could see as we approached was the massive gate pillars that held two 12-foot gates. They were open so we drove in and parked about twenty metres from what was obviously the main house.

All the houses in the compound, and there must have been about thirty, were built of mud blocks and roofed with palm leafs. "Will you wait here Sir," the immigration officer said, "we'll go in and tell him the good news."

I shut off the engine and got out of the Range Rover as we'd stopped under a mango tree to get out of the sun. Watching the comings and goings of the compound was interesting: children playing in the dirt with a football made out of rags bound together into a ball and tied with strips of rice sack. Women and men looking at me suspiciously and avoiding me like the plague.

A woman was drawing water from the well in the middle of the compound she reminded me of various stories in the Bible about women and wells. "That might be a way to talk to the father," I thought, "he'll be able to relate to it as things are probably the same here as they were in Jesus' day."

A shout brought me back from my musings. Looking across at the big house, I was just in time to see both 6 foot plus brothers legging it for the far end of the compound, followed by a white robed man brandishing a rifle.

I wasn't the only one watching as half the compound had stopped in their tracks and many of the men were grinning wickedly. At the time, I had been sitting on the bull bar, but without really thinking about it I'd slipped off and was slowly making my way round to the driver's door.

A roar came from behind me; "Tubab, Tubab stop! Every eye was on me and, as I'd guessed, it was the father who had shouted, I reckoned this was a good time to exit stage left. Several men surrounded the Range Rover, but I got the door opened when 'Wham'. I was hit on the side of the head, a glancing blow. I ignored it and tried to get into the car. "Biff" again I was hit, this time I saw it was a rock that a man was doing the business with. I punched him in the face, and scrambled unsteadily into the driver's seat and turned the key to start the engine.

Hands tried to grab me through the open window, but thankfully, the old 2.5 diesel started first time (for a change). I threw it into gear and headed at speed for the compound gates. Someone had managed to hold onto my jacket and hung on until the buttons tore off and he was unbalanced and fell to the ground.

Two young boys were trying to close the gates but the hinges were sagging and they both had to lift one at a time. I headed for the one they reached yet, when there was a Bang and a thud.

The old man was shooting at me and had hit the car somewhere. Bang again, just as I reached the gate and the back of the car slewed to the right. I automatically corrected and went through the open gate like a bat out of hell.

The old Range Rover was struggling, the rear tyre was been shot out, but there was nothing I could do about that now. I certainly wasn't going to go back and ask if they'd give me a hand changing the wheel.

It was about twenty kilometres to my compound and I knew I probably had concussion as there were three tracks in front of me and I was sure there had only been one when I came. I decided to carry on slowly as the Range Rover in constant four-wheel drive would manage the sand tracks with no problem, even with one wheel out.

I was feeling groggy and finding it difficult to stay conscious. Using the mobile, I tried to phone Fiona, but there was no reception here. Half an hour later, I tried again and this time got through. Explaining that I was hurt and bleeding, I said, "Have the compound gates open so that I can drive straight in." I didn't want anyone to see me in this state as there would be endless questions asked.

Fiona told me that she and Luke were at a white friend's compound about half a kilometre from ours and would be looking out for me. Jenny, our friend was a nurse and she'd be there as well.

Luke found me slumped over the steering wheel unconscious, the old Range Rover, was in first or second gear, ploughing through bush the side of the track. Luke (he'd be sixteen then) jumped on the running board, leaned in the window and pushing me away from the wheel, steered the car back onto the track then switched off the engine.

Jenny's husband had a minibus which he used in the tourist trade and I was bundled out of the Range Rover into it and taken to my own compound and then to bed.

Luke drove the wounded Range Rover to the compound while Jenny attended to my wounds.

I did indeed have concussion, but didn't need any stitches. I heard Jenny mutter in the usual nurse's compassionate way, "Always knew he had a thick head."

The next day we examined the Range Rover. The rear right side tyre had been shot out, as I'd thought. The other bullet hit and smashed the rear light cluster, so all in all it could have been a lot worse.

I was on my feet and on the mend the next day and Luke had the Range Rover back in service again. I was left wondering if my life was always going to be like this, and if it wasn't, how would I cope without the excitement, and did I have a massive character flaw.

It seemed to me as I thought about it that I always had to be in the thick of things and when I wasn't, I was looking for something outrageous to do. I think that's at the root of my fear of being crippled, I just couldn't stand being inactive. Truth to be told, I couldn't stand living even one foot away from the edge.

I don't suppose anyone who knows me would have been surprised that here I was, mixing with the men probably more hated by President Jammeh than even I was.

# GOT IT IN WRITING
## February 2010

It was early in the New Year that they brought former Inspector General of Police, Essa Badjie into Mile Two's confinement wing. He was in a bit of a state from the torturing, but didn't get a lot of sympathy which was unsurprising considering he had been one of President Jammeh's righthand men and a large number of the men in confinement were here because of him.

What was a surprise however was that he wanted to see me? "How do we do that?" I asked the guard. "One night when I'm on night shift I'll come and get you." What a strange thing, well I guess by this time nothing was strange anymore. "OK," I replied, "I'll just hang around till then, ok." The following week the keys rattling in the door woke me. 'NIA,' I thought, but no it was the guard I had spoken to the week before and with him was IGP Badjie. He looked like hell and although he had been thin while IGP, he was like a skeleton now.

He was sitting in the passageway by my door and he was crying. "I'm sorry Major," he sobbed, "it was me that had your wife arrested, please forgive me."

Well, I guess we talked for about two hours. He was nothing but a petty criminal who had been elevated to the rank of IGP by the President to implement Jammeh's wishes. I felt nothing but pity for him, he truly believed that he would die in prison as he knew too much of the President's dirty business. He confessed to me the whereabouts of forty-seven bodies. He told me about the murders of some high profile people who were 'disappeared' and where the bodies were.

It was almost unbelievable, but I knew it to be true when he told me of how the President sacrificed some of his own family to the dark forces (his words) so that he would stay in power. There were other things relating to arms smuggling with Babba Jobe (now dead, murdered by the dictators orders). Drugs, and support for the rebels, in the civil war across the border in the Casamance.

As the night wore on, I realised that the knowledge I had learnt about the President, was just the tip of the iceberg. The man was a monster. If I were a sensible man, I would keep my head down and avoid this murdering maniac of a dictator, but as many who know me will tell you, good sense was never one of my strong suits.

The guard agreed to bring Badjie the next night and I asked him to write down all he'd told me. He said he would and looked forward to it. When he had gone, I made up my mind to do everything in my limited power to get rid of this murdering despot. I had a mission; I loved missions.

2010 was very much like the end of 2008 and the whole of 2009. There were those who were surprised that I'd made it thus far and even some of the officers showed me some respect for surviving. However, there was only one reason I was alive, God, and God doesn't do anything without a reason. Ergo, I'd better find out what that reason was so that I could get on with it.

Throughout 2010 I went back and forth to court and the whole thing became a joke. The guards were happy for a day out; knowing as we all did that there would be no sitting. It became common knowledge that I had no case to answer after the judge threw it out of court. It was the President stopping my release.

Every week to ten days I'd be taken away by the NIA, and subjected to whatever they wanted to do to me, but with every nocturnal excursion, as my body grew weaker and more mutilated, my faith grew stronger. It seemed that through adversity I was able to have such a close relationship with God that as I write this I am tempted to say that I miss these times.

Our fellowship grew with each meeting, always held in the passageway outside my cell every Sunday morning.

# A FUTURE AND A HOPE
## February 2010

I got a visit, Wow, A visit from my friends, three wonderful brave women who are still in The Gambia. They had all decided to make their home there before Jammeh came to power, one Scottish, one English and one Welsh, (and no this isn't the start of a joke.) When they took me into the courtyard where the visits take place I was surprised to see what looked like fifty to fifty-five soldiers billeted in the courtyard. They had erected two large tents, and a kitchen, from which was coming a wonderful smell.

What happened next however was even more surprising. A Sergeant who recognised me stood up and shouted, "Officer present," and, as one, the squadies jumped to attention and saluted me as the guard and I passed. I was aware of several things almost simultaneously. Firstly, David Collie, the Director, who would never get a salute from the army, was watching from his office door. Secondly, I noted the reaction of the guard who was looking at me with an astonished expression on his face. Thirdly, was my own reaction: without hesitation, I returned the salute as if it was my due? It was only later that I questioned my response to what had happened.

The visit was only half an hour and it seemed to pass in half a minute, but wonderful for all that. There was my first news from Fiona and she had settled in with Iona our daughter. Photos of the family with Elizabeth in her school uniform. Yep, it was such a pick-me-up, just what I needed.

At the end of May 2010, a guard led me to block one where they served coffee and bread and this time there were sardines in the bread. Though I knew what the meeting was about, I had to enquire, "Where did this food and drink come from?" "Ah," said the CDS, tapping the side his nose and smiling knowingly, "things aren't always what they seem." The other men nodded sagely, but I was none the wiser. "What do you mean?" I said.

"Well major, it's like this, not everyone in the prison service is on the President's or the Director's side. How to you think your door is often open in the evening? Alternatively, you get some groundnuts or a mango from time to time. We have friends here Major."

I added my own sagely nod to theirs as we wrapped our loincloths about us and sat down. "OK, that's going to be helpful."

As the meeting went on, I outlined the plan I had been working on since the last meeting. "Right gentlemen, the last time we met we talked about the failure of the past. Today we are going to talk about the success of the future." That brought a smile to their faces.

"The first thing I have to say is, that you men are doing ether life or death sentences and let's face it, you've got nothing to lose and everything to gain. The second is that you have a common enemy, Jammeh, so that should bind you together." Again there came a murmur of agreement.

What has to happen is that you must break out of the prison taking all your men with you." There was a gasp. "Break out!" exclaimed the Major, "How can we break out? Jammeh's brought about fifty extra soldiers to guard us." "No," I replied, "these soldiers are in positions to defend the prison from an attempt to break in and release you guys. You will have two major advantages. Firstly, you know all these men and if they show me respect, still recognising my rank, then how much more will they respect you?

Secondly, as well as that, there are only ten men on duty at any one time and they have taken over the prison guards duties. What the President has in fact done is to bring in two light machine guns, several hand guns and fifty plus AH47s over and above the twenty held by the prison. So what he's done is supply you with enough weapons to stage a coup from Mile Two." You can arm over eighty men, think about it."

As one, their jaws dropped, but I went on, "You either see the glass half empty 'Oh dear, more men to guard us' or you see it half full 'Ah, plenty arms and ammunition'. What is it to be? As time went on and we talked about the details of making the break, of who among the prisoners could be best for which tasks, there came the inevitable question, who was going to be the leader.

It was at about this time that the guard came back. "Sorry Sirs, but my shift is coming to a close and my replacement is a Jammeh man, you'll have to get back to your cells." As we broke up and they ushered me out, I said over my shoulder. "Think hard about the leadership issue and always ask the unselfish question "who apart from 'me' is the most capable?" then the next time we meet maybe it can be resolved."

On the way back to my cell the guard said, "One day when Jammeh is gone you will be my boss again." I didn't answer but he obviously thought that I was getting involved in this coup plot, for that was what it was in order that the status quo would be returned, but what was my real motive? I'd have to think about that.

Sitting in the darkness of my cell I thought about getting involved and it has as they say "ever been thus". I remembered some of the times before I had the boat when we had to travel into the interior using an old Nissan Patrol I had. I sent a diary type email back to our friends and family when we got back from one of our trips.

# A WEEK IN THE LIFE

**From:** Fiona & Dave Fulton
**Sent:** Monday, November 03, 2003 6:54 PM
**Subject:** The Gambia! No problem.

### Sunday

The temperature is a reasonable 42$^c$, but the humidity is off the wall. We sit dripping in the lean to which serves as a church in the remand wing of mile two prison. Again, Fiona signals me that the old guitar has gone out of tune and who can blame it. I'm just amazed that she can notice the guitar from among the twenty four off key singers who come to the "Church service." The conditions in the prison are horrific, the cells are seven foot by ten and there are nine men in each cell, they seem to die for a past time either with malaria, beriberi or aids. Some of these men have been on remand for more than ten years without trial and if I am ever tempted to renege from doing "Church service" because I am exhausted, or feeling a little under the weather, then remembering their condition spurs me on to mile two prison.

> Amazing grace, how sweet the sound,
> that saves a wretch like me
> I once was lost, but now I>m found
> was blind but now I see.

They sing it as if they mean it. There are murderers who have given their lives to the Lord. Men who have had no visits for years, they have been ostracized by their families because they have become "Born again Christians" converting from Islam. The only time out of their cells is when we come to take "Church service."

> T'was grace that taught my heart to fear
> and grace my fears relieved
> How precious did that grace appear
> The hour I first believed.

I carry on playing, the infection in my fingers causing the skin to crack and bleed, but who cares, their eyes are closed, their faces intense.

> Through many dangers, toils and snares
> I have already come
> Tis grace has brought me safe thus far
> and grace will lead me home.

The sweat is running down my face, or is it tears? Whatever, the men start their African singing as I try to keep up on the guitar. The flies, I hate the flies, they buzz around the moisture, get in my mouth as I sing, inside my specs to my eyes, ears are a favourite place. Ever tried to swat flies and play the guitar at the same time?

> In the morning, early in the morning
> In the morning, I will rise and praise the Lord

My commitment is challenged yet again, because they do. They rise and praise the Lord. Why? Because it is quite probable that someone in their cell will have died that night.

I preach for about half an hour maybe more, bringing in repentance and salvation, because in the surrounding cells there will be those listening who don't know the Lord. I will talk about God being in control to men who hardly see the light of day from one week to the other. They say "amen'" AMEN for goodness sake!! I'd be shouting, "God if you're in control do something about my situation!", but they say amen. God bless them.

On a Sunday we will take three services in the prisons from 9am till about 2pm. Physically, emotionally and spiritually it is exhausting, but at least we don't have too far to travel and we can be home by 3.30 or 4pm. Next weekend Janjanburgh, or Georgetown as it was called in colonial times, now that's a challenge !

## UP RIVER TO JANJANBURUGH

### Thursday

Don't you just hate breaking down, calling out the AA or the RAC, the hours of waiting for recovery? The temperature gauge had been gradually rising and at last the engine had overheated and we ground to a halt. There is nothing or no one to be seen. We are on our own on the north bank road which is nothing more than a track through the bush winding 355 km from Kerrawang to Laminkoto there we will cross the river Gambia to Janjanburgh where we will (by Gods grace) camp in a tent for the night. Well, that looked doubtful for though I had water with me I knew the problem was serious, probably a cylinder head gasket gone. We had set off at 6.30am and crossed to the north bank on the early ferry. It was my intention to take the service at the barracks in Farafenni on the way up, maybe we could still manage it. I let the engine cool enough to start adding water as well as the last of my "stop leak" which was for extreme emergencies only.

Eventually we got on the way again with the filler cap off in an effort to stop the pressure building up. We made it to Farafenni which is about half way and I went into the barracks and took the service for about 100 men, mostly army but a few immigration. That went well and they want me to start another Alpha course in that barracks for soldiers who want to know about Christianity, Great. The car had only used 3ltrs of water in 190km so I decided to press on though the road conditions were getting much worse and often we were grinding along using 2nd gear and in four wheel drive for mile after mile, in and out gullies cut by the rains across the track and in one of those the exhaust was torn off. I suppose it could be worse, but I couldn't see it.

However thank God we did eventually arrive at Laminkoto, only to find there was no ferry. "THANK YOU GOD!!" I shouted and collapsed in the shade of a tree to watch for the ferry which we were assured would arrive sometime (what an encouragement). Fiona chatted to the locals who were awaiting the ferry and indeed had been there for some hours, but me! I just slumped there and fretted. (Some Christian huh?) We were all brown with the dust and I couldn›t even get any cool water to drink, but you never can up river, so what's my beef? Luke sat with me, "I knew it was a mistake" I said to him "we were always going to be short of money and now I have to fix the car before we can get back." Well, the ferry did come and just as we thought it was all over we got well and truly stuck in the mud up to the doors, (deep joy) and that took some getting out of. However we did spend the night in our tents by the side if the river on McCarthy island and I was privileged to see the most beautiful sunset imaginable before going to sleep that night.

## Friday

We had brought up with us cwt bags of split peas and lentils for the prison, as there is a real problem with nutrition in the prisons and Beriberi is a real killer. We delivered the food in the morning then set off to find a welder to repair the exhaust. In fact it needed remove and rebuild which took most of the day and a lump of our cash, but it least it was fixed. Friday was particularly bad for mosquitoes and we were all bitten quite badly, which is a concern as malaria is a big problem on the island. Of course the kids were more concerned with the discomfort of a hundred bites than anything else. The car was the priority on Friday and while it would need some serious ministry when we got home I think I have been able to manage it by tightening down the head a little more, so after another wonderful sunset we thanked God for a better day.

## Saturday

After our breakfast we headed off to the prison along the mud track which was a serious four wheel drive job, (I can't believe I used to enjoy off roading)

We took the service and enjoyed two and a half hours with the men, many of whom were first time attendees. I then went off to Basse, another 150km further up river to take the service in the barracks there. After the service three men who had become Christians three months ago asked for baptism. Quite a step for them as they will be thrown out of their compounds and one of the men who is married will have his wife and two sons taken away from him. That was an encouragement, but it was a long way to go just to hear something I could have heard about on the phone.

## Sunday

We headed back early because I wanted to take it easy with the car and the ferry crossing from Barra to Banjul is often difficult. Praise God it was a hot but uneventful journey back down to the coast. The Nissan went well and we arrived in Barra at five pm. Small problem though, there were about forty cars and twenty one trucks in front of us and there were only two more sailings that day with five cars and four trucks per ferry. It didn't take O levels and A levels in math to work out that we were stuck overnight in Barra, known as the armpit of the Gambia and that's saying something. Anyway, just as I was getting out to pay for my ticket a port official approached me and saluted me. Sir (I was in full uniform) please come to the front of the queue. Praise God I had priority because of the army.

On the way back I have to confess that I was a little down, we have such an opportunity to win souls for the Lord and I had to go into debt to get up there. Then the mobile rang, it was a Christian soldier stationed in Basse, "Sir," he said "when you left one of the men, a Moslem, gave his heart to the Lord, we've been trying to phone you but you were out of range." So it was worth it, worth the study, worth the sweat, worth the bush driving, worth the breakdowns, worth the debt, worth the discomfort, worth the mosquitoes, worth the work I'll have to do on the car.

## Monday

I'm having today off, well nearly off. It's not my thing this email business and I am apprehensive whenever I sit at the keyboard. I'd rather face the bush with all its hazards than a computer. However, my work is not over, indeed, the more I go to the barracks and the prisons the more Fiona goes to the female wings of the prisons. the more we are able to reach more people with the Gospel. People are getting saved, and baptised, people are getting healed as we pray for them. BUT, why does there have to be a, but? We are stuck, because of inflation every trip up river now costs about two hundred and fifty pounds and we just don't have it. Everything has doubled in the last four months and the ministry is going to be stagnant if more funds are not forthcoming. I know some of you reading this are already supporting the work here and we thank you from the bottom of our hearts. However if anyone feels God's prompting to support the expansion of the work here in The Gambia, please let us know and Fiona the email specialist in the family will give you details.

May God bless you, David Fulton.

# PRESIDENT JAMMEH DRUG BARRON

Well life might not be as exciting here banged up in prison, but it still had its challenges, namely, staying alive. The next day there was a buzz going round the prison that two and a half tons of the President's cocaine had been uncovered just outside Banjul. Of course, we all knew of his involvement in the arms and drugs trade, but two and a half tons, wow! Speculation was running wild and although the President denied any knowledge of it, declaring to all and sundry that, they would hunt down the drug runners, he fooled no one. We heard that the International Drugs Agencies from UK and the USA were in The Gambia looking into it.

"This is it," everyone was saying, "the President's going to be arrested." I had little doubt that the Drugs agencies were very well aware who owned the cocaine and who was behind the smuggling, but there was no way that Jammeh would put his hands up to this.

The prison was, and still is a rumour factory and they were flying about thick and fast. However, everything stopped when nine men were arrested and brought into the confinement wing at Mile Two. They were a mixture of Venezuelans, Dutch and Nigerians, with a Gambian woman thrown in for good measure.

Most of the men were Roman Catholic and while on remand, technically they should have been able to see a priest. I say 'technically' as there was no chance of it ever happening in Mile Two. However, I was there when a guard explained that while not a priest, as they understood it, I was nevertheless a Chaplain and that it seemed was good enough for them.

One at a time, they came to me for advice and I did the best I could, but more significantly they started to give me information that I wasn't sure I wanted to hear. They told me all about the smuggling of cocaine from Venezuela to Holland, via Guinea Bissau and The Gambia. They told me in detail about the involvement of the Presidents of Venezuela, Bissau and specifically of Jammeh in The Gambia and of their fears for their lives. Now that, I could understand and what an opportunity to tell them that if one knew of a certainty that he was going to heaven, then there would be no fear in death.

I was sure that they wanted to know what the prognosis was as far as I could guess. That was a difficult one, as I believed that the only thing that kept them from disappearing was the fact that the international drug agencies knew about the arrests and were watching what was going on with a close eye.

What I did know however, was that if they stood trial in The Gambia they would probably receive the death sentence. Jammeh had made it clear that it was his wish to pass a law that would allow anyone found with 250g or more of class 'A' drugs to be put to death. Now, this meant "My wish is your command" – if he wanted it then it would happen. He appointed a former lawyer Edward Gomez to be Attorney General of The Gambia in order to get his various nonsense ideas made law.

I was surprised at this for many reasons, the main one being that Jammeh himself was the drug king of West Africa and when it came on top for him, as it surely would one fine day, he'd be subject to his own laws. Arguably, I could see that he could be making a smokescreen for himself, in that his own people, many of whom were illiterate would think 'he can't be involved in anything that he was so obviously against'.

One of the other things that surprised me was that Edu

Gomez, who was a nominal Christian, had joined forces with Jammeh and his evil ambitions. I knew him prior to my captivity as a reasonable and likeable man, but it seemed that he had changed his allegiance and it only accentuated my despair about the 'nominal church.' What was it that the Apostle John said in Revelations 3:16 about being lukewarm in your faith? He said that God said, "I will spew you out of my mouth." Look out Edu, that's all I have to say.

Well, no it isn't all I have to say, the Bible also says in Joshua 24:15 "Choose you this day whom you will serve." Well Edu, if you are reading this, the good news is that God is a God of new beginnings and if you repent then he can fix it.

Anyway, these drug smugglers were telling me all this stuff, which would have been dynamite in the right hands, but I was in prison in solitary confinement, ill and regularly tortured what could I do? What I decided was to get a message out to the British High Commission. There was only one way I could do that: bribery and corruption, smuggling the information through prison officers. Now that could be an interesting debating point in a moral forum or Christian group, but I doubt if there would be any meeting of minds, between us.

In some ways it has been thus since I started this captivity, since I realised that I wasn't going to walk away from this place and I'd have to do something about it personally. The Church needs to know what the reality of Christianity is for thousands upon thousands of Christians. Some people in extreme circumstances have to make decisions that other Christians living in their cholesterol-lined comfort zones would find appalling.

So what should I do? Should I try to use the information to inform on the President and his evil regime, or should I say like the Muslims "Inshallah" (if God wills). Should I advise and even help to plan an insurrection within the prison against the President?

I'd given up the 'GAP' wearing, flat packed life to live for Christ in this Muslim country. We'd made the decision to put ourselves in harm's way, to do the right thing and I wasn't going to back down now.

There comes a time when Christians have to stand up and

be counted. Christians hid Jews from the Nazis during WW11. Christians smuggled slaves out of the Southern states of America to save their lives and bring them freedom. Christians have stood and planned against slavery and indeed all sorts of evil throughout the ages. So regardless of the consequences I was up for it.

I asked Sanneh to find me a sheet of paper and to be able to speak to a man called Faal, who despite being a prisoner was also an Imam and well respected by everyone in the prison and especially by the guards.

Within half an hour, Faal was at the hatch in my cell door. "What can I do for you Brother Dave," he asked through the open space. I lay down and we talked face to face in whispers. "I want to get a letter out to my High Commission," I said, "it's important, can you help?"

He didn't ask why, or what, he just said, "It'll take a fifty dalasi bribe (£1), do you have any money?" "Not a Butut" (a hundredth of a dalasi), I replied. "Hmm, what have you got?" he asked. "Some soap and a few shaving sticks," I replied. "English soap?" he asked. "Yep," said I. "Ok, I'll see if I can sell them," and with that he left.

Sanneh managed to get me two sheets of lined paper and I asked him to tell the drugs guys to come to see me one at a time if they could. I compiled a dossier over the next week that was damning, conclusive, and signed by every one of the men involved in the President's drugs dealings.

During that week I was taken to the NIA one night and again hung on the rack and beaten, but strangely enough I felt that I was at least fighting back and because of the information I would pass on to the BHC the President would soon be discredited and we'd all be free. Told you I was a dreamer.

Faal returned a day later and knocked on the door. "Come in," I shouted. That got a laugh, how wonderful it was that men could still laugh even in these conditions. "I can sell four bars of English soap for 50 Dalasi," he said through the hatch. I had removed the block behind which I had accumulated the soap and shaving sticks that I'd managed to wangle out of new guards without giving the old ones back. Handing the soap to him I said, "When can it happen?" "Soon," he replied and was gone.

The door opened that afternoon and it was the inmate medic who'd come to see me with some painkillers. My left thumb had been dislocated after the last nocturnal visit to the NIA and I couldn't get it back in. "No need for these," I said to him, "I've got no feeling in my left hand now: you can do what you like to it.""Keep them hidden," he replied, "if you don't need them, then someone else will and I'll know where to come. I stole them from the Director's office when I was in there treating his syphilis." "His what," I exclaimed, "syphilis? It couldn't happen to a nicer man." We laughed till we were sore.

# PLANNING A COUP

It was about a week later on a Sunday that I was taken to cell block one for our meeting with the coup plotters. It was the strangest of feelings: here was a guard who saluted me, asked for the note that I was passing out. Then showed me to a meeting with former senior army, navy and immigration officers to plan the overthrow of a government, in a maximum-security prison, while supposedly in solitary confinement 24/7.

It was like living in a novel, like being the central character in an adventure book and all the while fighting to keep myself alive. I'm reluctant to say this, but I was enjoying it. As the saying goes, "Enjoy what you can, endure what you must." Yes, that summed it up quite well. On arrival at block one, we were again given our respective kilts to wear. Obviously being a Scotsman I called my piece of blanket a kilt, I suppose to the others it would have been a loincloth. There were the obligatory handshakes all round.

"Welcome Sir." said the former CDS. "Please be seated." We all sat and as coffee and bread were arrived, he went on, "Today we have plenty of time and we have questions to ask you, so relax and enjoy your coffee." "This sounds a bit ominous" I thought but I'd determined to enjoy what I could. "Sir," he began, "since our last meeting we have all been in deep discussion and the same thing has cropped up time after time." Looking directly at me he asked, "Why are you willing to risk your life to help us when we are mostly Muslims and you are a Christian?"

After saying, this he was silent, and everyone was watching me intently. "Good point," I replied. "I guess there are many reasons and I'll try to list them one by one. However, I probably won't be able to explain them, so don't expect me to:

1. I want to because I believe it's the right thing to do, not necessarily as a Christian, but as a person who can help.
2. It's my belief that Jammeh could and should be stopped.
3. I have friends who Jammeh has had killed and justice needs to be done and seen to be done.
4. He and his evil government have put my family and myself through so much I want some payback.
5. As a Christian, I have to make a stand against evil. The Bible says, 'Faith without works is dead.'
6. Selfishly, it seems to me that this is a way that I and we can escape from Mile Two.
7. Again selfishly, I want to stay with my family in The Gambia, and I can't if Jammeh and his Islamic extremists are still in power.
8. If we succeed and you guys are in government and one of you is President, then I believe I will be given the chance to do my Gods work here with your approval as you are not extremist Muslims, and Hey! You'd owe me.

There was a mixture of nods and laughs, but I got my point across. Nobody trusts a do-gooder and the fact that I seemed to have some personal motive satisfied them. What I didn't say was that I needed to be involved, I needed the excitement, I always had to have that adrenalin rush, to live again on the edge. As I've said before and will no doubt say again, it's probably a character flaw.

"We have then one more question to ask you," he said. "Will you lead us?" Again, that silence, followed by a look of expectation on the faces that were turned towards me. I let the silence grow louder and louder until they could no longer stand it. "It's taken a lot for us to ask you Sir," said a major, "we all wanted to lead but as you so rightly said the last time we met, we just don't trust another tribe. Will you lead us?"

"Gentlemen," I replied, "I can't begin to thank you enough for what you have said this afternoon, I am honoured. However, the answer has to be "No." There was a groaning from the men, but I put my hand up to silence them. "I have to say no because it just wouldn't be right, I'm a white Scotsman for goodness sake. It's you guys that have to take the credit for this not me. It's the way you'll restore your credibility. If I were to lead you, then you'd be accused of bringing in a mercenary and a few enquiries about me might confirm it."

"There were some among us," said the CDS waving his hand specifically at a former ambassador to Bissau, "who thought that might be the case and we agree, but will you help us?" I wouldn't be sitting here if I wasn't going to help," I said, "so let's get started, let's put all our thoughts on the table and we'll take it from there."

The meeting went on for some time and after another mug of coffee and more bread, I could see my diet going out the window, but I was starting to enjoy the good life again. It all came down in the end to a simple plan. Each of the men would solicit help from their individual tribesmen within the prison, people they could trust. With a rough headcount, we reckoned on just over one hundred men in the confinement wing, so there would be about one hundred and twenty men and officers in all. A Sunday was the best day to do it, as there were no senior prison officers working then. In addition, the soldiers ware so laid back now that they were off home or out with their girlfriends on a Sunday afternoon.

Outside the prison, the roads would be quiet and the population of Banjul would be down the beach swimming or playing football on the sand. We needed to know when the President would be in the State House as we planned not to kill him and have another coup, but to arrest him for crimes against humanity and other things. So this wouldn't be a coup that could be criticized by the international community, rather, we'd be arresting a known murderer, drug baron and gun smuggler. Therefore, instead of criticism we'd gain some brownie points.

As many of the soldiers sent to guard the prison had relatives in captivity and were subordinate to us in rank, we were sure that they would willingly hand over their weapons or maybe even join us, so in theory we'd have plenty of men, plenty of weapons. There were two 3-ton prison trucks, a minibus and a pickup belonging to the prison, so transport for up to one hundred men wouldn't be a problem.

Banjul is on an island, as is the prison and the State House also. The only way onto the island is across Denton Bridge and that was easy to defend. The plan was to overcome the guards, which should be easy as there were only four on duty in the confinement wing on a Sunday and then those men who were going to be part of the force, would be released from their cells. That would give us about one hundred and twenty men 99% of whom were former senior officers, and would still hold their rank in the eyes of the ordinary squadie.

We would strip the guards of their uniforms and four men of the same size would don them. Two of them would then escort the most senior officers out of the confinement wing without raising any suspicions, to speak to whoever was in charge of the army detail guarding the prison. While these negotiations were going on, the other two imposters would escort more men to where the soldier's arms and ammunition were stored. They would overpower anyone who tried to resist them and arm themselves.

If all went well with the talks and it was generally agreed that it would we'd move to the prison administration office and armoury where the prison AK 47s and the guards' mobile phones were handed in and stored. Within fifteen minutes, we believed we'd have the prison in our hands, the vehicles fuelled and running and all the other prisoners and guards locked up.

The minibus would turn left at the gate and reach Denton Bridge with fourteen men; they'd be in uniform so as to arouse no suspicion. While only armed with two LMGs and five AKs they would be rearmed when they overcame the four soldiers and two policemen stationed on the mainland side of Denton Bridge. Once the bridge was secure, they'd re-cross it to the island and stop all traffic from crossing. Again, the chances were good that when the men stationed there saw that a move was being made on the President they'd join us – who wants to be on the losing side?

This move would ensure there would be no reinforcements from other barracks on the mainland and no one would leave the island to raise the alarm.

Of the second and much larger group, six armed men would remain at the prison to maintain security (as the last thing we wanted was seven hundred prisoners breaking out and going on the rampage). The rest, about one hundred, would turn right on leaving the prison and head for the State House and the barracks in Banjul. En route, the CDS and other senior officers would be using 'liberated' mobile phones to inform the British High Commissioner and American Ambassador and other people we'd want on our side that something was afoot and we, as they say in The Gambia, "were on it".

When we were at the barracks and State House there was no plan, save to get control of the armoury and take the President into custody. Again, in keeping with the looking at the glass half-full theory, we talked about what to do when we had secured the President and as many ministers as resided in Banjul.

There had to be a credible alternative to Jammeh and it had to happen quickly. I suggested that the Vice President should form an interim government, which would show the international community that we were not a bunch of coup-plotting thugs, but respected the constitution of The Gambia.

We would ask the UN and the EC to supervise elections within ninety days. However, as the APRC, the President's party had misappropriated public funds to the tune of five million dollars while Jammeh was in power; there was no viable way for them to operate as a political party until there was a refund of the money. This of course would never happen.

In general, we agreed that MR Jallou (not his real name for

obvious reasons) would make a good President. He had lived in the West and was well travelled, plus he had dual nationality and was an xxxxxxxxx citizen who had fought as a soldier in Desert Storm. He was highly qualified and had a degree or two in stuff that I hadn't a clue about. Lastly he had been prominent in government prior to his confinement here with us.

The great thing about this decision was that xxxx was my friend; there was something of a wow factor when I thought that my friend was going to be the next President of The Gambia. We all understood that there was a lot of work to do before this could happen: there were people to contact; alliances to be made so that nationalism would be put before tribalism. As if on cue, the guard came in and told us that it was time for shift change and I took me back to my cell.

The few hours out of my cell and in the company of men who had expected a better life than this, unsettled me. I was starting to think on my feet again, questioning things. What was I getting out of all this intrigue, this flirting with the affairs of The Gambia's future? I guess if I'm honest I was fighting back, I was doing what ordinary people in first world countries can't do, making a difference. If the truth's to be told I was also enjoying the opportunity to use my brain, my experience, and to help, not just myself to get out of this hell, but to help people who had become my comrades, even in a strange way, my friends.

# A THORN IN THE BHC's SIDE

I think I was coming to the realisation that the British Government in the shape of the British High Commission weren't coming to the rescue, not now, not ever. I can't say that it was a great surprise. It was only Fiona that they were interested in, an innocent British woman held in a Gambian prison wasn't good press for the Government with an election coming up.

Anyway, I had always been a thorn in the side of the High Commission with my stand against FGM and threatening to expose suspected British paedophiles living and operating in The Gambia. I've had letters written about me to the BHC from a group of suspected paedophiles and the BHC believed them and I was told "not to rock the boat". In fact in May 2004 I was asked to see the High Commissioner and shown a letter which was signed by about fifteen British ex-pats, most of whom I only knew by name.

The Islamic Council also complained to the BHS about me and the Commissioner took their side. Well, that tends only to make me look at what the Apostle Paul did and I quoted him to them. "I preach Christ and Him crucified." As my 23-year-old son would say, "End of."

I came across an email that I sent after such a visit.

You must be fed up hearing all my prayer requests, but this is an important one. I was called to the British High Commission today to answer charges brought by the Islamic council. I have been accused of using my rank and uniform to gain access to the services in The Gambia.

They say that I have been over zealous in my work and I was a threat to country. All of this is of course quite true, but not in the way they think. It is a little worrying that these people are on my case again, because they have the power and influence here.

I have decided therefore to only wear my uniform in the barracks for a little while, giving me a lower profile. However, no way am I going to be intimidated into cutting back on my work, indeed I will soon be going up river when the boat is repaired so the work will increase. I would ask though for your prayers regarding this issue, for our safety and freedom to minister to the services.

PS For those who were praying for Sgt Barr, the good news is that he has had a successful operation and is recovering well.

Yours Dave Fulton.

It wasn't long after I sent that email that we had a visit from an English couple Martin and Tina, who spent about five months a year in a house they rented in The Gambia.

They had been to Tanzania on holiday a few years earlier and while there, they met a British man called Rob, who was working as a teacher and trying to set up a residential school for girls. He seemed quite a pleasant person, but after our friends returned from a trip into the bush, they found Rob deported as a paedophile, and his passport stamped "DEPORTED."

As they talked, we had a coffee and they went on to say that they thought they saw him the previous evening having a meal in the tourist area of Senegambia. Martin just ignored it, but Tina decided to approach him, as they believed that he'd have no knowledge of what they knew about him. She introduced herself and Rob was chatty and open. What concerned our friends most was that he said that he was Deputy Headmaster at the International School that our children, Iona and Luke, were attending. Of course, it goes without saying that we were also concerned and I was determined to make my own enquiries and deal with the situation the next day.

What we were unaware of was that Luke was listening from the top of the stairs and it being an open plan house he heard every word. He'd be about fourteen years old at the time and the next day he imparted his bit of scandal to his friends. Then of course, it went through the school like a bush fire. I got a phone call from one teacher then another, then eventually the Headmistress. "Can you come and see me," she said, "I'd like to meet you privately away from the school." We arranged to meet at a cafe on the tourist strip that evening. She came with her husband who worked for some international agency, the UN, or WHO or something of that nature. I was pleased to see him as we were meeting in the open, she was well known, as indeed was I.

I told her the story as I had heard it and said that I'd get some corroborating proof. There was an emergency school board meeting set for the Friday, which was in two days, so I had to get my finger out and substantiate the claims. Emails went back and forth from our friend Martin to people he knew in the security forces in Dar es Salaam. None of them detailed what he had done, but one from the Chief of Security who had been on leave at the time said, "If I'd been on duty then, I would have had him taken to the river and staked out on the mud for the crabs to deal with."

We also got documentation that he was on the 'suspected Paedophile' watch-list in the UK, so I was surprised that he got into The Gambia in the first place with "Deported" stamped on his passport. As is my wont, I went to Immigration and had a talk with the Deputy Director and he arranged for an immigration officer to call on him.

I attended the board meeting in uniform, (I still felt uncomfortable in front of teachers) with my proof and there was no doubt that he was that man who was at their school. The problem was that to operate as an international school there had to be a certain number of international teachers and *he* enabled them to fill their quota. If they dismissed him, they wouldn't be able to fulfil the expectations of the parents.

I went ballistic. "If you don't do something about him, then I will and every parent in the school will know you are employing paedophiles in this school and I will be the first parent to remove my children and demand my money back." Silence reigned; it was probably the mention of money. Unsurprisingly, it did the trick.

"We'll have to suspend him as from Monday," said the Headmistress. "And report him to the police," shouted a woman I didn't recognise. "At the moment he's done nothing wrong in this country," I replied, "and if the police got to know about this, then so would half of The Gambia. Do you want that?" "I think we should speak to him over the weekend," said one of the board members, a Lebanese businessman, "maybe if *he* knows that *we* know, he'll resign and save any embarrassment." I thought that was the most sensible statement made that evening, and so it was agreed. On leaving there were a number of people who thanked me, but there was also a few whose looks would have taken a few inches off the polar cap.

On Monday, I received a call from Immigration Inspector Faal: he wanted me to come into the Immigration headquarters as soon as possible. I was in Banjul Barracks that day anyway so within an hour I was with the Director of Immigration.

After the usual greetings, he told me that they had interviewed the British teacher Rob, and discovered that he had cut out the page of his passport, which had the "DEPORTED" stamp on it. They had given him one week to leave the country and they knew he was on the Friday flight. I suppose my son's expression covers the whole episode: "Sorted."

# ABANDON SHIP

I managed to get my letter smuggled out but to this day, I've never been told if the BHC ever received it and if they did, if it was helpful. Shortly afterwards we heard that one of the drug guys who was one of the kingpins and close to Jammeh was taken to hospital. A few days later, he and his family were smuggled out of The Gambia and rumour had it that it was the BHC that was behind it.

I had been in captivity for one year eight months and I was still alive despite everything. There was no doubt in my mind that my faith had played a large part in my survival thus far. Strangely enough, I was not the only one who gave God the credit, both Christian and Muslim agreed on this point. I have to say that one of the advantages of talking to 'non extremist' Muslims about Jesus was their openness and awareness of the existence of God. Back home in the UK people have shelved God as an irrelevance, a nonentity, prayer is only for when your back's against the wall. Anyway, not only inmates, but also officers commented that as a Tubab in these conditions I should be dead, but for God . . . True, true.

One chap lay outside my cell and knocked on the door. "Do you remember me?" He asked. I leaned over gingerly as at that time my body was covered with infected boils. "Sorry fella," I replied, "don't know you from Adam." "I'm the one who didn't rescue you when your boat broke down in 2004." I laughed, "My friend, lots of people didn't rescue me when my boat broke down in 2004." Yet he persisted, "I was the one who tried with the speedboat." Ah, it started to dawn, I remembered. "I thought you had drowned," I said as I peered through the hatch to get a look at him. "No I survived," he explained, "but I'd borrowed the speedboat and ran away when it was wrecked." "I often wondered about you," I said quite relieved.

When he left, I recalled the incident and the email I sent out when it was all over with a smile. Yes, God was keeping me alive in prison, but it also took an act of will and he chose well when he chose me for The Gambia, coz I have the gift of stubbornness, not a spiritual gift to be sure, but very necessary where I was.

# AN EMAIL

From Dave & Fiona Fulton 20/04/2004

"Comfort zone" is a bit of an "in" word, especially at missionary weekends. Will you leave your "comfort zone", go into the world and preach the Gospel? I got a sort of revelation on Thursday night that I had the meaning wrong. Maybe it's only me, but I had thought it related to luxury e.g. two car family, detached house, meals out at will, hobbies, constant water and electricity, Sainsbury's every Friday, bottle of nice plonk with a meal and watch Satellite TV, a holiday every year ( how could we do without that).

Yes that is what I thought was the "comfort zone." However, not so, one's "comfort zone" is where one feels comfortable, a prisoner who is scared of leaving prison with its routine and safety, the paraplegic who gets all the benefits going and the wheelchair has become a symbol of his "brave fight."

The working wife who feels that having children will lower her status in people's eyes, a missionary who is reluctant to push the boundaries and has lots of excuses why not to. Yes, comfort is not about external things, but rather a feeling of safety in what one knows, in routine, and I suppose in success however one measures it.

Well, as most of you will already know I was asked to take on the position of Chaplain to the Immigration Dept. here in The Gambia and God healed my neck and provided a boat (both my arguments against it) in order that I go up river to reach the outposts where the men and women were. However, there was always some very good reason to delay the day. Two weeks ago, a godly woman who felt that there was some blockage regarding the progress of the ministry to the Immigration people contacted me. I was perplexed and told Fiona who immediately agreed and said that we were the blockage. She didn't want me to go and leave the family unprotected and I guess vulnerable, and I didn't want to leave my "comfort zone." We repented.

Tuesday at 8 am, I set out with Luke my 13-year-old son and the former skipper of the boat. We had been steaming for about five hours and everything was good when Luke went down from the Flying Bridge to check the gauges. He came running back up and reported that there was smoke coming from behind the saloon steering wheel. I went down and when I lifted the engine room hatch the saloon was enveloped in smoke. I stopped the engine and we waited till the smoke cleared.

The weather was fair, wind force two, current 3 knots with a two-foot swell and we could just see both banks, each two km away. Something bothered me about the smoke and as I thought about it I realised that it wasn't exhaust smoke, nor was it burning oil, but a sweet smell. So when the smoke cleared I went down into the engine room.

The automatic gearbox hydraulic oil was gone, and I realised that the smell was that of a melting oil seal and after an hour of investigative work there was indeed a melted oil seal. To the unversed in engineering, that means trouble with a capital T.

I decided to drop anchor, but after a look at the chart rejected that thought as below our keel was 153 metres and I only had 49 metres of anchor chain so it would have been wasted energy and my mind was already in survival mode. We were on the border of radio range and just in and out of cell phone reception,

I composed a text which Luke sent telling my wife Fiona to pray and to contact a friend, Anthony, who could come with it and another rescue boat, (having said that, there is no rescue boat in The Gambia something I intend to rectify). However, I had worked out that if my old boat (which had a big engine) could come we could wait till the tide turned (the river being tidal up to 300 km) and could get back with the tide. Our friend went to Banjul and told the people there of our plight and one fellow who thought he could make a killing out of a Tubab (white man) in distress took a speedboat and came to us.

I couldn't believe it when at 4pm this fellow arrived in a speedboat offering to tow us back (my boat weighs about seventeen tons) and when I realized he was drunk (obviously a good Muslim) I sent him on his way.

However, by this time the wind had freshened to force 3 with three foot waves. I said to him to send help and gave him 2000 Dallasis (£40) and a shirt as the wind was cold. I also tried to give him a life jacket, but he refused saying he was a good sailor and I have insulted him by offering. He set off and we awaited our rescuers.

Tuesday at ten we went below to try to get some sleep, quite exhausted, but not too worried as we had drifted into a place where the anchor was holding.

Wednesday 6am. First light and not a lot of sleep later, I took our bearings and according to the GPS the anchor wasn't holding and we had drifted 2km up river with two and a half km to the north bank and one and a half km to the south bank. I felt that was acceptable, but was surprised that no help was within sight. Drinking water was getting low but food was plentiful so I restricted the fresh water to drinking only and washing and cooking would be river water, which was really seawater.

All day we waited and at five in the afternoon, a small boat arrived, not to rescue us (it couldn't) but to look for the speedboat that had never returned to Banjul. I sent the former skipper Lamin back with it as the weather was deteriorating rapidly and we needed a large vessel to pull us now. This left Luke and I on board. Luke was great, he obeyed orders without question (why doesn't he do that at home?) and was a real asset. By 8pm, the wind had risen to force 5 on the Beaufort scale and the waves were 5ft high, it wasn't good. Luke made us some food. I'm not sure, what it was, but there were eggs, pasta, and plenty of ketchup. (Ta Luke!) It was a long night; we were drifting towards the South bank at about three and a half knots with the anchor down but dragging.

 It was then that we noticed that she was acting a bit sluggish and the stern was letting the waves up and along the gunnels. We were on the flying bridge signalling every two minutes with torches, in case Lamin the former skipper was searching for us where he left us and we should have been. So again, Luke went below and this time reported that there was a foot of water above the floor in the stern cabin.

Call me "Mr Picky" if you like, but, I would have sworn that the water should have been below the cabin floor. I switched on the bilge pump, but it wasn't coping with the influx of water. Luke and I started bailing, emptying the water into the head. Luke seemed to be talking to himself and I asked him if he was OK. "I'm talking to God dad" he replied. "Oh" I said, "what's God saying?" "He says to keep bailing" was his answer, and who was I to argue with that.

After an hour, we were down to the floor and I was able to lift the carpet and floorboards to ascertain the problem. The exhaust pipe under the stern cabin floor had broken and the waves over the past two days of wallowing had pushed water up the pipe and under the floor. Eventually because of the weight of water in the stern, the exhaust was below the water level and the water came pouring in unchecked by a special one-way swinging door inside the pipe but nearer to the engine.

The exhaust pipe is 4" in diameter where the bilge outlet is 2", I think that is what is called a losing battle. (Something else I intend to remedy). It was pitch dark and just a tad stormy, but someone had to go over the stern and plug the exhaust and when I suggested to Luke that he was younger and fitter than me, he told me that I had lived most of my life anyway, so I had less to lose. (Sometimes that boy can be a real smart bottom).

Anyway, time was a-wasting and I cut a 2ltr plastic bottle in half and went over the rail. I managed to get it positioned when a wave took me down the port side, but I was able to grab a fender and pull myself up. However, on my second attempt the bottle went in, was driven home by the water pressure, and stopped the leak. Luke and I were then able to bail out the remainder of the water by hand as the battery was now flat (note for me, "spare battery"). Luke was able to sleep, but I spent the night signalling into the darkness to where I hoped our rescuers were.

I have to say at this point that one's prayer life went into overdrive and I knew that Fiona had contacted people who were also praying. The chances of the boat going down were high, as a plastic bottle was all that was keeping us afloat and the wind and the waves were too high to use the dinghy. So I made the decision that I would have to raise the anchor and let the boat drift onto a mangrove island which was about three miles away according to my reckoning.

We grounded on the mangroves at high tide at 2.30am and by 4am, we were left high and dry as the tide receded, and then I managed three hours sleep till dawn.

Thursday 7am. Light found us about 15 metre from the river on top of the mud and mangroves with a 20ft fibreglass boat lying off. Lamin had come, he had seen our signals in the night, but it was all he could do to keep his boat under control. He waded knee deep through the mud to get to us and I told him we were abandoning the ship in order to formulate a rescue plan. Lamin, Luke and I got into the small boat and headed back to Banjul. We arrived at 2.30 pm and I started to solicit help from other boat owners and by 3pm had organized three boats to leave Banjul at seven the next morning. It was with great sadness that we learned that the speedboat that had come out to us on Tues afternoon had been found overturned with no sign of the man. Luke and I got a lift home to a grateful family. I slept.

Friday 8am. We set out from Banjul, three boats including a large pirogue and arrived at our grounded boat at high tide. We tried pulling her off, but to no avail, but one of the three (the most powerful of the boats) damaged her prop on the anchor chain and had to limp home. It was becoming obvious that this was it, there was already talk in Banjul that the boat was unsalvageable and I knew if we sailed away from here I wouldn't get anyone to return. So I got the men together and told them my plan.

We would wait till low tide and remove the mangroves from around the boat and down to the water. All told there were nine of us, including Luke and me (you didn't think Luke was going to be left behind, did you?) That operation took about two hours and then I told the men that we were going to dig a channel from around the boat to the river. As you can imagine that was met with shouts of joy, well shouts of something anyway.

Luke and I were first at it and soon shamed the rest into working and by the time the tide was coming in it was dark, but we had it done. At 8.30 pm, she floated and we managed to pull her out the channel we had dug and this time the shouts were joyful. We started the long slow tow back to Banjul.

Saturday. We had to moor alongside a wreck near Banjul harbour, as we couldn't go any further for lack of fuel for the towing boats. However, at dawn we managed to get some more and came to her mooring at 11 am where Luke and I gave thanks to God for his deliverance. I realised that I had been complacent in some areas especially prayer covering. Now there is some work to be done.

It turned out that the defective oil seal was Nigerian, but how could I tell? So I am now going to replace all the engine and gearbox seals and the exhaust pipe along with some other safety measures before I set out again, by God's grace in two weeks.

I am far from being a super spiritual person, but some things have been brought to my attention. The weather. None of the local fishermen have ever experienced wind at force five and waves over five foot high on the river and had I been a super spiritual person I might be tempted to believe that this was a deliberate attempt to stop me, or even kill me.

Well let it be known to the principalities and powers, that it's only one-nil with the other half to play, and if that is the case I know I'm on the right track and "greater is He that is within me than he who is in the world". High tide on Friday evening was 5cm higher than forecast and many people said "how lucky".

I, unspiritual though I am have to say "Thank you Lord." To those who Fiona managed to contact and were praying, I say thank you, I owe you one, come out to The Gambia and have a Gambian experience. AMEN Dave.

# SHOCKING

I had been reminiscing on this when the door opened. It was very early morning, (not that I could see outside), but it was the presence of Shades that gave it away. He was standing in the passageway looking as uncool (as my kids would say) as ever.

It was the usual procedure, dressed, cuffs and leg irons, all in silence. This time though I sensed a feeling of anger towards me and I wondered if they had got wind of the conversations that had gone on in block number one. That made me tense, and all of a sudden, he recognised the change of atmosphere, which heightened his tension. "What is it today," I asked Shades in an effort to defuse the situation, "Will it be good NIA or bad NIA? Or maybe I'll be a chimney-sweep today." He grinned and said, "Whatever it is, it'll hurt you more than it'll hurt me." I was staggered; this was more words than Shades has ever put together in the seventeen months I've known him.

The same old Toyota pickup was there. That old Hi-lux deserves a medal. These things must me the most durable vehicles in the world, if the NIA in The Gambia can keep it on the road then I have to take my hat off to it. Anyway, I wasn't the only one to go with the NIA that night, three of the drug traffickers came stumbling and shuffling towards me. We all nodded to each other, it's not easy to shake hands with them chained behind our backs.

"What's going on Pastor?" asked Gazi who was in his late sixties and lived in Holland but was a native of Suriname in South America. "We're off to the NIA," I replied, "haven't you been there before?" "No sir," he said I don't suppose it'll be nice." "Right first time", I said, "it won't be nice."

They shackled us to one another and we shuffled up to the pickup and managed to get in the back with some difficulty. Gazi had very bad eyesight and his glasses were as thick as the bottom of a Coke bottle. "You need to help me, "he whispered to when we were in the pickup. "I'll tell your High Commissioner everything about the cocaine shipments and who's involved, I've got records of the Presidents involvement going back years."Well now's not the time to talk about it," I replied, "see me when we get back." "If we get back," he whispered. I agreed, "If we get back."

Pulling into the NIA headquarters compound, I noticed that for a change I wasn't their main focus of attention. Obviously it was the drugs issue that was uppermost in Jammeh's mind, but it was sad to see them bullying Gazi, at his age he should have been treated better. One NIA officer took off his glasses and threw them to the ground. When he complained he was beaten. I feared for his survival, but maybe the international attention on his case would ensure that for the time being. The drugs guys were taken away while I was left with Shades and he had no idea what to do. "You'd better come with me," he said, prodding me towards the Babba Dinka cell. I'll keep you there just now." Well, that was fine with me, at least I had a reprieve and who knows, maybe they'd forget about me.

I pretended to trip and when I rolled about trying to get up, I picked up Gazi's specs and stuffed them down the back of my shorts. Shades got me to Babba Dinka and unshackled me before opening the cell and pushing me in without getting me to undress. Once again I was struck by the stench of the place and the reception I got. Most of the men in there when I was there last time were still there.

"Is that you Major?" someone said in the darkness. "None other," I replied, "Who are you?" "It's me, Modu," he said with an incredulous edge to his voice, maybe even verging on hysteria. "Sorry," I said consolingly, "I didn't recognise your voice." In fact, I had no idea who he was but this wasn't the time for irrelevancies, the poor guy was on the edge.

"I'm still here," he went on. "Sorry to hear that," I replied, not really knowing what to say. "I'll die here, you know," he went on, "can you help me?" What do Gambians see in white people, especially the British, that they think we can help them. I was tempted to say, "Yes, of course I will" but that would have been a lie – I couldn't even help myself.

After a minute or two of silence he whispered, "Tell your Government I'm here. I can help them if they help me," Now that got me wondering, "Who was this guy and how could I find out without him knowing that I didn't recognise him." You may think that isn't important, but in the Gambian culture one is expected to remember everyone and his dog. The Gambians have fantastic memories. I would guarantee that this fellow has a phone book in his head, while I struggle to remember my wife's number and as for our anniversary . . .

"Do you know the High Commissioner?" I asked him probingly. "Know him," he said excitedly, "I've been to the High Commission often when I was Minister of Finance."

"Ahh," I thought, "I think I know you now," but I let him continue. "I've even had lunch with him; he's shaken my hand and said that there was no better man to guide the President than Modu Camara." That's what I was waiting on, now it all fell into place, probably if I'd been able to see his face I'd have recognised him, but now I knew. "Well Modu" I replied, "I'd like to say that the British government will help you, but they, being British, don't rock the boat. They've done nothing for me, maybe they've tried, but nothing's come of it, I'm still here with you in Babba Dinka."

In Babba Dinka with him and about fifteen others with nothing to do but talk, and talk we did. I wasn't surprised to find that every one of the men were political prisoners, but I was surprised to discover some of them had until recently been close to the President. We talked about some of the atrocities that they had done in the name of the President and how he had put them in Babba Dinka. "This is terrible," I said. "Not as terrible as what we've done in his name," said a former soldier. "We were the Green Boys, President Jammeh's own men, but we know too much and now we're here."

The man started crying, but no one consoled him, he cried to his Muslim god, but his god left him crying. "I used to be a Muslim," said a voice in the darkness. "What are you now?" I asked. "Oh, I'm a Christian the same as my uncle," "Your uncle?" I questioned, "Who's your uncle?" I asked, "Inspector Bah he replied" he was an immigration officer in Barra.

"I knew your uncle," I told him, "he's a good man." "He is now, but wasn't a few years ago," the man replied. "Aren't you the very man who saved him sir?" "I remember I led him to faith in Christ," I replied, "but only Jesus can save someone."What do you mean?" piped up another voice, "Well, I'll tell you what happened. It was about three years ago . . ." and I told about the incidents reported in the email below.

# EMAIL
## 20 July 2006

This month I went (as you probably know) up river, but what you don't know is it wasn't the great success we hoped and prayed for. Again, the boat let me down; I really didn't realise how many things there were to go wrong that could disable the boat. There I was David Fulton "Captain under God of the good ship Nautilus1" with my son Luke (a good lad) on the open flying bridge leaving Denton Bridge for the journey up river.

The Gambian Pastor who was coming with me chickened out and maybe when the rain started to sheet across the boat and the wind tried to blow us off course I should have done the same. I think it might be a personality flaw, but when within seconds of the storm, soaked to the skin, lashed by the force 8 gales, I was standing at the wheel on the flying bridge laughing and whooping at the storm. Lamin my Gambian 1st mate (when I'm on board, 2nd mate when Luke's with me) cowered below decks with every flash of lightning, Yes! This is living, "Thank you God."

 Eight hours later we had almost reached the first of the villages and immigration outposts when the engine started revving and the boat started slowing down. Quickly, Luke dived into the engine room (well when I say room, that's a slight exaggeration: I can just manage to get in it without burning myself on the nasty very hot bits). The drive shaft splines had stripped, you know the ones, between the 3 to 1 reduction ratio gearbox and the UJ prop shaft coupling, "yep, that one".

As you can well imagine, I thought, "Oh goodness me, whatever next." However, my priority was to cover the next ten miles in the outboard to the village and outpost and get on with what I came here to do. The outpost was fine, I did a Bible study with the men and women who were stationed there, saw little David, the son of the immigration officer who died after I delivered her baby. Little David needs prayer as he is not growing as much as he should. He is just over a year old, but the size of a four-month baby. I was given some clothes for him some time ago but they are still too big. He is healthy and eating solids, but not growing. He has had tests but no one knows what is wrong. They were grateful that I had made the effort, especially in the rainy season.

The village was more difficult as I wasn't able to take the Jesus film, TV battery and inverter in the small boat in the rain. However, one of the officers came with me to the village to interpret and we talked to the local people. I told them I would be back another time with a film about Jesus on the TV for them to watch. Film? TV? Steel boat? All a mystery, but I will be back!

The prop shaft could not be fixed to enable us to go on, but I was able to do a temporary repair, which meant we could travel in reverse. After spending the night at anchor with squadrons of mosquitoes as shipmates, we limped back to Banjul backwards, (not an easy task).

Now for the good news, after a few days back home I had a call from an immigration officer who got saved about 7 weeks ago. He told me his entire family (9 in all) wanted to accept Christ. I was a little sceptical as prior to his conversion this man was a renowned bully and maybe he was making the family follow his lead. I have to confess my reluctance to travel in one of the canoes the 10 miles to where the family was. You see, before one-steps into the canoe one has to pay in advance and upon receipt of payment one is handed what looks like a pint mug. "Ah!" thought I, the first time I travelled that way, "onboard refreshments, that'll do for me by the way" No such luck, I mean blessing.

It is for baling out the water and believe me bale you must. Trousers rolled up to the knees, socks in the pockets and shoes hanging by the laces around my neck I, along with 15 others baled as if our lives depended on it, which they probably did. The 4hp outboard only broke down twice (which I'm reliably informed was a minor miracle).

*Well, we made it and to my amazement, they were ready to accept Jesus as their saviour as a result of the changed life of the officer and family member who they now admired and respected. Anyway, I had the privilege to lead the family to the Lord.*

*It is my intention to travel up river as soon as the repairs are carried out.*

*God bless you. Dave.*

"That was my uncle," he shouted, "he told me about you, you paid for our church to be built." "I paid for it, but it was money given to me from Christians in the UK." "It's closed now," he almost cried, "they closed it."

There was nothing to say, I was devastated. We had planted two churches; one on the North Bank of the river called The North Bank Church and the Veranda Church in our compound and now it seemed that they were both closed down. Had it all been for nothing? Where would the new Christians go?

The cell door opening interrupted my thoughts and in the light of the passageway, I saw the three drug guys being unchained then one by one thrown into the cell. Before the door was shut I looked about me and there were in fact sixteen other men with me and now with the new arrivals we were twenty in all in a cell, probably about fifteen feet square.

Gazi was moaning, sobbing. He was talking in Dutch and I couldn't understand what he was saying. Crawling over to him I asked, "What did they do to you?" I guess it was because I spoke in English that he replied in the same without thinking about it. "They beat me and filled me with water." I knew then that he had gone through what I hadn't yet, and hoped I never would.

"My glasses," he cried, "I can't see anything without my glasses." "I have them here," I told him, "but put them down your underpants till you get back to the prison, they'll only take them away."

I guess we were there for about two days, at least that's what I worked out by the food we were given. It was a real anomaly that here we were in the place of torture, but they fed us quite well. Someone would go out and buy Tapalapa bread filled with anything from meat and onions, beans, salad or chicken. We'd get one each with water. Many of the men didn't want to eat and so I ate theirs.

If I had a seat I'd have been on the edge of it in anticipation of them coming for me. However, it seemed that I'd been forgotten and I wasn't going to remind them I was still here. The door opened and a short fat man who I vaguely recognised but couldn't place was thrown in. "You, you, you and you," shouted the guard pointing to the three drugs guys and myself, "out," which of course we did and then we were shackled and marched off.

Before the door closed, I heard a man shout "Bun (pronounced Boon) Sanneh, you bastard," and the sound of a scuffle in the cell. *"Aha,"* I thought, *"Bun Sanneh that's him, I hope they give him a hard time"*

Bun Sanneh had been the head of the drug squad and he had a reputation for being very corrupt. If he wanted your house, he'd come with a squad of drug enforcement officers, search it, and miraculously find drugs, which of course he'd planted. Your house would be confiscated and he'd pay a nominal amount to the Government to buy it. I knew he wasn't the most popular man in The Gambia and I got the feeling he was just about to find that out too.

When we arrived back in Mile Two the guard asked me if I

could help Gazi as he was in pain. "The director won't send the medic," he told me while handing me a sheet of paper. "I think he's hoping that Gazi will die." I took the paper, which was a computer printout and read:

Source BBC

## At least two tonnes of cocaine with a street value of $1bn has been seized in The Gambia bound for Europe

In addition to the huge haul of drugs, the Gambian authorities have arrested a dozen suspected traffickers, and seized large quantities of cash and arms.

Gambian investigators made the first arrests then called in British agents to gather forensic evidence.

West Africa has become a major transit hub for trafficking Latin American drugs to markets in Europe.

Drugs cartels are taking advantage of the region's poverty and weak security and judicial systems.

Agents from the UK's Serious Organised Crime Agency – the rough equivalent of the US FBI – helped discover the haul of highly concentrated cocaine behind a false wall in a warehouse basement an hour's drive from the Gambian capital, Banjul.

Numerous revealing computer records were also found.

One investigator closely involved told the BBC: "We're excited about this one – we've got all the elements here."

The BBC's Mark Doyle in Banjul says some of the Gambian officers involved in the bust are clearly pleased, if saying nothing in public for now.

............................................................

Below is the story the Freedom Newspaper radio had reported about the major cocaine catch in The Gambia well before the BBC story. Please read on . . .

## Breaking News: Gambia: MAJOR COCAINE "CATCH" IN GAMBIA

## MAJOR COCAINE "CATCH" IN GAMBIA

### Lebanese Timber Factory Transformed Into A Cocaine Zone

### As Joint Security Team Raid Land Proprietor In Trouble

By Staff Reporter Bakary Gibba, Banjul

The impoverished nation of the Gambia is gradually becoming a safe-haven for drug cartel networks – notably drug dealers from South America, Guinea Bissau and the country's indigenous local citizens who used the West African country to traffic cocaine and other dangerous drugs, the Freedom Newspaper can report. A massive joint security operation Friday, June 4th led to the confiscation of a huge consignment of cocaine – that was hidden at Muktharr Trading Store – situated between Bonto village and Pirang in the Kombo East District, West Region of the Gambia, intelligence sources said.

Muktharr Trading is engaged in timber sale in The Gambia. The company is owned by a Lebanese born business tycoon Mr. Muktharr. Mr. Muktaharr is a close associate of President Yahya Jammeh. His company is partly responsible for the country's dwindling flora and fauna.

The raiding team which consist of Military, police, NIA and officials of the National Drug Enforcement Agency – known as (NDEA) received a tip off that a large consignment of cocaine were hidden at the Muktaharr timber factory. This led to the confiscation of the drugs. Though, no one has claimed ownership of the confiscated cocaine, investigators said.

The owner of the timber factory is helping police with their investigators. He has denied having knowledge about the said cocaine even though it was found in his business property, police said.

The Friday raid, said a member of the raiding team is one of the country's biggest cocaine catch ever in the history of the Jammeh administration. The official said he suspects that there is a bigger network infiltrating Banjul as a drug transit point.

"The proprietor of the Muktaharr company is very close to the President. I'm sure the President would be upset to learn that Mr. Muktaharr's factory has been transformed into a cocaine zone. We are still trying to gather bit and pieces as to the whereabouts of those responsible for smuggling of the large quantity of cocaine into the country," said a source close to the team investigating the incident.

According to our source "cocaine is now rampant in the Gambia. We have more cocaine in this country than marijuana. This is a disturbing situation. Someone out there is benefiting from the cocaine trafficking. There are powerful officials involved in the deal that I can confirm to you."

It would be recalled the arrest of the former anti narcotic chief and other NDEA officials led to the discovery of the cocaine zones across the country.

Of recent at Kuloro in the same area, some high profile arrests were made. The Eco-Tourist Centre Sita Joyeh was raided and some Spanish and Gambian Nationals were rounded up who were accused of cocaine trafficking.

Posted on Tuesday, June 08, 2010 (Archive on Friday, July 30, 2010)

Posted by PNMBAI Contributed by PNMBAI


"Wow" I responded "I can see you're not a Jammeh supporter my friend, can I keep this?" "Yes but I didn't give it to you, OK?" "Thanks I said and put it in my cell.

The guard took me to Gazi's cell, which was the same size as mine but was about eight feet high and had a small window. He was lying on the floor with a swollen face but no cuts. However, the thing that concerned me was his belly; he was clutching it and rolling about. His stomach was so distended he looked about nine months pregnant.

"How do you feel my friend?" I asked "Sore," he replied, "my stomach so painful."

"I'm sorry to say that I really don't know what to do," I said as I knelt down beside him. "Does it feel like it's full of water?"

"It feels heavy and as if I've had too much to eat," he groaned, "and it sometimes cramps." I turned to the guard who was standing with some orderlies in the passageway. "Do you have any laxatives or food that would make him go to the toilet and shit?"

There was a general shake of heads, but one guy said, "Faal the marabout (witch doctor) will know what to use." "Can I speak to him? I asked the guard. I don't like the look of Gazi, he's an old man and not fit, we don't want him to die, do we?"

Now this is where I will hang my head in shame. I didn't think for one moment that this would help Gazi, but I'd had constipation for a week and as my mother used to say, "If you see the stick, cut it." Well maybe I would have the cure for my constipation. Faal arrived with instructions for the guard to go to the market and get some leaves and a small 5 Dalasi bag of sugar. I guessed he was going to make one of their infusions, maybe I'd let him take it first, sort of, try it out?

I was still with Gazi when Sanneh came back with an old but reasonably clean Mao jar brimming with a steaming amber coloured liquid. "Is that a Whisky Toddy"? I enquired jokingly. "No," said Sanneh in all seriousness, "it's an infusion." (I really have to curb my witticisms with these people.) "OK," I said, "let's do it."

Gazi started to sip it and almost gagged at the taste, but managed about a quarter of it down his neck. "Enough," he spluttered, pushing the hot handleless container at me. "This cure is worse than the affliction." It was then the guard handed me the

272

sugar. "Oops," I said, and added it to the still hot drink. Putting it gingerly to my lips, I sipped. "Mmm," I said, "not bad." "You can have it," said Gazi, and I did, and it did the trick, but we won't go into that right now.

# TWO FACES OF EVIL

Back in the cell, I was finding it difficult to understand what was going on with me. I was supposed to be in solitary confinement, but here I was, helping to plan a mass prison breakout as a prelude to a coup and the arrest of the President of The Gambia. I was the confidant of international drug smugglers and the personal enemy to the country's President. As I said before, I felt as if I was in the middle of a novel by John Le Carre, and I was enjoying it.

What did that say about me as a Christian? Oh, I could always justify what I was doing, we're all good at that, but was it right?

I had the opportunity a week later when my cell opened and the guard told me to sit in the corridor. This hadn't happened before so I was somewhat apprehensive. They told me to put on my shorts and t-shirt, which again was out of the ordinary. There were two seats by my cell door and I was now staggered. I'd never seen proper seats in the confinement wing. What was going on? I have to confess to being confused, but as is my wont, I sat on one of the chairs without waiting for permission, fully expecting to be beaten off it. However, they left me there, much to the surprise of those inmates who passed on their way to empty their paint tin toilets.

Then along came a man in prison garb except instead of shorts he wore long trousers of the same blue material with a broad white stripe down the outside seams. He marched up to me and offered his hand. "My name is Fatty and I'm an Imam." With that, he sat down on the other seat. "I want to talk to you reasonably about signing the confession that will enable you to go back home to your wife and family."

I interrupted him. "What are you doing in prison if you are on the side of the Islamic Council?" "Ah," he replied, "That's a long story and I don't want to go into it at present."

At that moment, Sanneh was walking up the passageway towards us. He was facing me and approaching the Imam from behind. Without breaking step, he pointed to the Imam and vigorously shook his head from side to side. I took this as a signal not to trust the man, which only confirmed my own feelings.

"I haven't been asked to speak to you, I'm on your side," he lied through his teeth, "but I know all about what you do here, you're a good man, (shows how little he really knew) and I want to help you."

Of course, I didn't believe it for a moment, but the longer I was out of the cell, the better for me, so I kept the conversation going. "What good things have I done that you think I'm worth helping."

"Well", he said holding up one finger. "We know that you have supplied your village with water from your bore hole." Another finger went up, "you are always giving the local people their injections when they have malaria." A third finger rose up and he went on, "You and your wife paid for and supplied medicines for prisoners and helped them when they came out." Yet another finger rose up, "Your wife worked with aids people, and . . ."

Before he opened his hand and my head started swelling, I cut in. "That wasn't the main thrust of our work in The Gambia, was it? Our work here was as Christian missionaries, not as "do gooders." The bible says that "Faith without works is dead" and so as Christians we not only brought the love of Christ to people, but the compassion of Christ also."

At last, he was able to hold up his outstretched hand, but this time in a gesture to stop me talking. "Ah, now that's the problem, that's the reason you've found yourself in here. You have stood on many toes, as you English say. Even your embassy has warned you to stop, but you ignored them and that stubbornness could get you killed."

There was a pregnant pause as we stared at each other, and I broke the silence first. "Is that a threat?" "Oh no," he quickly said, "More of a warning." "Well, it seems to me," I replied, "that some Christians are called by God to be downright stubborn and bloody-minded. The Bible is full of Christian evangelists killed for preaching the Gospel; even the Apostle Paul was beheaded. He said when questioned, "I preach Christ and Him crucified." So I'd be in good company, wouldn't I?"

"You're a fool." He shouted. This time I held up my hand to stop him and said, "It's true. As a British preacher once said, "I'm a fool for Christ, whose fool are you?""

Now, I didn't mean that to be offensive, but he took it that way and stood up so violently that he stood on my toes and his chair fell back. "I am only trying to help you and you throw it in my face." I just sat there, stunned at the transformation in his face. From being a reasonable congenial fellow, his face had morphed into a mask of hatred. It was easy to see that perhaps he wasn't really on my side after all.

"Guard," he shouted, "guard, get me out of here." I guessed we weren't going to be exchanging email addresses or Christmas cards this year. Oh well, no great loss.

Back in the cell, I reviewed our conversation and was surprised at what they knew. I knew I'd been followed by the NIA, but it seemed they'd had quite a lot of detail that I didn't think they would have been interested in, was that good? I doubted it.

The next night, as if in response to the Imam's visit they dragged me from my cell round about midnight. No surprises, it was the NIA again with Bin Ladin for company. There was something sinister and evil about that man. Looking back, I can joke a little about calling him Bin Ladin and about how he looked, but the man exuded evil to such an extent that even now it sends shivers down my spine.

After the usual trip to the NIA headquarters, they shoved me down some steps to what they euphemistically called the interrogation room. This time I had my hands cuffed behind my back and attached to the leg irons by a rope.

I noticed a change that day, I wasn't asked to sign anything either before or after the torture. I truly believe that they had given up on that. They realised that I wasn't going to sign anything, but they were still going to extract their pound of flesh, and they did. I wasn't able to walk for two weeks.

It was the first week in July 2010 when I was unlocked and given a bucket of water and a razor. The guard said, "Your High Commission has come to see you." While I could hardly walk it didn't take me long to wash, shave and dress. I shuffled along on bruised feet to the conference room where Lin, one of the High Commission staff sat. I could see by the expression on her face that it wasn't good news and I was right. After the obligatory greetings she said, "I'm sorry to tell you David that your mother has been taken into hospital in Scotland and isn't expected to live."

I felt numb: my mother was well into her eighties and was a committed Christian. I believe the emotion I felt most was one of sadness that I was in captivity in The Gambia and not with her at the last. "Thanks for coming Lin," I said. "My mum's going to a better place where there'll be no more worry about me, no more pain in her body. She heading for heaven and it wouldn't surprise me if I'll be seeing her there soon." She was more emotional than I was and promised to let me know of any developments.

My mother passed away in the second week of July 2010. I was not heartbroken because as I've said I knew where she was. That did however create some talk, as when one of the men had a bereavement there was all sorts of weeping and wailing. Quite a few men noticed my reaction to her death and that started many interesting conversations, one of which led to one guard coming to faith in Christ. I believe that mum would have been delighted at that.

I was starting to sense a moving of sentiment away from people supporting the Establishment against me. Not just in the inmates who had formerly been antagonistic towards me for whatever reason, but from the officers who believed that surely, enough is enough, I didn't deserve this. This sea change didn't affect my treatment in prison, as the Director David Colley was still calling the shots there, but it was nice to get some encouragement from unexpected quarters.

In the prison, there were rumours of an amnesty on July 22nd, the celebration of the coup in 1994 when Jammeh came to power. I didn't believe it for one moment, but there were signs that it might just be true. We heard that a list was taken of all those who were political prisoners and I was included in that list. Despite myself, I was starting to get a little optimistic. While I was telling others not to get their hopes up, I was thinking that maybe the President was going to make a gesture that would give him some brownie points with the international community.

Many times men would stop by my cell and questioned me on what I thought and each time I told them that there would be no amnesty, while hoping I was wrong.

On the 21st of July, The guards informed me that I was due in court on the following day. Everyone including the officers knew that this was a public holiday, indeed the biggest celebration in The Gambia bar none. Despite believing that nothing was going to happen, as there would be no court sitting that day, I looked forward to the day out.

July 22nd came with an air of excitement, for me seeing the outside world again and in the prison as men eagerly anticipated their imminent release. They allowed me a shave and shower before they took me to reception where I dressed in my own clothes. I could hardly believe how much weight I'd lost as my shirt hung on me like a sack and I had to hold up my trousers as they were miles to big now.

On the way to court, I absorbed the preparations for the July 22nd celebrations with disbelief. What I was seeing was worlds apart from where I'd just come from. People were dancing in the streets, soldiers were everywhere in their ceremonials, drilling and generally being pompous. The bunting and flags were out in Banjul because other West African presidents were expected.

Didn't they know what was going on behind the walls if the NIA building? On the other hand, did they just choose to ignore it, stick their collective heads in the sand and hope that it would go away? Well, as expected the court was shut, not a soul to be seen anywhere. My escort lost no time in taking the pickup to the harbour side and parked behind a rusting old crane. My handcuffs were unlocked and I was able to swing my bound legs out the door and sit in the sun.

Out came the cigarettes and the Tapalapa bread with sardines. While they smoked, I ate and for a short time, I felt that the world wasn't such a bad place after all.

All good things must come to an end, as the saying goes, and we headed back through the festivities to Mile Two where the contrast was obvious. In the prison, July 22nd went off like a damp squib. Men who had gone as far as to make plans for the last half of 2010 were depressed. They knew that their families outside, had counted on their loved ones being set free, they were gutted, and I learned that my mother was being buried that day.

I was disappointed but not surprised, nothing that Jammeh did, surprised me anymore, but after the depression had worn off, I sensed a mood of anger and defiance instead of the usual "Inshallah".

# ON THE BRINK

Given everyone's disappointment I half expected that I would be unlocked the following Sunday and given my kilt with a metre of string to hold it up. "Briefing time," the guard said. I recognised him as the guard who'd stood stag on the previous "Government in waiting" meetings.

On arrival at cellblock, a group of stern faced men greeted one me. "Welcome major," said the former CDS, "you were accurate in your assessment of our situation here. This President will need removal by force, and he is getting rid of anyone he perceives as a threat. What was it you diagnosed him as?"

"A paranoid schizophrenic," I answered. "Yes that's it, the man is mad, he has to go and we have to do it. Will you help us Major?" I looked around at the expectant faces. "Yes I will," I said, "but only with regard to planning and maybe enabling."

"Enabling? What do you mean enabling?" he said. "Well, I might be able to help with support in some way. For example, I could contact the British High Commission and the American Embassy when you guys are involved in the operation. They know the President is a monster and will be happy to have him out of the picture and The Gambia return to a stable country again."

"We were hoping that you might have had second thoughts and lead us," said one of the men. "We would follow you as you aren't from any of our tribes. It seems that we can't agree on who should be the leader, indeed we all want to be, but it's not going to happen, is it? The only thing we agree on is that we all trust and would follow you, sir."

"Again I am honoured by your confidence in me, but let's say I did lead you and let's say that we arrested Jammeh. You'd still have this tribal distrust and I'd doubt if you'd allow me to be President."

When the laughter died down, I continued. "Gentlemen, you have to do this. We've done the rough planning, and now you realise that President Jammeh, like his role model Mugabe, is never going to step down, and like his friend Gaddafi, he will get rid of anyone who he perceives as a threat.

"I've said it before and I'll say it again. You all have a common enemy, none of you has anything to lose, but you have everything to gain. Therefore, you have to go for it. You have to put nationalism before tribalism.

"In my country, Scotland, we have the same system as you, except instead of tribes we have clans. Hundreds of years ago, we fought each other, only coming together on occasion to fight the English. "Now we are united, we have put our country before our clan. We even became part of the United Kingdom (UK). This country of The Gambia could be a wonderful place under the right management and you are it, so get off your backsides and do it!"

I hadn't realised that I had raised my voice, but when I stopped my tirade there was a silence that spoke volumes to me. I'd expected nonsense arguments, but there was a thoughtful air about the silence that I was content to leave alone.

"Thank you sir," said the CDS to the accompanying nods of the others. "You have said the right thing. There were those among us who doubted your motive, but it's clear to all that you don't want power, you just want change." "And freedom," I added, "I also want to get out of this place." "Amen," said one, "Amen" chorused the rest.

It was time to leave it to them: they were servicemen, soldiers, sailors, police and immigration, in theory they should be able to do it. I hoped so.

# BEFORE THE COUNCIL

About a week later I was taken again on a nocturnal visit to what I thought was the NIA. There was the usual nonsense with the handcuffs and leg irons, but this time an Imam had come to get me, and when I got to the prison courtyard, there was a Pajero to transport me.

"At last," I thought, "a bit of respect. I wonder if this is a good thing or what?"

Nothing was said and as we came to the outskirts of Banjul, we turned right at the arch, away from the NIA headquarters. It wasn't long before we stopped at the large double gates of a high walled compound. The driver honked his horn and the gates opened inward. We were in a compound about fifty square metres, with a concrete building three storeys high, which I was told were the new offices of the Gambian Islamic Council. Several enormous satellite dishes, crowned the flat roof. The place looked more like Jodrell Bank.

There was also a mosque in the compound, a grand affair with a green dome and massive loudspeakers pointing to the four corners of the earth.

"Looks as if there's money in being an Imam," I joked, but needn't have bothered, as I was met with blank faces and pushed towards the main door. We stepped into an ornate reception room decorated after the Middle Eastern style. There were rugs hanging from the walls and scattered about the tiled floor. What I took to be another Imam in long flowing white robes gestured me to a well-padded upright chair by a large desk.

He seemed calm and well mannered: I suppose that if I were to describe him I'd have said that he seemed to be a gentleman.

"Please be seated," he said, "there's no need to be afraid, you'll come to no harm here." Sitting down I replied. "Afraid? I'm not afraid; my dad's bigger than your dad." I really should stop trying the one-liners on these people; all I ever get is a frown of incomprehension.

"Excuse me?" he questioned, "what do you mean?" Never one to miss a chance I said, "My God, the father of Jesus Christ is the only God. Your god, Allah, will lead you to hell.

"Stop this heresy," he shouted, "do you not realise what trouble you're in? I am the one who has the power to put YOU through hell."

Surprisingly calmly, I replied, "The Bible talks in 1 Samuel that even King David, who is your Prophet Dowda, said that he'd be in serious trouble if he harmed the Lord's anointed. And my friend, today, whether you appreciate it or not, I am the Lord's anointed and if you don't repent and follow Christ it's you that's going to hell."

"Whack" and I was on the floor. "Infidel, Colonialist, Christian bastard" he shouted and with that lashed out with his foot. So much for the gentleman.

They dragged back up on my chair and the Imam, having gained his composure sat down opposite me. "You have been a nuisance to us," he said in a measured voice, "and don't flatter yourself that you have been anything more."

"It has never been my intention to take any credit for anything I've been able to do," I interrupted. "The only one who gets any glory is my God, and if you had any sense you'd get down on your knees and ask Him for forgiveness."

To give him his due, he held it together, albeit with some difficulty. "You have been doing Christian evangelism outside the military and that's outside your area of authority. What do you have to say to that?"

I hadn't any idea what he was talking about, I was held captive because I had some success in leading Muslims to faith in Christ and now this man was telling me that I had the authority to do that, but only in the Military. "What do you mean?" I asked, obviously puzzled. "You took other missionaries into the bush to try to convert Gambians with your lies," he shouted and with a flourish, he produced what he believed to be damning proof. "Who are these people?" He shouted again and a slid a picture over to me.

He showed me photos of people from the Veranda Church. We were taking a service in a village on the edge of the mangrove swamps.

"This brings back happy memories," I said, "Do you have any more? "More" he said quietly, "Oh yes, your own people have put a noose about your own neck." "Around your neck," I corrected "Anyway what more?" He shoved three pieces of paper across the desk and with astonishment I began to read.

# A GLOWING REPORT

Much has been said in the media regarding the shocking trial outcome of a British missionary couple in the Gambia.

Now for the first time, friends, relatives, and co-workers have spoken out about the humanitarian work they were doing in The Gambia.

Though they were said to have been carrying on seditious activity, David (60) & Fiona Fulton (47), over a decade, undertook effective humanitarian work in the Gambia, for the benefit of the people and the country – a place they loved to call home!

The family, David, Fiona and their two children Luke and Iona initially went to The Gambia on holiday. Fiona recalled how *"We stood on the beach, and I just knew that we would be called back here to serve God." It was "that" feeling "that this was the place of our calling." Some few years later, when Luke and Iona were 5 and 8 years old, they sold their home in Torquay cut all ties, and "came out in Faith."*

They rented a small house initially until they were able to buy a piece of land at Serekunda and slowly, over the period of their time in the country, built their own house, which is still not finished.

Prior to the mission field, they had worked in conjunction with Prison Fellowship, visiting prisoners and their families in the UK. This work continued for some time in The Gambia until, after its establishment, it was passed on to a local person and David was then invited to become Chaplain to the Armed Forces and was given the honorary rank of Major. He also was later invited to chaplain the Immigration Service.

Their home was open to all as it served as the "Veranda Fellowship" – where a small group of ex-pats and Gambians met – on the Veranda. It grew so much they eventually had to build an extension. Here they supported one another and all were welcome. Those who worshipped included those rejected by society and whose previous lifestyles were based on despair. All were given the same warm hospitality and cared for one another. It was here that many folk came to know the Love of Jesus poured out – not by preaching or evangelising, but simple Agape love supporting each other as a Christian family; no condemnation for the past but a new life turned around to a Godly lifestyle where folk could once more become part of the community and be accepted. The total funds of the Veranda Fellowship at the end of the year (unlike many Churches) stood at £51 – everything that came in went out as gifts to the poor and needy.

The home at Serekunda was the first port of call for neighbours for any problem. They were the first to turn to for help, be it transporting someone to hospital or in providing water from their own bore hole to neighbours and friends.

The home was also a refuge to ex-prisoners who were found work, the homeless, and women who had suffered domestic violence came to find sanctuary. It was also the base for many visiting friends and missionaries – who can testify to the humanitarian work of the Fultons

Those who visited were often invited to take part in Prison Services. One missionary , Mary , recalls a trip when they held a service in a prison corridor "up country" Janjanburi. *"It was a simple service with prisoners in shorts sitting on matting in a corridor. I sat on an orange box. We only had a handful of copies of Mission Praise but we all managed . . . I streamed tears of compassion for those men who were so open to receive the love of Jesus. There was no evangelising, no hard sell; we simply praised God and the Holy Spirit came. I understand the following day one of the prison officers had made a commitment to God, simply from the compassion he saw."*

Some 6 years ago, knowing there was a need, through the Fultons own generosity and physical labour and an appeal to a UK Christian organisation, the prison at Janjanburi and one other had a facelift with repainting – providing also much needed occupation and an improvement for prisoners.

It was in the area of Janjanburi too that the Fultons were able to acquire a piece of land, donated by a grateful recipient of the Fultons' love and concern, which was cleared to use as an agricultural project for the training of ex-prisoners who would live there and provide food for their own use and to make profit to encourage self-sufficiency. Though one family moved in to live and work there they did not manage to sustain their work on site and sadly the enterprise closed.

Another Christian who visited The Gambia with 34 people in 2003 on an educational holiday recalls how helpful the couple had been with factual knowledge about the people, the country, and its culture – "and *as a result we began to appreciate and love the country and the people. David arranged with the Governor of Joshwang prison for us to go there on a Sunday afternoon for worship and praise with the Christian prisoners. David took the service and Fiona played the guitar. Later the Governor gave us a tour of the prison and showed us the ways in which the prisoners generated income to cover prison costs. We were a bit shocked at the strong smell of sewage, and were told it was because they had no money to have the cesspit emptied, so we had a whip round and collected the £90 charge. The Governor was delighted and gave each of us a coconut and had her photo taken with the group. None of this would have happened without David arranging it* "

Fiona had her own ministry to prisons. She, along with her daughter Iona, taught life skills to the women prisoners, especially in the prison in which she now finds herself as a prisoner, Mile 2 in Banjul. They taught knitting, sewing and other skills the women could pick up and use later in life. She also visited the juvenile wing in one of the other prisons and taught them to read and write in English, which most of the boys had never had the chance of before. The Veranda Fellowship also organised a Christmas party for the lads in the wing. It was not uncommon for them to provide medicine for prisoners when they visited a sick inmate.

Dave Fulton was/ is part of the Gambian nation, respected by all.

Like their neighbours, many other folk in the Gambia turned to them in times of crisis-like the village whose water supply was contaminated and the villagers at risk of typhoid from using water from the mangroves for washing and cooking. They had to travel 2 miles to collect fresh water to drink. Hearing of the need Dave had tried to arrange for a fresh water supply to be piped in, though this turned out not to be possible.

In the event of an accident or when someone's car had broken down David was always ready to help out and as a trained mechanic he was also able to pass on this skill, training others to enable them to earn their living.

In order to make monthly visits up country there was a long arduous road journey. One visiting missionary recalls how as they went through the villages the police, soldiers and folk on the street would come up to the jeep and shake his hand in recognition. This couple touched many people's lives through their kindness and Christian love

On such journeys, crossings of the River Gambia could be precarious, particularly on the upper reaches. On one trip the propeller of the ferry became entangled; knowing he was a mechanic, it was Dave who was asked to rescue them and stop the ferry being carried down river. He dived in Crocodile infested water to untangle the rope which had fouled it, with a soldier with a rifle keeping an eye open on board! David was a 'man of the people' who cared about anyone needing any type of help.

About 3 years ago, David raised from supporters in the U.K. the £20,000 needed to buy a boat to enable him to be independent in making journeys to the remote immigration outposts and villages. Such journeys were often fraught with difficulties and potential danger but were continued by David despite this.

In order to serve the people of The Gambia the couple and their children made huge personal sacrifices. Theirs was not a luxury lifestyle they lived simply and by faith, 'praying in money as needed' not only for themselves but also for other families, whom they also helped, supported and worked alongside.

At Christmas 2007 David encountered a lapsed Christian who begged him to come to their village on the river bank on the outskirts of Banjul. Here they found the unloved and the neediest of the needy. Their only income was from Oyster catching. Some had diseases and were in need of medicine. The whole Fulton family, with visiting Missionary friends went to the river bank village and took food and held a Christmas service for them. They prayed for the sick, and then each Sunday after, visited them and provided what help was needed.

Fiona has provided physical, practical, and emotional support and aftercare for the families of people with terminal illness, often being the only one to make someone's last days on earth special, and showing the family that someone cared and they were not ostracised. She also visited the sick in hospital and in their homes, often buying special food for them. Iona did voluntary work in the Children's Ward of the Royal Victoria Hospital in Banjul, the capital.

As a family they travelled the length of the Gambia distributing clothing, toys and medical supplies some of which they had brought back especially from the UK, some given by visitors

Examples of their care are the way in which Fiona encouraged a single mother-to-be to be self supporting by buying her a large bag of rice which she could sell on to make a profit; sponsoring at least 2 children through school and 2 abandoned mothers through computer training courses.

Often they took into their own home ex-prisoners and former soldiers and other unfortunate people helping to re-habilitate them, sometimes creating jobs for them as watchmen or gardeners. They also encouraged them to become self sufficient (as in the previously mentioned banana plantation ) and, for example, provided a fishing boat and engine to start a fishing co-operative and setting one person up in his own business selling juices to tourists. They helped illiterate people with form filling and teaching them to read and write.

David and Fiona kept their Christian friends and supporters in the UK informed of their work and the needs that they found through regular emails and urged those in the UK – friends, family, and churches – to support their mission work and pray for those in need of help. On more than one occasion, UK Christians were asked to pray for injured folk who needed to make a long and hazardous journey to Senegal – with the costs of the travel and medical treatment borne by David who had asked those he emailed for financial support on their behalf.

One such act was in 2008 when a soldier had become impaled on a railing – he was driven to Dakar by David and with skilful surgery survived. In the autumn of that year a member of the Army who was training to take over as a Chaplain was run down by a lorry. His back was broken. Much prayer went up in the UK and he was taken by road to Dakar, and an orthopaedic surgeon (a Christian) flew over from the UK to operate. As a result of this skilful surgery the man lived and will be able to walk again.

As a missionary David was called on to, do many things – apart from undertaking an 11 hour Alpha course in one sitting! He married a young couple who had become Christian. At the ceremony the wife then began contractions and it was evident her baby was about to be born. David had no skills in such matters and as this was a breach birth, he was only able to take instruction from a Banjul doctor on his mobile. The baby boy was delivered with the aid of all that he had available, a razor blade and some string. Sadly, the mother was not able to be saved but the family christened the baby David. At 18 months, he appeared undernourished and lacked growth. David was able, yet again, to get him to specialists in Dakar, and a Christian surgeon who flew out diagnosed a digestive tract problem. He was treated and is now doing well.

In the last ten years David and Fiona's purpose in The Gambia has been to serve the people amongst whom they lived in any way that was needed and with the active support of friends and Churches in the UK who have provided funds for their humanitarian work and supported them in prayer. In giving this part of their lives in this way, they have themselves experienced hardship and illness. Luke and David have suffered from Cerebral Malaria and they have all experienced diseases common in Africa. On several occasions David has been assaulted, sometimes severely and causing injury, the boat has been sabotaged and their home broken into on several occasions. In spite of these and other difficult times they have remained true to the call they felt upon their lives to serve the people of The Gambia and to present the Christian message to any who enquired of them or wished to join in the opportunities that they gave for people to attend Alpha courses or watch the Jesus film, both in the town and in the remote Bush areas.

They have accepted that in some of their emails to friends and supporters outside The Gambia they made comments reflective of their understanding of matters within The Gambia which they failed to consider sufficiently carefully. In particular, they did not take account of the way in which those comments would be understood within The Gambia and that, with that understanding, those comments might cause hurt and distress and be understood under Gambian law as amounting to seditious comments. It is for that reason, now appreciating the effect of those comments within The Gambia that they have apologised unreservedly to The President, Government and people of The Gambia for any hurt or distress caused. On advice from their Gambian Lawyer they changed their plea from not guilty to guilty, having been advised that this would achieve a lesser penalty. In the event they were sentenced to twelve months hard labour and each fined the equivalent of about £6,300. They are currently held in Mile2 prison. Christian friends and supporters are praying that The President of The Gambia will, in spite of his evident disquiet at the detail in the Magistrate's judgment put forward at the trial, exercise clemency in favour of David and Fiona and take action that will enable them to be released from prison and return home to the UK.

## EDITORS NOTE

(If the fines are not paid immediately then they will serve an extra 6 months.) Additionally family and friends have to raise £2500 for lawyer's costs, and other expenses which are incalculable as it depends on how long they remain in prison and whether their assets can be capitalised.

The information in this article was provided by people who
have worked in or visited the Gambia and who have known
the Fulton's work over many years and is largely from those
persons own eyewitness experience.

WOW! As I finished reading, I was aware that my neck and
shoulders were numb. While this resume only scratched the
surface of what we did in The Gambia, I could see how what had
been written could, as they say, be used in evidence against me
given the twisted way they perceived things.

"No more wise noises," he said, smirking. "I need to read this
again," I said. "Take as long as you like," he replied, rising from
behind the desk, "you've got years to think on how your so-called
friends dropped you on it." "In it," I corrected him as he walked
out, "one gets dropped in it, not on it."

I was left on my own to re-read the document. It was pretty
accurate apart from a few mistakes which were unavoidable. I
smiled when it was said that Fiona played the guitar, I doubt if
she'd ever picked one up. It was 'me' on the guitar and after hearing me practice I doubt if Fiona would ever want to try.

One thing that did strike me was how I'd forgotten how much
humanitarian work we had done as a matter of course. In fact,
that document didn't tell the half of it and I had to laugh when I
thought of the nights I went to different compounds in our village
giving injections every six hours to people suffering from malaria.
Other times I'd be stitching people up after they'd been in fights
or had an accident. Where were all these people now? What did
they think of my incarceration? Did they stand up for Fiona and
me? Ah well, best not to go down that road, they probably kept
their heads down and who could blame them in this evil country.

Getting up I shuffled round the room and found a calendar on
the wall. It had been such a long time since I'd seen one that I
was drawn to it like a magnet. It was open at the month of August
2010 so I had to assume that was the current month. I counted
back from Sept 2008. Twenty-two months, was that all? It seemed
more like twenty-two years. I had no idea what date in August it
was, but I was elated at having survived thus far. Some would say

"against the odds" but it only went to confirm to me that God was in control and that he had a purpose for me beyond this captivity.

I guess about half an hour passed before the Imam returned. He was dabbing his lips with a white napkin. "Have you eaten?" he asked with a smirk. "Thank you, but I'm on a diet at the moment, but maybe later."

Sitting down he placed both elbows in the desk and leaning his chin on his knuckles he said in a serious conspiratorial voice, "I'm going to speak to you like a Dutch man." Again, I interrupted. "I think you mean, like a Dutch uncle."

"I know what I mean," he shouted as he lost his cool again. "I swear by the mighty name of Allah that you will never see your family or freedom again."

"Did you get round to reading the book of 1 Kings Chapter 18?" I asked. "Now, I might be wrong but I think you should read it and take special note of verse 40. Don't challenge me or my God. Now, I think I'll take you up on that offer of food thank you."

I could tell he was a trifle annoyed by the way he stormed out. I can't say that I felt especially proud of myself, but the guy was so smug, so sure of himself that I felt it wouldn't do him any harm to have some food for thought.

I must have been there a further hour when a boy of about twelve came in with a tray. I smelt the food before I saw it. There on a real plate was Chicken Yassa, rice, and a jug of local lemonade and a glass.

The saliva was running out of the corners of my mouth when he put it in front of me and left. I looked at it in disbelief, then with doubt. Was it poisoned? Should I eat it? I prayed, "Lord I believe that you can protect me from poison so I thank you for this food, may it do me only good and no harm, in Jesus' name, Amen."

I took my time eating it. Yes, I made it last at least two minutes. I was crunching the bones and drinking lemonade when the Imam returned.

"I don't think I am going to have any influence on you, am I," he said. "I hope you enjoyed your meal, if what is planned for you happens, you won't have many more. Goodbye Major," and with that he turned and left the room. I never knew his name, I never saw him again, but I think on the whole he was a good man.

What a strange episode that was, somewhat confusing, but the first time in a long time that I'd been treated like a human being, let alone ate a good meal. I was taken back to Mile Two and left to my thoughts, about what seemed to be a warning, or was it a threat?

# DESPERATE

That month of August I was taken to court for the reading of my judgement on my appeal. It came as no surprise to anyone that yet again there was no sitting. This time the judge was up country, but again it was a day out for me.

A week passed without a visit by the NIA. In some ways, it was worse, as the anticipation of the nocturnal visit was always there. However, my body was able to recover to some extent during that time and some extra food was being smuggled to me from time to time.

One day there'd be a handful of peanuts, the next a mango, maybe a bit of boiled cassava and a piece of bread. I know it doesn't sound much, but to me it was lifesaving and for the most part it was my Muslim friends in the prison who brought it.

My birthday was coming up, September 10th and for some strange reason I felt my spirits drop. I wasn't ever that enamoured by birthdays, Fiona's the birthday person as are the children, but for me they just came and went. I believe it was because I am a twin and as such, the money set aside for birthdays was split between us. Also we were born after WW11 when things in the country were tight and birthdays weren't that important. I guess it was because there was nothing else to judge the passing years by, and I really didn't want to spend too many of them in this place.

Nevertheless, as I have said to many people in here on many occasions, "God's in control" and that was good to remember. Now having said all that, and I really meant it, it was about this time that I began to plan an escape. Oh, I know what you are thinking, but maybe this was what God wanted. Well that's what I told myself.

It started when Ramadan was in full swing and some of the Moslems were smuggling me food from their extra rations. I felt it was now or never.

I hadn't been tortured for well over a month so I had no fresh injuries to recover from and with the extra food I felt my body getting stronger. Added to that, the rainy season was coming to an end and the humidity was lessening. I started to do press-ups and half squats in my cell until I was exhausted.

The next public holidays were scheduled for the end of Ramadan, the 8th, 9th and 10th of September and if things went as they have been doing, then I'd be scheduled to go to court on one of those days. That was my target, I'd get away from the escort, and it would be then or never. I always worked to targets: I'd set my mind on something and go for it. Now I had my approximate date and my target.

I was well acquainted with the topography of The Gambia and I knew that I had to get out of the country immediately. I also knew that the President and all those who wished me harm would have travelled to their villages for Ramadan, at least the day before.

I would have to get to the British Embassy in Senegal, there was one in Dakar which I'd seen before. If I got away at the court, there was little or no chance of using the ferry to cross to the north bank. Firstly, I would have no money and secondly, that was where they would be looking for me.

I knew there was no chance of swimming the river in my physical condition; it was about 6km wide. If I could get to Denton Bridge then I could get out on my boat, but no, they'd be watching for that. They might be stupid, but they weren't daft. No the north bank was out and my boat was out, what then? I'd have to get across the river at Denton Bridge to get off the island where

Banjul is situated. This was not an easy of task as my whiteness stands out like a sore thumb.

I'd have no transport and no money, so that was a problem I had to start working on immediately.

Sanneh came round with my bowl and as he pushed it through the hole in the bottom of the door, I asked him, "Sanneh how do I go about getting some money in here?" "You need to have something to sell," he replied, "'I'll come round later and we'll talk about it."

Sell, what did I have to sell? I took the block out of the wall to see what I had; three new razors, seven bars of Imperial Leather and a new toothbrush. Hardly Harrods, but who knows?

Sanneh came round to collect the bowls and asked, "Major, what do you have to sell?" When I told him what I had he said, "Put it all in the empty bowl and I'll see what I can do."

It seems ludicrous now to think that I was reluctant to part with these few material possessions, but they were all I owned in the world. Then with a smile, I remembered the words I've spoken from the scriptures from Job 1: 21 at well over a hundred funerals. *"Naked came I out of my mother's womb, and naked shall I return thither; the Lord gave and the Lord hath taken away; blessed be the name of the Lord."*

I put the stuff in the bowl and Sanneh disappeared. It was the next day before I found out I was rich. Sanneh came with my bowl of food and inside there was a small clear plastic bag with three hundred and twenty five Dalasi in it. I immediately took out the block from the wall and hid it, as to be found with money in the prison was serious stuff. Later that day I was told that I was scheduled to go to court for my judgement to be read on Wednesday 8th September.

When I told Sanneh he said that he'd find out from a guard today's date so we could work out how far away it was. He returned and it was with regret in his voice that he told me that it was in ten days' time and it was the last day of Ramadan, a public holiday. "I'm sorry sir," he said, "they've done it again." "Sanneh," I whispered loudly, "come down to the hatch where we can talk."

He lay on the ground outside my cell with his head against the opening. "Sanneh I don't intend to come back. It's obvious they are trying to keep me till I ether starve to death or I'm charged with, and sentenced for spying. So I have to use this opportunity to escape, it'll be my last."

There was silence from behind the door and then he said, "I will help you. You will need help." "Listen," I argued, "I don't want to get anyone into trouble, I can do this on my own." "Trouble?" he replied, "I have a death sentence, what more trouble could I have? No I will help you, we will help you, so prepare yourself to eat and build up your strength," and with that he was gone.

I didn't have to wait long before a cooked cassava and a handful of groundnuts were pushed through the hatch along with a litre of water in a plastic bottle.

I had no idea what time it was, but it was quiet outside so a guess of 21.00hrs wouldn't have been far wrong. I settled down to my feast, but before anything else I thanked God for his live saving provision and looked to Him to open whatever doors he would when I got to court.

I used some water to wash my hands, as this was no time to go down with some dreaded lurgy. Then taking my time I slowly ate the lot. I could see my stomach had swollen with the food and water. After praying, I sang Amazing Grace at full volume and some other men joined in, and then I fell asleep.

# I HAVE A DREAM

That night I dreamed. I was out of prison hacking my way through the jungle with a machete and being chased by prison officers with dogs. They couldn't see me, but they fired short bursts from their AK47s in the general direction of the noise I was making.

Waking up in a sweat, I wondered if God was speaking to me in a dream, was he telling me that it was too dangerous to try to escape. On the other hand, was he telling me that when I did get away I'd always be a step in front of my pursuers? Here we had both ends of the spectrum. Was I to call it off, or to go for it? I am no great philosopher or Bible scholar, but I believe God made us and He accepts us just as we are. Me? I was made to walk on the edge, so I'll plump for the latter. I'd go for it.

The noise outside the cell told me that it was about 07.00 and I'd slept the sleep of the just. A bowl slid through the hatch and inside was a mess of steaming hot porridge made of cassava. I was doubtful as to its origin and didn't tuck in, but Sanneh came to the hatch and threw in a small plastic bag. "Enjoy a hearty breakfast," he whispered and was gone.

Inside was sugar mixed with powdered milk. I emptied the lot into the bowl and stirred it around with the handle of my toothbrush.

It was wonderful, well almost wonderful – when I dug into it with my fingers there was some movement there, however I thanked God for the food and ate the lot, living protein and all.

Another amazing thing happened. At about ten, that morning the cell door opened and the guard told me I was going outside to do hard labour.

I got dressed in my prison uniform of a t-shirt and shorts and he led me out to join a work detail. Most of the men I knew from the main yard when I had worked there as Chaplain. They were visibly shocked to see my condition and as a man ran towards me to help me stand. I hadn't realised just how bad I looked and indeed felt until I compared myself to these guys.

The sun was high and hot, and while the others weren't too happy about it I was ecstatic. I held my head up and basked in the heat of it. I felt it revive me that I was being built up again. With the extra food and water, the exercise, and now fresh air and sunshine, something was going to happen and I was going to be fit and ready for it.

We went into the back of the ubiquitous pickup and we headed towards the beach behind the rundown shell of a former tourist hotel. The Idea was that we climbed the palm trees by the beach with a machete and cut down the palm branches.

Well there was no way I could climb the trees in my physical condition and to my surprise, the guards didn't expect me to. While they stood guard with their AK47s, I gathered up the cut branches and then bundled them all together. It was a relaxing time and after about two hours, there was enough to take back to the prison. Spontaneously I stripped off my clothes and ran into the sea.

The guards started shouting, "Come back Tubab, what are you doing?" I ignored them as the salt water soothed my body and deliciously stung the sores and skin infections. "Which way is America?" I shouted back from about one hundred yards out. "Come back," they shouted louder, but to no avail. Then the other prisoners stripped of their clothes and with whoops of laughter ran into the sea.

Of course order was restored after a while when we just frolicked about with no attempt to escape and even the guards joined us. I know it doesn't seem much, but to me it was another victory and another rung up the ladder towards freedom.

When we got back to the prison, I felt better than I had in a long time and was sure the time was near for my escape. I started to exercise again, ten squats, ten push-ups, ten sit-ups. I laughed at how pathetic it was, but determined to increase them by one every day until I was fit again.

# ROLLER COASTER

The day came for my September court appearance scheduled for the last day of Ramadan, which everyone and his dog knew was a public holiday. However, I was ready for any eventuality and by that time, I considered myself reasonably fit.

As I've said before, with no yardstick to gauge my physical state with, it was easy to convince myself that I was as fit as a fiddle. In faith, I gave away my belongings: my towel, four bars of soap, two razors, a blanket, a lighter and my homemade chess set. This was it, I wasn't going back. Any opportunity and I was off.

My Muslim friends wished me good luck and God's blessing by the Christian ones.

They took me out of the confinement wing to reception to get my own clothes. "Hey! " I said to the reception officer. "My wife sent me in some new clothes that fit me; I want them, not these"

"OK sir," he said and went in search of the stuff Fiona sent to me when she got back to UK.

While I waited, I was holding the trousers by the waistband and I noticed that it was thicker than it should be. I examined it further and found packets of what I guessed were drugs stuffed around the full length of the waistband. Just then, the guard came back carrying a new pair of black, size 30" waist trousers and a new black medium shirt. Rather than make a fuss about what I found in the trousers I dumped them behind a rubbish bin and put my new clothes on. I felt a million dollars.

It was while we made our way to the pickup that I noticed that there seemed to be a lot of prison officers about for a public holiday. "What's going on?" I asked my escort, "I thought there would only be a skeleton staff today, isn't it a public holiday?"

One of the guards laughed. "It should have been, and all the senior officers have travelled to their villages, but last night the Imam didn't see the moon so we have to fast another day" Failing to see the significance of this I asked him, "Why are you laughing when you have to do another day's fasting?" "Oh," he replied, "I'm off duty tonight and I can be with my family for the feasting."

As we drove along, I wondered how it would affect me, as everyone travels a day early to his or her villages for the feasting. We arrived at the appeal court in Banjul and to all our surprise (my guards and me), the court was open. There was no Press outside and as we walked into the courthouse, the place was empty. The two guards and I sat twiddling our thumbs. I hoped that the High Commissioner would come. I hoped to see some friends there, but the cavernous place was empty.

This didn't look good for me to get away, I needed crowds of people and I needed to mingle with noisy tourists, even join a tourist safari trip. Empty wasn't good. "God," I prayed, "empty isn't good, could you do something about it?"

We must have been there for about an hour and the guards were beginning to make noises about heading back to the prison. "Good morning David," came a voice from a side entrance. It was Lamin Camera, my lawyer. "Lamin!" I exclaimed, "Glad you could make it is it going to happen today at last?"

"I don't know," he replied, "it seems that everyone who's anyone has travelled, so we'll have to wait and see."

Five minutes later a uniformed policeman came in and sat at the prosecutor's desk and started taking papers from a briefcase. Lamin walked over to him and all I could see was them in a huddle, before the door at the back of the court opened and in walked the clerk of the court.

Wow, things were looking up, three out of four, but I was looking for a full house.

Time seemed to drag, but I didn't waste it. As I sat on my own, I prayed and prayed that God would do something. I felt weak physically, but so strong emotionally and spiritually, I was so aware of God's presence, something was going to happen, but what?

"All rise!" It was the clerk of the court, and as I got to my feet, in came the Judge.

As he sat so did we all. The clerk continued, "The appeal of David Fulton against conviction and sentence by the state of The Gambia." While saying this he gestured me to stand in the dock.

Lamin Camera my lawyer stood and said, "Your honour, I submitted the documents regarding the appeal of Mr Fulton almost one year ago and if the court please can this appeal be dealt with today?"

"I am fully aware," said the judge, "of the intrigue and manipulation regarding this case, so if you will allow me to proceed Mr Camera." With that, he raised his eyebrows and turned to me.

"Mr Fulton, it was my judgement to acquit and discharge you from this court. However my learned friend the public prosecutor told me," and he inclined his head in a mock bow to the junior prosecutor who looked totally out of his depth, "That if I passed that judgement he would appeal against my judgement. Then, Mr Fulton you would have been taken back to Mile Two where, by the look of you, you would die."

I stood there holding myself up by the rail on top of the dock, unable to do anything but nod. "So," he continued, "I am fining you 15,000 Dallasis and ordering you out of the country as soon as possible. Failure to pay the fine will result in you going back to prison. Do you understand?"

I still couldn't speak, but my head nodded fit to fall off. His gavel dropped and he stood up abruptly and left. I was dazed. Lamin was dazed and left to celebrate Ramadan with his family shaking his head in wonderment. The guards were dazed but smiling for me, and the prosecutor scuttled out of court, no doubt contemplating his bleak future and cursing whatever demon, he worshipped for his bad luck in being on duty that day.

When the shock wore off, I realised that God had just done a minor miracle, but I also realized that some more miracles would have to happen if I was to walk free and get out of the country alive. Firstly, I'd have to find 15,000 dalasi to pay the fine, and apart from the guards and the clerk of the court I was on my own.

"Can I use your mobile?" I asked one of the guards who I knew quite well. "My credit is small," he replied reluctantly. "It's OK," I reassured him, "If I get through I will get my people to give you a 100 Dalasi phone card." That brightened his face as he handed it over.

It was then that I cursed the system of putting names on the mobiles and never having to use numbers. "Lord," I prayed I don't remember any phone numbers, can you help?"

A number came into my head and I dialled it. "Hullo?" said a Scottish accented woman's voice. "Betty," I shouted, flabbergasted. "David," she shouted back down the phone. "Where are you?"

"I'm in the court and I've been freed, but I need 15,000 dalais to stop me being put back inside again. Can you lend me the money?"

"I don't need to lend you anything; I'm holding your money in case of any eventuality." I cut in. "Can you get to Banjul court as soon as possible, I have to pay this before everything shuts down for Ramadan."

"We'll be there in half an hour," she said and before she cut the line, I butted in again. "Can you also bring a 100 Dalasi phone card for the officer who let me use his phone?" With a quick "No problem" she hung up..

The moon hadn't been seen which put back the end of Ramadan. The Government had moved the public holiday. Everyone who mattered was in court and hadn't travelled to their villages. The judge satisfied the prosecution with what I believe to have been Godly wisdom. The guard gave me the use of his phone. God put Betty's telephone number into my head, she was at home and she was holding my money.

I said out loud, "thank you Lord for what you have done, I look forward to what you are about to do. Amen"

It took an hour for Betty and out mutual friend Caroline to arrive. My money that they were holding was in pounds sterling and they had to change it to dalais to pay the fine. However when they arrived there was plenty of emotion. Tears of joy were the order of the day, and I have to confess I felt one or two rolling down my cheek.

Betty gave the guard his phone card credit which broadened the smile on his face. Off they went with the clerk of the court and reappeared quarter of an hour later waving the receipt for 15,000 and we headed for the prison pickup, which Caroline and Betty followed.

I had to go back to Mile Two to be processed and given my release papers and when I arrived there was confusion as to what to do. There were no senior officers in the prison. Like so many others, they assumed that this would have been a public holiday and went home. However, the sergeant who did the administration was there and reluctantly prepared the appropriate paperwork and I was handed my "Get out of jail free card"! Yes!

I was then taken back to the pickup and left Mile Two prison for what I prayed was the last time. I say that because my next port of call was the immigration headquarters where I ought be held in custody until I was deported.

Now that presented major problems. Firstly, if President Jammeh was informed that I was out then he'd immediately put into place the plan to have me arrested for spying. The same went for the Islamic Council and the NIA.

Looking at things from a natural perspective, I didn't stand a chance of getting out of the country. However, (what a wonderful word) I was aware of the prayers of hundreds, if not thousands of Christian's worldwide and the scripture came to mind, "If God be for us, who could be against us."

It was with that verse in my ear we arrived at immigration headquarters. It was strange to be there again, the place I'd taken so many "Church services". The guards didn't know where to go and the place seemed empty because of the Ramadan mix-up. "Follow me," I said to them and led the way to the Director of Immigration's office.

# THE ONE IN CHARGE

The door was ajar, so I knocked and stuck my head in. Behind the desk sat a man I knew well, Inspector Faal. With the guards, pushing me from behind, I moved into the room. "Looking up he exclaimed, "Is that you major?" "None other," I replied as he came round the desk and gave me a bear hug.

"We were all so sorry for you and your wife," he began as we sat down, "but I helped your wife at the airport when she was deported. Ask her and she'll tell you."

"I hope to get the chance too," I said, "but to do that I'll need your help"

"My help, he queried. "Yep," I went on, "I need my passport back now and I want to be out the country before anyone knows it's happened."

He turned to the two guards who were standing behind my chair. "You two can go now, tell your senior officer that I am dealing with the major" The men saluted him and then turned to me and saluted me, shook my hand and said, "You are a good man sir, go with your god," and with that they were gone. I was almost on the verge of tears.

It was then Betty came in and I introduced her to my friend. "Betty this is Inspector Faal." "Not inspector," he interrupted, "Commissioner." "I noticed the scrambled egg," I said grinning, "Congratulations."

"I'm in charge of Immigration over the Ramadan holidays," he said proudly, "so let's see what can be done my friend." It's at times like that when one can see God standing there with a baton in His hand orchestrating things, it's marvellous.

Betty was still her bubbly self, but there seemed to me after what I'd been through a feeling of unreality. Freedom, friends by my side, people talking of how they could help, I wasn't used to this but I could get used to it.

"OK," said Faal, "in theory you should be held in the Immigration cells until you are deported. However, if someone can stand surety for you then I will let you work out your own exit from the country. "I'll stand surety," said Betty before I got a word in edgeways. "That's great," Faal replied, but I'd need your ID card as guarantee."

With a flourish, Betty produced her all-important ID card, without which she was vulnerable in The Gambia. I was trying to attract her attention to silently mime not to do that, for like Baldric; I had a "cunning plan".

However I wasn't noticed and Faal jumped at what he obviously saw as a wonderful way to help me. Taking Betty's ID card he wrote a receipt for it and announced with a grin from ear to ear, "Major you are free to go with your friends."

"What about my passport?" I exclaimed, "I need my passport."

"Well," said Faal, "for the time being it's locked in a safe at police headquarters," and looking at his watch, he continued, "and as everyone has gone to their villages for Ramadan, there it will remain."

"This is a disaster!" I exclaimed. "I need to get it now, now, what can you do?"

He looked at me calmly, "This evening when my duty finishes I'll go to see the man who holds the keys and we can get your passport tomorrow."

"Tomorrow," I almost shouted, "is that the best you can do?"

"I think it best that the police don't connect your release and me asking for the safe keys," he smiled knowingly. "Just let me get your passport tomorrow, come back to this office by 9am."

I looked at Betty and she nodded. I'd have a lift to Banjul, so I agreed.

So much for my cunning plan to get out of the country through the jungle into The Casamance then on to Guinea Bissau. If I escaped while Betty had given her ID as guarantee, she'd be in serious trouble and I couldn't have that. How quickly I took my eye off the conductor.

Making our way out of the Immigration Headquarters on our own was weird. For the past two years, I had been the object of close attention wherever I was. In prison my fellow prisoners were either looking at me with awe that I was still living, or with incredulity that this was the white man that stood up against the President. I was the object of particular attention from the NIA during our nocturnal journeys. Then if I went to court, there were reporters and onlookers and of course, I was the centre of attention again. Now, as we walked into the dusty street, nobody paid us the slightest bit of attention and I wasn't sure how I felt about that, it was unsettling. That was for sure.

We got into my friend's car and I itched to drive, but common sense prevailed.

As we headed through the crowded streets of Banjul, the ladies talked excitedly about the phone call catching them unawares and their journey to the court. Most of it went over my head as I was contemplating the next hurdle of getting out of the country without the secret police catching me. I love challenges, but this time I'd have preferred an easier one.

# FRIENDS AND HELPERS

At my friend's house, I had a bath, steaming hot, the first for almost two years. Aah! All my skin rashes and sores screamed out in delicious pain – the kind that was healing and was good for me.

Stepping out from the bath, I saw myself in a full-length mirror and was so shocked that I gaped. I looked like someone who'd just stepped out of Belsen Bergen. My face was gaunt and my ribs stood out like scaffolding, I had sticks for arms and legs, I was shocked.

Yet help was at hand. When I was dry and dressed, I joined my friends and Betty said, "How would you like Mince and Tatties for dinner?" "Wonderful," I replied, "I'd like nothing better."

Betty's husband John said, "Sit down here, I've got a surprise for you." The computer screen was in front of me and I thought he was going to show me some photos. However as it happened I was on Skype and there was my family. Wow! It was almost too much to take in. I could see them but for some reason they could only hear me. I was actually quite grateful for that as I was embarrassed about my appearance and I didn't want my family to see me crying.

I didn't realise it at the time, but that night Betty and John gave up their bed for me and I slept the sleep of the just in a bed that was bigger by far than the area of my cell. The next day, after a full Scottish breakfast, (that's like a full English breakfast without giving a tip), we set off to Banjul to collect my passport.

Faal seemed to be the only person at Immigration Headquarters and again he greeted me like a long lost son. I exclaimed as he hugged my frail frame. "I have your passport," and with a flourish produced the valuable document.

"Many thanks," I said examining it. "I see there is no deportation stamp on it." "No my friend," he replied, grinning, "Neither you nor your wife have deportation stamps, indeed, you won't even be on the computer."

"Ah!" I said, "The only fly in the ointment is that Fiona's name is on your computer."

Crooking his finger at me, he gestured for me to come to his side of the desk. Using the mouse, he scrolled down the computer screen full of names until he came to Fiona Fulton. He clicked the mouse then moved it to the top of the screen where it stopped at the 'delete' sign. Then with a look of satisfaction, he clicked it and Fiona's name disappeared.

"Voila!" he shouted, "Deportation? What deportation?"

It was my turn to hug him, "Thanks my friend, Fiona will be delighted." "One last thing," he said, "when you get to the airport come to the Immigration office and see me, you might need some help."

# DAVID WHO?

The next stop was the airline office. I thought that this was going to be particularly difficult as the NIA had a link into their computer. They could monitor who was coming and in my case leaving The Gambia.

We drove out of Banjul for what I hoped was to be the last time and as we crossed Denton Bridge, I caught a glimpse of my boat drawn up on the hard mud as the tide was out.

It took about an hour to get to The Gambian Experience office, and when we arrived, a friend who worked there greeted me. She was all over me in the nicest of ways, "Oh Dave," she murmured, "What have they done to you, you look awful." "Thanks," I replied, "always the encourager, aren't you?"

Taking me by the elbow, she tried to lead me to her office, but I stopped her. "The NIA told me that if I fly out they will stop the plane and I'll be arrested for spying in front of the GRTS cameras."

"Let's see," she said kindly, "where there's a will there's a way," and with that, I allowed her to help me inside. Seated at a desk in the office was a man I had never seen before and he never gave me as much as a glance. "So, where are you wanting a ticket to sir?" she asked me in a businesslike manner. "London Gatwick", I replied. "Can I see your passport?" "No problem," I said as I handed it over.

Opening it, she looked at it for a moment then with her thumb over my surname; she asked her colleague, "Issue a ticket for this man will you?"

Looking at what he could see on the passport he said "David Borland" and started to type on the keyboard. (Now Borland was my mother's maiden name and is my middle name). It was the work of a moment, and a single ticket appeared for Mr David Borland to fly to London the following afternoon, Friday 10th Sept 2010, coincidentally my birthday, and exactly eleven years to the day when I arrived in The Gambia, 10th Sept 1999.

It was with a light heart we left the office and I was able to examine the passport to see how this came about. There it was, Fulton was above my two given names and for all to see was written David Borland.

That night my friends took me to a Chinese restaurant in the tourist area. While I enjoyed the meal, it turned out to be too rich for my delicate stomach and that night I was up at the toilet. To be honest I think it wasn't only the food that made my stomach do somersaults.

The next day, Friday 10th Betty and Caroline took me to the airport that thronged with tourists heading home. I thanked them profusely as we said our goodbyes and I headed to the Immigration office. As good as his word Faal was there. "I'm glad you could make it," he said jokingly but I could see that he was relieved. "Give me your ticket and passport and I'll get you booked in and get your boarding pass. You stay here."

I waited on tenterhooks, as a little demon whispered in my ear. "He's gone to get the NIA, make a run for it." However, (what a wonderful word that is) he soon returned with my ticket, passport and boarding pass. Phew!

"Don't go through security," he cautioned, "they've installed cameras since you were chaplain here." "You know the internal corridors, use them to get to the airport bus and you'll be OK."

We embraced and as I made my way through the labyrinth of passageways, I couldn't help but marvel once again at how things were working out. I emerged on the tarmac as the bus was loading the first load of happy holidaymakers and I joined them. Another white face in the crowd with my carry-on, that was me, I was almost there.

I had been given my mobile phone back and it had been charged at Betty and John's and as the plane started to fill up I put in the number of the British High Commissioner and left it on with my finger poised over the button.

I was in row 22 in an aisle seat and after what seemed like an eternity, the engines whined loudly. While everyone else was switching their mobiles off, I made the call.

"Hello? Is that the High Commission?"

"The British High Commission duty officer speaking, how can I help you?"

"My name is David Fulton, I'm sure you've heard of me. I'm free from Mile Two prison and flying out of The Gambia in a few minutes on the Monarch flight. I am travelling under the name of David Borland. Please inform those who need to know at Gatwick, thank you."

With that I turned my phone off and sat back as the plane started to taxi slowly to the end of the runway. Turning at the end, we stopped and the wait seemed to be interminable. All sorts of things went through my mind, had my call been intercepted by the secret police? Had they refused the pilot permission to take off and were they speeding to arrest me?

It must have been fifteen minutes we sat there my heart in my mouth and praying quietly, as I've never prayed before. One of the cabin crew stood up and started reciting the safety instructions. I knew this was only a ruse to fill the time while the NIA got their act together and despite the AC I was sweating like a pig. When the spiel came to an end and the stewardesses strapped themselves in I was almost beside myself with worry, to the extent that I was looking at some way of getting out of the plane.

The woman next to me took my hand and said, "I was frightened of flying once but really there is nothing to worry about. I'm sure the man in charge knows what he's doing." It wasn't flying I'd been frightened of, but what she said pulled me up. How quickly I'd forgotten who was in charge here. God had done it this far and he wasn't going to let me down now.

The engine noise rose to a crescendo and the pilot released the brakes. Soon we were thundering down the runway and in the air. There is no way that I can describe the relief and thankfulness to God and the thousands of people who had prayed for this day.

When the seatbelt light went off, one of the cabin crew came up to me. "Mr Borland?" I looked around me before I realised that I was travelling in that name, "There is a seat at the front where you will have more room."

I followed her down staggering from one chair back to the next, until I sat in a seat with extra legroom. "Is there anything I can do for you?" she asked, "Two things," I replied. "Can you let me know when we leave Gambian airspace and when that happens can you bring me a large whisky, Dr Johnnie Walker if you have it?"

It only seemed a few minutes when the airhostess returned and stood beside me holding a tray. As I was sitting and she was standing, I couldn't see what was on it. I looked at her and she was grinning from ear to ear, but not looking at me.

The public address system came to life. "This is your captain speaking; we have just left Gambian airspace." The hostess leaned over, opened the lid on the arm of my seat and swung the tray out. Then set in front of me two miniature bottles of whisky, a plastic tumbler with ice and said, "Compliments of the crew".

I guess for the first time for two years I was totally relaxed, I was going home.

I thought of the challenges that lay ahead; Health, physical, yes, but probably mentally and emotionally as well. Financial problems too as I was going back penniless. However, (and how I love that word) my God had seen me through thus far and I could trust him for the future.

I fell asleep and when I awoke about two hours later there was an old song by Elvis Presley going through my mind, which I sang quietly to myself.

> In this world of fear and doubt
> On my knees I ask the question
> Why alone this heavy cross I must bear
> Then He tells me in my prayer
> It's because I am trustworthy
> He gives me strength for more than my share
>
> Known only to Him are the great hidden secrets
> I'll fear not the darkness when my flame shall dim
> I know not what the future holds
> But I know who holds the future
> It's a secret known only to him.

That was it in a nutshell.

AMEN

# GLOSSARY

Alpha Course – An introduction to Christianity by the Rev. Nicky Gumiel

BHC – British High Comission

CDS – Chief of Defence Staff

DIG – Deputy Inspector General

DPM'S – Disruptive Pattern Material (Camouflage)

FGM – Female Genital Mutilation – Practiced by some African tribes

Flying Bridge – Open cockpit with duplicate steering/controls

GRTS – Gambian Radio and Television Service

LMG – Light machine gun

MRC – Medical research Council

Mufti – Out of uniform – Civilian Clothing

NIA – National Intelligence Agency (Secret Police)

OIC – Officer in command

Port – Nautical term for left hand side

SOS – Secretary Of State

Starboard – Nautical term for right hand side

Tubab – The Gambian name for a white person

WEC – World wide evangelisation for Christ